THE SHADOW
IN THE SUN

ALSO BY MICHAEL SHAPIRO:

Japan: In the Land of the Brokenhearted

THE SHADOW
IN THE SUN

A Korean Year of Love and Sorrow

MICHAEL SHAPIRO

Introduction by Susan Chira

Atlantic Monthly Press
New York

Published simultaneously in Canada
Printed in the United States of America
First edition

Library of Congress Cataloging-in-Publication Data

Shapiro, Michael, 1952–
    The shadow in the sun: a Korean year of love and sorrow /
    by Michael Shapiro; introduction by Susan Chira.—1st ed.
       ISBN 0-87113-357-1
       1. Korea (South)—Social conditions. 2. Civil rights
movements—Korea (South) I. Title.
    HN730.5.A8S48   1990   306'.095195—dc20   89-77933

The Atlantic Monthly Press
19 Union Square West
New York, NY 10003

First printing

For my parents,
Herbert and Lorraine Shapiro,
and for my
brother, James, and sister, Jill

Acknowledgments

I could not have written this book without the help of a good many people.

I am especially indebted to Edward and Genell Poitras, who were so generous in sharing the wisdom gained through a generation spent living in and caring for Korea. It was Ed Poitras who introduced me to the concepts of *han* and *jong.* I could never hope to know all that the Poitrases know about Korea. I am just grateful that they were there, time and again, to point in the right direction.

My interpreter, Bae Yu Chung, was a patient and wise guide. She was also uncommonly adept at drawing out the most reluctant subject. Among the others who assisted in translation were Sumi Chang, Stella Song Hee Kim, Jeanne Han and Jennie Kim.

In addition to the people interviewed for this book, there were a good many others who offered their time in helping educate me about Korea. I particularly want to thank Chi Jung Nam, Cho Song Kum, Choi Jang Jip, Scott Kalb, Sean Goldrick, Jang Jung Soo, Hahn Changgi, Han Bae Ho, Kim Mol Yong, Eunice Yoo Sook Kim, Richard Kim, Kwon Hyog Myon, Father Jack Trisolini, Father Basil Price, John V. Daley and Yi Moo Sul.

Amnesty International and Asia Watch provided, through their meticulously researched reports, the sort of evidence about official abuses and wrongdoings that for so long were so difficult to come by in Korea.

One of the pleasures of being in Korea was the company of the foreign journalists who covered the country. I am grateful for their friendship and for the time spent together at what seemed like one too many student demonstrations and political rallies. My thanks to Tom Ashbrook, Tony Barbieri, Nathan Benn, Jacques Boyer, John Burgess, Peter Cave, Charlie Cole, Roger Crabb, Greg Davis, Bob Deans, Kim Ferraro, Boyd Gibbons, Barry Hillenbrand, Clyde Haberman, Simon Holberton, Fred Hiatt, Bradley Martin, Peter Maass, Karl Schoenberger, Jim Nachtwey, Lew Simons, Dan Sneider, David Watts and Ed White.

I am grateful for the patience of my editor, Ann Godoff, but even more so for the ambitious ways she thinks of books. I am grateful, as well, to my wise and incisive agent, Barney Karpfinger. Miles Corwin, Sam Freedman, Donald McNeil and James Shapiro read the manuscript and provided invaluable advice.

The introduction to this book was written by my wife, Susan Chira. The beginning of her discovery of Korea, through her reporting for *The New York Times,* preceded mine. Her passion about the country was infectious. The joy in writing this book was in discovering Korea with her.

Contents

Introduction

*B*Y all rights, South Korea—this engaging, infuriating, improbable country—should not, cannot, exist. To the north loom well-armed brothers and enemies, maddeningly similar in stubbornness and xenophobia but startlingly different in their choice of political and economic systems. Within South Korea's borders a deceptively homogeneous people square off at countless provocations, real or imagined. Politics, regional rivalry, lineage and education will divide South Koreans as quickly as a perceived national slight will unite them.

Yet in barely three decades this tiny, contentious, resource-poor nation has transformed itself into a burgeoning economic power challenging American manufacturers of cars, computers and consumer goods. Korean immigrants began showing up in American cities as successful shopkeepers, greengrocers, entrepreneurs and businessmen.

While Korea's neighbor and nemesis, Japan, was undergoing a similar transformation, the West paid scant attention until crises broke out—first war, and then trade war. But Americans assumed that Japanese society mirrored theirs, that the Japanese were rebuilding not only roads and buildings but also their culture to make them more like those of the United States. We are only now discovering that the Japanese have instead fashioned their own distinct economic and political systems.

Now South Korea is embarking on an uncertain but crucial experiment—how to fashion a democracy from dictatorship in a nation with a tradition of hierarchy and absolutism. And Americans have a chance to pay attention early, to see what this economic power-house comes up with.

Like the Philippines, Taiwan, Brazil and Argentina, South Korea is testing whether the transition from dictatorship to democracy—in some cases, under the stewardship of the same military leaders who presided over absolutism—can work. The verdict is not yet in. But the struggle is riveting.

South Korea's is a task made harder and more complicated by its own long-standing conflicts. This is a society where rulers have brutally repressed dissent while desperately seeking legitimacy, where subjects at once revere authority and resent it, where people practice extraordinary self-control and let loose with equal intensity.

My first glimpse of these anomalies came in December 1984, during three days of whirlwind meetings with senior economic policymakers. The 1988 Olympics were far ahead, the Hyundai car had not yet conquered the American market and South Korea was, as usual, on the periphery of the American imagination.

A period of relative political quiescence was drawing to a close. A populace long silenced by terror was beginning to grow bolder as the government gradually lifted some of its controls. With police banished from campuses for the first time in years, students were demonstrating. Although intelligence agents continued to arrest and torture them, labor organizers were stepping up their efforts.

South Korea's economy was booming and as a colleague and I were whisked in and out of the offices of the nation's top economic advisers, I caught a hint of defensiveness underlying the proud recital of South Korea's accomplishments. Once in a while, amid the litany of impressive statistics and the talk of containing inflation, I would raise the issue of politics. A pained smile would appear on the officials' faces, as if I had talked of sex in church. As economists, they assured me, they had nothing to do with the political side of President Chun Doo Hwan's government. But they rejected as unfair any hint that the state was repressive. President Chun had ended his earlier ban on political activity for several opposition politicians, allowed them to form a genuine opposition party and would permit legislative elections later that winter.

In the same breath they denounced political opponents as deluded Marxist revolutionaries or troublemakers naive not only about politics but also about economics. Officials, many with graduate degrees from the United States, often spoke of "democratization" and insisted they were preparing an untutored, volatile populace for the responsibilities of democracy. South Korea had prospered, they said, because political turmoil had been kept to a minimum. The code word was *stability*.

Indeed, South Korea did not feel like a totalitarian state. Even in its harshest days it was never as regimented as the Soviet Union or China or its neighbor to the north. Koreans are not a people easily cowed. They did not slink past the ubiquitous policemen standing guard at the entrances to Seoul's myriad underground passageways or blink at the sight of riot police massing outside university campuses. People poked sly fun at President Chun, saying they would regularly turn on the nightly news ten minutes late, after the requisite footage of the stern-faced president touring the Demilitarized Zone or accepting wreaths from children.

On days when the headlines were full of their leaders' dire warnings of impending social chaos and imminent crackdown, shoppers continued to crowd open-air markets, where sellers squatted beside mounds of peanuts, red peppers and garlic. They traded jokes and insults, their lined faces speaking of cares more pressing than who was in or out of power.

For those South Koreans who saved their fervor for the workplace, life was getting better. More had television sets, refrigerators and a roof over their head; fewer went hungry. But stepping over the line meant swift reprisals—warnings from the local policeman if you were lucky; sudden arrest and torture if you were not.

South Korea's dictatorship was a curious blend of terror and tolerance, grimness and absurdity. It was a regime that did not hesitate to deploy thousands of Darth Vader–helmeted riot police to hold back a few thousand marching students and politicians who did not like the government. Its intelligence agents could spirit opponents away and torture them at will, march errant journalists into headquarters and beat them up, tap phones and open letters.

It could also police ideas. Communism is illegal in South Korea. To protect the public from its pernicious and dangerous ideas, the state screened and banned thousands of songs, books and movies. Writers and students were imprisoned for advocating vaguely defined "anti-state" ideas, even for writing novels or poems that could be construed, because they had workers as oppressed heroes or alluded to historical rebellions, as anti-state. Thus to have Marcuse on your bookshelf could be evidence of anti-state intent and students and labor organizers who wrote about class conflict or imperialist oppression were dangerous radicals out to destroy the state. Government officials educated in the West rivaled the most adept philosophers in the logical contortions they marshaled to draw lines between what was anti-government, and thus permissible, and what was anti-state.

The military leaders did these things, but they took pains to justify them. South Korean officials seldom tired of complaining that Korea got a bum rap, that the world's attention focused on them while their neighbors practiced far harsher forms of totalitarianism. To some degree they were right. Singapore's leaders simply locked up and tortured young professionals whom they branded dangerous dissidents. They crushed opposition movements and dismissed the world's opprobrium. Western ideas of democracy, Premier Lee Kuan Yew said, had no place in Singapore.

Not so in South Korea, where leaders constantly invoked democratic ideals even as they enforced authoritarian realities. In February 1986, a year after the opposition won an unexpectedly strong showing in legislative elections, Kim Dae Jung, its canny chief strategist, launched a brilliant and simple move. What could be more innocent than a petition drive, merely asking the Korean people whether they supported changing the constitution to permit direct elections? But the government, knowing that the public yearned for direct elections after years of rigged plebiscites, did not dare permit the drive. They deployed thousands of riot police, placed nearly three hundred legally elected opposition politicians and their aides under house arrest and bundled others into vans, letting them off miles from downtown Seoul—all to prevent a political meeting to discuss the petition drive.

This confrontation yielded vivid pictures and front-page articles and I got an early lesson in Koreaspeak. Two government officials called on me at my hotel for a polite dressing-down. I was wrong to use the phrase *house arrest* to describe the confinement of opposition politicians to their homes by rows of policemen. The government was merely thinking of them, keeping politicians in their homes so they would not commit a crime by supporting the banned petition drive. Reporters should call that *preventive detention.*

Moreover, I had failed to divine the real motives behind the opposition petition drive. This was no exercise of free expression, but a plot to overthrow the government. The officials handed me a two-page note entitled "Misleading Terms Used by the Foreign Press in Reporting Recent Developments in Korea." "There is some concern," the note read, "that the two terms 'house arrest' and 'petition drive,' taken out of context and read in an information vacuum, will lead to the conclusion that Koreans are being arrested for simply filing a petition and this is not true."

Korea's leaders cared what others thought of them and, true to their Confucian heritage, cared how history would judge them. Such scruples, as other dictators have discovered before, make it more difficult to cling to power.

In 1984, when I first went to South Korea, President Chun and his advisers were busy polishing their image for posterity. It was just four years earlier that Chun had shocked and terrified the nation into submission by sending troops to crush a civil uprising in the southwestern city of Kwangju. Like Tiananmen Square for the Chinese, Kwangju represented the ultimate, until then unthinkable, brutality—that troops would mow down South Korea's own people. Chun moved decisively to quash rebellion and bring the country under his control. He rounded up thousands of vagrants and political activists in camps, where at least fifty people died after being forced to crawl over broken glass and join work teams to build roads. Chun slapped student leaders into "reeducation" camps, set professors to report on students and installed government-controlled student organizations. He forced newspaper publishers and television station owners to merge, consolidating his control over the press. He banned hundreds of opposition politicians from politics and toughened laws against union organizing.

Koreans put their heads down, went back to work and clammed up about politics. And so after a few years Chun began to let up. He ended a curfew that had been in place since the Korean War, allowing night life on South Korean streets. He abolished required school uniforms and withdrew police from campuses. He lifted the bans on some opposition politicians and allowed Kim Dae Jung, whose very name prompted apoplectic rages among government officials, to return from his American exile.

For a man capable of such ruthless brutality, Chun had a curious vulnerability. He wanted not to be liked but to be justified by history. He pledged from the beginning that he would step down after one term, unlike other postwar Korean leaders, who seized power and did not voluntarily yield it.

In the Confucian philosophy that dominated Korea for centuries, the ruler had absolute power but lost the mandate of heaven if he turned to tyranny. While Korea's rapid industrialization eroded some of its Confucian heritage, Korean political rhetoric remained infused with Confucian ideals. Chun wanted the mandate, not only from the Korean people but from a world that had long dismissed or exploited his country. In his quest for the legitimacy that eluded him, he made occasional bows to public opinion. Yet when Chun lifted the lid, the steam shot out, scalding his hand. He kept trying to shove the lid down again, but his burns got worse every time.

The real turnaround came in February 1985, when Chun allowed elections for the legislature and the unbanned opposition politicians began to organize. The election was blatantly weighted against the opposition, with rules restricting rallies and forbidding its members to criticize the government directly. But the government won only 35 percent of the vote, with the major opposition party capturing nearly 30 percent. Now the opposition had a clear popular mandate, as well as some institutional legitimacy and protection. And it had Kim Dae Jung, who worked as a strategist behind the scenes, although he was still banned from open political activity as an unpardoned criminal on a suspended sentence. The government had branded Kim an instigator of the Kwangju rebellion and had sentenced him to death in 1981 but yielded to pressure from the United States and instead allowed him to live in exile.

He and Kim Young Sam, his opposition rival, launched the petition drive for direct elections in 1986. Stung by unusually harsh criticism from the United States and spooked by comparisons with the Philippines, where Ferdinand Marcos had just been deposed, Chun suddenly reversed himself. He had long insisted that any constitutional revision be put off in the spirit of Grand Harmony until the Great National Task of the 1988 Seoul Olympics. But he said he would discuss constitutional changes.

All through the winter and spring the issue remained deadlocked as the opposition parties held out for a referendum rather than voting on constitutional revision in the legislature, where the government still had a majority. Then the opposition upped the ante again, staging rallies and calling for direct elections in major cities. The rallies drew tens of thousands of people, the biggest crowds since the demonstrations of 1980 that led up to the Kwangju massacre.

Stunned by the resurgence of political protest since the 1985 elections, the government began clamping down. For the most part officials left elected opposition legislators alone. But they banned books, launched dragnets to capture student leaders suspected of subscribing to such dangerous dogmas as class analysis, tortured Kim Keun Tae and other leading labor activists, arrested opposition clergymen and beat up journalists who violated press guidelines on what they could publish. In the fall of 1986 Chun deployed tens of thousands of police in a massive show of force to crush planned opposition protests.

The deadlock on constitutional revision continued. But ordinary Koreans, who had generally left political agitation to the professionals, were shocked out of their silence when news emerged of the torture death in January 1987 of Park Chong Chol, a student being questioned about the whereabouts of some of his politically active friends. That winter hints of large-scale corruption, long rumored, began to surface. In April, perhaps sensing his increasing vulnerability, Chun acted. He abruptly forbade further discussion of direct elections until after the Olympics. And on June 10 he presided over the anointing of his handpicked successor, Roh Tae Woo, at his party's presidential convention. Without any changes in the constitution, Roh was all but guaranteed of winning the December 1987 presidential election. Pictures of the two men, holding their clasped hands high above their heads in an arrogant tableau of victory, flashed through Korea.

The nation exploded in protest. Students, clergymen, opposition leaders and, for a change, ordinary people took to the streets in cities across the country for three weeks of continuous demonstrations. Rumors flew that the military, for the third time in three decades, would step in to crush the protests. A chastened but savvy Roh Tae Woo backed down, prodding Chun to agree to all the opposition's demands and setting the stage for the first free elections in sixteen years.

It was a stunning reversal. But few Koreans, even those in the opposition, felt triumphant. For it was after June 1987 that an even more difficult task began—how to move toward democracy in a society suffused with authoritarianism: in politics, at work, at home, in school. Repressive laws, interpreted and enforced by prosecutors and judges swayed by those in power, belied constitutional guarantees of civil rights and civil liberties. Intelligence agents could investigate and interrogate political dissidents at will. Police could jail without retrial people with criminal records. A National Security Law mandated harsh penalties for "anti-state" organizations, a term so loosely defined it could and did cover some opposition groups.

Democracy may have been the chant on protesters' lips, but those protesters had little more understanding of the ideal than did the rulers they fought. The same students who stood so bravely at the barricades enduring tear gas, beatings and even torture in the name of democracy would tolerate no deviation from their political line. The same opposition leaders who spent their lives in and out of jail because they dared speak out against dictators brooked no opposition from their followers. In the offices and factories where Korea's economic boom was built, the boss's word was law and workers leapt to attention when a superior entered the room. Few Korean children would dream of defying their parents when choosing a mate or a child's name. Many of democracy's most basic tenets—the belief that the public can be trusted to hear heretical ideas or make wise decisions, the faith that losers will have a chance to try again, the concept of a loyal opposition—are undermined by an elitism and an ethic of control with deep roots in Korea's past.

For centuries Korea was a society in which everyone was rooted in a village, bound by the village's moral codes and fixed hierarchies. At the apex stood the king and the court, where the losers of ideological or factional battles lost everything: position, privilege and often their lives as well. A small group of landed aristocrats ruled absolutely over a large peasant population, including many slaves, owned outright by the landed gentry. A Confucian ideology imported from China and enforced more rigidly in its adopted country than its native land extended from the king's court to the smallest village, freezing Korea in time.

Even in the most rigid days of Confucian orthodoxy conflicts that would later shape South Korea's fledgling democracy boiled below the surface. The reserved aristocrats spent their days studying Chinese classics or painting delicate landscapes in faint hues. Farmers and servants formed a vibrant culture of their own—of whirling dances punctuated by cymbals and drums, of folk art painted in bold shades of blue and red, of open expression of emotions that horrified their aristocratic rulers.

The ravages of Japanese occupation, civil war and economic growth destroyed that society but not all of its values. Those who would fashion a democracy had to contend not only with the unresolved conflicts of the past but also the unsettling legacies of South Korea's phenomenal economic success.

In less than a generation South Korea achieved transformations that took centuries in most Western nations. An overwhelmingly rural population moved to the cities, creating new slums overnight. The government led Koreans on a forced march toward industrialization, compressing all the upheaval and degradation of any industrial revolution into a few decades. Most workers endured Dickensian conditions, but the economy flourished and the lucky workers graduated from bicycles to motorcycles, from shacks to cramped company apartments. Economic planners nurtured and directed growth, using tax breaks and low-interest loans to steer entrepreneurs into export-oriented industries. A push toward heavy industry—construction, shipbuilding, steel, automobiles—and a more recent investment in high technology—computers, electronics, telecommunications systems—drove South Korea past such regional rivals as Taiwan to challenge Japan and America.

The desperate struggle, at first to survive and later to excel, left little room for the old precepts. Upstart entrepreneurs catapulted past their neighbors, winning wealth, power and political influence regardless of their antecedents. The young did not always bow to the old. Workers began to grumble about the gaps between the haves and have-nots. New foreign patrons, the Americans and the Russians, exposed Koreans to alien ideas like democracy, egalitarianism and Marxism.

South Korea in 1987 was a society unsure of which traditions to preserve and which to scuttle. What was democracy and how could it be adapted to suit Korean culture? What was too much freedom and what too little?

These conflicts boiled over after the lid was finally blown off in June. A wave of strikes swept across the country as workers tested the limits of the new order and pressed for their fair share of South

Korea's prosperity. Caddies walked off golf courses. Students sacked professors' offices and demanded that those who had supported the government resign. Chun unsuccessfully struck the old chords, warning of conspiracies and extremists and social chaos.

Helped by a split opposition ticket, Roh Tae Woo won the presidency in December and set about creating a new man-of-the-people image. But little of real substance changed until the opposition parties won an unexpected and crucial victory in April, forcing the government to share power with the opposition for the first time. Old rhythms held sway, but new ideas burst upon a nation in ferment. No one knew just how Korea's experiment would turn out, but for a change people were tuning in. The June demonstrations had dominated the U.S. television news, with their shocking, vivid scenes of a Darth Vader–helmeted riot policeman, his clothes in flames, retreating before a band of students; crude Molotov cocktails exploding, sending flares over nighttime Seoul; elderly housewives with their hair decorously permed screaming at riot policemen and beating them with their handbags. Viewers had heard commentators asking whether Seoul was a safe place to hold the Olympics. And as the Games approached, as Korea became something more than the setting for "M*A*S*H," people began to watch and wait.

SUSAN CHIRA

October 1988: The Closing Ceremonies

*I*N central Seoul, on a boulevard wide enough for tanks to pass, sits an unintentional monument to bitterness. Koreans call this bitterness han. Han is the result of injustices perpetrated by, among others, parents, friends, siblings, a colonial ruler, an occupying army, past governments, the present government, and those who in crucial moments failed to display sincerity.

When I mention the building to Koreans they say, "Yes, that would represent han." But they see no need to make the designation themselves. The monument is a long and squat stone building with a pillared facade and green dome. It was, for thirty-five years, the headquarters of the Japanese colonial government. The Japanese, late entrants into the colonial game but nonetheless quick learners, situated their headquarters so that it blocked from view the Kyongbok Palace, where Korea's kings had lived for centuries. In this way Koreans were to understand who ruled them.

There is now a reconstructed Kyongbok Palace and guided tours are conducted in Korean, English and Japanese. But you still cannot see the palace as you look up this wide boulevard because standing in its way is the heavy, gray vestige of Japanese imperial rule, rule that forbade the speaking of the Korean language or the use of Korean names and which pressed eight hundred thousand Koreans into slave labor.

I ask Koreans, "Why was that building never torn down?" I am offered explanations about Korea's having been such a poor country that the cost of demolition would have been too great or that with so much rebuilding to do, the nation never got around to it. I bring to this question the assumption that so obvious a reminder of misery would be an early target for eradication. I thought this way until a Korean friend told me that I was applying my idea of the building as a monument incorrectly: We live with the building, she said, the way we live with our bitterness, our han. It is a fact of our lives.

I have been in South Korea on and off for much of the year and have begun to feel as if I were locked in a small room with a manic-depressive, feeling the alternating pulses of ebullience and melancholy. I long for the comfortable gray of the in-between, where a bad day can be dismissed as a bad day and not proof positive of the inevitability of tragedy. But in Korea everything matters. There is winning and losing and no such thing as the contest well played. Winners take the spoils and gloat, while losers nurse their bitterness. Losers have nothing. Winners are not forgiven.

Life feels relentless. The alleys of the outdoor markets are jammed and the goods a jumble and the burly young men who do the hawking stand on wooden platforms, stomping and clapping. Old women squat on the pavement, selling dried fish, and do not move when the motorcycles rumble past, their loads piled ten feet high. Crippled young men, shriveled legs wrapped in strips of rubber, wheel themselves between the pushcarts, singing for handouts. Machinists and glass cutters work on the sidewalks and people step over and around them and over and around the cassette-tape peddlers, whose pushcart speakers provide an accompaniment of sentimental saxophone music. Beggars holding infants perch on the steps of the overhead walkways and those who do not keep up with the pedestrian traffic are in danger of being trampled underfoot. At lunchtime the businessmen eat fast and then hurry to the coffee shops with the blacked-out windows, where they can rush down a cup while fondling the breasts of the young women hired for just that purpose.

On thoroughfares now insufficient for the traffic cars honk their horns whether they need to or not. Buses cut off taxis, which cut off trucks, which cut off the polished black limousines with telephones in the backseats. Drivers lean out their windows to curse. Often they fight. They get out of their cars and begin the ritual shoving. The fight is like a schoolyard fight—"Oh yeah . . . Up yours . . . Your mother . . ." Shirts are grabbed and words exchanged and traffic will back up for a block or two with everyone else honking his horn. When Korean men get drunk, which they do often at the end of the day, they will first slow-dance with each other. Then they fight.

The passion makes Seoul feel like the most dynamic place in the world. There is always conflict, always the dramatic display. But the conflict is not resolved. It builds and builds and gets stored away, but not neatly enough to allay fears about its suddenly bursting. A quarter of the nation's 40 million people live in Seoul and the city feels as if they are all marching at the same time. They are all marching toward the same place, competing for the same spot, elbowing each other out of the way, sure that they are being cheated of their rightful place, all the while accumulating hurt feelings over what was done to them along the way. If they do not win, then they will lose and if they lose, they have nothing. Each day in Korea somebody is fighting and losing to another fellow, who is always wrong and who will not be forgiven.

The han does not go away. Successive generations tried and failed to resolve the bitterness. The generation now at the universities, however, believes it has the answer. Its ideas are clear—rid the nation of the military men in power; keep the foreign powers out of Korea's affairs; return the nation to the unified, independent state it was a long time ago. This generation has never mentioned the Olympic Games, which end today. For a long time I made the mistake of thinking that the Olympic Games might help end the bitterness. But I have learned that the Games are a show for the rest of the world, as choreographed by a government that sounds like an effervescent caterer reminding the help to smile when the guests arrive. The world's approval will not erase the han.

Though the students are sure of what is necessary for eradicating the bitterness, they are less clear about what they are trying to rid themselves of. Han, like love, is a feeling universally recognized but resistant to definition.

There is the han of the police state and the han of progress. There is the han imposed by outsiders—especially the great powers, most especially the United States. And then there is the han that is not acknowledged, the han of the hatreds and cruelties the Koreans will inflict upon one another. It is not acknowledged because it is not supposed to exist. Unlike love, han is always imposed.

* * *

I have waited until the finish of the Olympic marathon and then gone to the airport. At the duty-free shop the Russian athletes crowd the jewelry counters. I check my watch and board early. I had planned to wait for the closing ceremonies, the fireworks and the day-after reflections. But I am drained by Korea. I am exhausted by its moods.

The two weeks of the Games had begun so well. On the night before the opening ceremonies I went to the Seoul city hall plaza, where a crowd had gathered to see the Olympic flame. Families lined up in front of the flame for snapshots. Buoyant music played. It was midnight and children were out with their parents. This was not a party for the guests. The endlessly rehearsed choreography would begin in the morning and people would be expected to be on hand, helping out and looking their best. This, however, was their moment. And in the early hours of the first day of the Seoul Olympics, Korean people pressed close together, beaming, staring at the fire that had come to their country.

Nothing was going to go wrong. The Games had been planned for seven years. Stadiums were built. The subway was dug. Seoul's murky Han River was dredged. Neighborhoods of old houses with sagging tile roofs were leveled and replaced with high rises and parking lots so that Korea would look like a wealthy country. Cabbies were given rudimentary English courses by radio—"May I show you my brochure of hotels?" Derelicts were rounded up and deposited in places where the foreigners could not see them. Street vendors were told to pack up their carts for the duration of the Games.

The nation's Olympic team was sent to army boot camp to heighten its competitive spirit. The anti-terrorist squad practiced responding to hostage takings and attacks on the main stadium. The security guards were taught to be friendly and smile when they inspected bags.

The sun shone for the opening ceremonies and in the days that followed it rained only once, and then only briefly. There was no boycott. There were no terrorists. The Games that were hoped for and worked for and planned to the last seemingly insignificant detail had come together and South Korea was showing the world that it was no longer a place to be overlooked.

But the good feeling did not last. The mood turned sour. The change came abruptly. And as so often happens in Korea, it started with a fight. It was a fight much like the fights I'd seen most every time I'd come to Seoul. There were fights between two drivers accusing one another of cutting each other off; there were fistfights between men and women. People stood around and watched for a while. But then the combatants would grab each other by the arms or collar and lock each other in an impossible knot. They'd be left to curse and snarl at one another until the police came to break them up.

But the world got to watch the fight that sullied the Games. It was played again and again on the television so that everyone would get to see it. The fight began when a Korean boxer lost a boxing match to a Hungarian because a judge from New Zealand penalized him. Perhaps the judge was right. And perhaps he was not. The Korean's seconds reached a quick consensus. They charged the ring. They pummeled the referee. A Korean security man pulled off his jacket and joined the assault. The Koreans looked as if they wanted to kill the man. The boxer sat in a ring corner for over an hour to protest his loss. The referee fled the country. The next day brought contrition and statements of shame.

The day after brought anger and accusations that the foreigners had deliberately humiliated Korea. Couldn't they see that the referee was wrong? *Doubtless* was the operative word. Doubtless the referee was incompetent. Doubtless the American broadcaster, NBC, was biased in its coverage. Doubtless the Korean boxer and his countrymen were the victims of unsympathetic coverage. NBC people vrere advised to hide their credentials for fear of reprisals.

People talked about the fight and analyzed it and stewed over it. And when asked why it wasn't dropped, why they couldn't just enjoy the rest of their party, they replied that that, of course, is what a foreigner would say, doubtless an imperialist foreigner, callous and insensitive to the feelings of the Korean people.

I had heard it too many times in too many different instances and I did not want to listen anymore. So as soon as the marathon was over, as soon as it was clear that radical students would not toss firebombs at the runners, I hurried to the airport to catch the last flight of the day. I did not want to wait until the morning.

In my moment of flight I almost forgot a time when I could not wait to come back to Korea, when the passion now so wearying felt so magnetic, the pull so strong that it could draw me back again and again.

* * *

I had first come in May of 1985, arriving, by chance, the week that students occupied the United States Information Service building in downtown Seoul. Korea excited me. Life here had an edge: students tossing proclamation leaflets from windows bedecked with banners written in red; the phalanx of helmeted riot police; plainclothesmen smiling menacing smiles; the rumors of an assault on the building and the threatened group suicide.

I came back several times a year after that, sometimes for work, sometimes just because I liked the place. I was living in Tokyo, which had none of Seoul's vibrancy, none of its life. In the capital, Seoul, people spoke in loud voices and ate spicy food that made their breath reek of garlic. Men put their hands on your leg when they talked and women laughed with their mouths wide open. You were inundated with opinions. If you asked one person what he thought and happened to be writing things down, someone else came over, and then another and another, and very quickly you had maybe twenty or thirty people standing around you hurling points of view, correcting one another, interrupting. Then someone would laugh and so too would another. Sometimes they laughed at me, especially when I attempted my few words of poorly pronounced Korean. Nothing was feigned, not pleasure nor anger nor even contempt.

At night young men walked hand in hand, as did the young women. They congregated, by sex, at the food carts that sat where the buses stopped along boulevards. The exhaust fumes were thick and noxious but the women ate rice cakes and the men sucked down clams and everyone talked at once. When the nights were warm, the men spread newspapers on the ground and with jackets off but ties still knotted poured soju—a cheap rice wine—for each other and got very drunk. When the time came to go home, they sprinted for the departing buses, dodged each other, calling out their good-byes.

I learned a little as I went along, hearing unfamiliar names and stories of tragedies that I was sure I must have known of but probably forgot. I heard names like Chun Doo Hwan and Kim Dae Jung and Kim Young Sam. No one talked much about Roh Tae Woo then. I heard about Kwangju. I heard about the 1979 coup that followed the assassination of the president, Park Chung Hee—Park I knew; he'd been around for eighteen years, long enough for the name to crop up. And I heard, again and again, about Kwangju, the officials' version and the dissidents' version and the Amnesty International version, which seemed to combine enough of the others to sound the most plausible. And I was more than a little ashamed to admit that I did not remember that in the spring of 1980 the South Korean army put down a civil uprising in the southern city of Kwangju by killing between 191 people—if you believed the government—and 2,000— if you believed the dissidents. Hundreds seemed the best guess.

Still, Korea was for me a country with no face, save for the increasingly familiar one of the families that ran the vegetable stands in Manhattan, where I had lived. It was a country, or rather two countries, stuck in my imagination between Japan and China, which meant that it did not register. I heard that the South Koreans made good radios and cars. And I also watched "M*A*S*H."

When I say I learned a little as I went along, I mean that I came to know a bit about a few things—preparations for the Olympics then several years hence; the sorry fate of the Korean professional boxing business (who wanted to go to the fights and risk having a chair thrown at your head when you could now go to the ball game or, better still, stay home and watch either on your TV?); and the sudden wealth of young American men who had come to Korea in the Peace Corps and were now working as investment bankers (there was money to be made in Seoul and the people who knew something about making money were getting themselves in place). But that was little more than a smattering, as insignificant as trying to draw deductions about Korean social mores from an evening spent watching American men and Korean women dance around each other—both literally and figuratively—in the Sportsman's Club in Seoul's Itaewon bar district.

None of it prepared me for June of 1987, when my education began and when a curiosity born of several pleasing visits blossomed into a fascination with a people whose passion drew me in with a strength equal to that with which it could drive me away. What began as an education about a revolution of rising expectations, however, became instead a lesson on the nature of those passions— passions that could drive a society and make it stand stock still, that could make it capable simultaneously of love and hate, that spilled from one to the next so quickly that I as a Westerner, seeking clarity, seeking one or the other, was lost between them.

"Can you live with happiness and sadness at the same time?" a Korean friend once asked me.

"No," I replied, thinking the answer obvious.

But he said, "We do."

I had spent this seminal year in the nation's life looking less at events than at a succession of dramas. Some were of consequence to the nation; others mattered only to the protagonists.

These were dramas without the clean lines of beginning, middle and end. Something happened and then something else followed and feelings were aroused. The dramas sustained themselves through two seemingly contradictory but nonetheless companion passions: the bitterness of han and the love called jong. Han alone would have made Korea a dull place, angry, resentful and self-pitying. But jong was han's equal.

Jong transcended affection. It was a bond, an unspoken understanding that connected people at the hip, for now and forever. Jong could feel warm and inviting and it could feel like a hug from a strong man showing off his strength. If han was the instrument of estrangement, then jong was the glue—an analogy Koreans themselves drew when they talked of the "sticky jong," love coupled with debts that could not be forgiven.

Jong was the fifty-year friendship that ended at death, the grandson washing his grandfather's back in the bath, the endless handshake, but it also was the mother moving in with her son and daughter-in-law because that daughter-in-law's cleaning and cooking were payment for years of the mother's doting on the son. Jong could smother, but it was also the necessary leaven, because the bitterness never seemed to go away.

Han was not static. It bubbled and surfaced in words and responses and then slipped from view. The motion paralleled the nation's capacity to embrace its bitterness while at the same time trying to wrest itself free. Part of feeling han was trying to be rid of the feeling. Korea had a dance for this. It was called salpuri and women danced it because it was said that women's han was the greater—the centuries-old han of being forced to stay indoors by day and wash the clothing at night, the han of a slave's existence. Salpuri was danced in white and the only prop was a white scarf. It was danced slowly and intricately and unless true feeling was displayed, the dance was meaningless. Salpuri well danced was a catharsis, a short-lived exorcism of han.

"Han is a tangled emotion," a university student named P. C. Chung told me before a march to the border to unify the nation. "We want to untangle this han."

Yet in the remarkable year before the Games began—and in the months just after they ended—I found myself wondering whether I was, in fact, seeing the beginning of the "untangling" of the han. It was as if the nation were collectively caught up in the game Korean mothers had for centuries taught their idle restless daughters. The daughter was handed a mass of knotted string and told to take it apart. When she was done taking it apart, she was told to tie it back together.

The collective unraveling began in June of 1987 and it had not stopped. After the June demonstrations came the August strikes, three thousand of them. After the strikes came the presidential election forced by the June demonstrations—the first chance the nation had had to freely choose its leader in sixteen years. After the presidential election came the National Assembly election—the first time the nation's military-backed governments were forced to share power. Political prisoners were freed; the torture ended; the press was freed. The past was unearthed, so the nation could begin to see the roots of its bitterness.

There were stops and starts, but the unraveling continued with such relentlessness that I wondered whether the process could ever be reversed, whether the knot might be wound anew. The unraveling took place in the seats of power, in the factories, coffee houses, sweatshops, cities, villages and farm towns. It took place between the rulers and the ruled, between bosses and workers, men and women, parents and children, lovers and friends.

Korea's winter of 1988 was bitter cold. But in spring, as the land thawed, the pace of life quickened. The ferment continued through the summer and into the fall, with the Games serving only as a brief interruption. In those twelve months I witnessed dramas on two levels: the national and the personal. Beneath the dramas that would change Korea as a nation there were seemingly lesser stories of men and women wrestling with the pain of bitterness and the occasional suffocation of love.

Between the election campaign, the strikes, the talks between North Korea and South Korea and the student demonstrations, I met, among many others, a man caught between his parents and the woman he loved; a father agonizing over the torture death of his son; a woman mired in a country town, selling coffee and squeezes; a rich man lamenting what he'd lost in his quest for respect; an elderly man in search of a family unseen in a generation; a fortune-teller; an aging dancer; and a sweatshop girl confused by love.

The changes that transformed Korea from police state to budding democracy not only made the year so important; together with the smaller, disconnected struggles they revealed the soul of a nation caught between absorption with its past and a compulsion to outrace the world into the future.

As compelling as I found the present, I too became consumed by the past, because it was in the past that the han was buried. I wanted to know the nature of the bitterness, because then I might know whether it could ever disappear.

The year began for me in the city of Kwangju, where the han was deepest. It ended in Seoul, on a quiet mountainside on a day so tranquil that the drama of the year felt as distant as the city far below, a city with a heavy stone monument in its heart.

WINTER

*I*N winter a hard freeze settles over Korea. The cold air blows down from Siberia. There is heavy snow in the mountains. The city streets are dusted with snow and the alleys are covered with ice so thick it will not thaw till spring.

Winter is a season for long underwear and imitation down jackets, for thick gloves and heavy sweaters worn indoors. It is the season of the charcoal peddler pushing his cart laden with bricks the size of coffee cans. The bricks heat the older houses and restaurants. In winter the best seats in the restaurants are near the space heaters whose tin chimneys run across the ceiling and out the window. At home the warmest place is on the floor. The charcoal heats the hard, yellow floors from below. People eat on the floor, watch TV on the floor, sleep on the floor. Sometimes, in the old homes, there are cracks in the floors and the carbon monoxide seeps through. Three thousand people would die during the winter of carbon monoxide poisoning as they tried to stay warm on the cold nights.

In the winter of 1988 an enlisted man opened fire in his barracks with an M-16, killing three men and injuring three others. He was angry with his corporal for berating him.

In Seoul the government shut down the play *Prostitution* after the producers refused to eliminate the explicit sexual language from the script. The changes were suggested by the Korean Ethics Committee of Public Performances, a group with government ties. Parents had picketed *Prostitution*, claiming it was harmful to their children. They carried signs reading STOP STAGING PORNOGRAPHY. The closing of the play enraged the artistic community, which feared that it might

23

foreshadow a return to the days, not long before, when all scripts were reviewed by a government censor. But a few weeks after *Prostitution* was closed, the ruling party introduced a bill eliminating the last of the censorship requirements.

In Puchon a retired electrician confessed to sending a parcel bomb that seriously injured the parents of a young man who had been sleeping with his wife. The electrician said that he only wanted to see his wife again. The wife, a beer hall owner, had been gone for months.

A survey of students at Seoul National University, the nation's most prestigious school, reported widespread anti-American feelings among the freshman class. The overwhelming number of students surveyed characterized the United States as a "deceptive" country. The students said that they learned about America from books, newspapers, professors and upperclassmen.

A riot policeman deserted his unit after declaring that the riot police should be disbanded because they were an instrument of authoritarian rule. He disappeared after making his statement at the office of the National Council of Churches, a dissident organization. The policeman had been a student at the Korean Baptist Theological College. Many college students performed their army service in the riot police—rather than as enlisted men—although this sometimes meant having to fire tear gas at their classmates. The police sent the deserted policeman's uncle to plead with him to surrender. But the policeman could not be found.

The winter of 1988 began with the presidential election, an event unimaginable a year before. The election culminated the revolution that began in the streets in June, spread to the factories in August and then grew in passion and intensity on the campaign trail throughout the fall.

The election capped a vibrant fall. On chilly Saturday and Sunday afternoons the candidates appeared at outdoor campaign rallies. Hundreds of thousands of people attended these rallies. They gathered in city squares or in fields at the edges of the cities. There were parades with marching bands playing "Danny Boy" and "Bessame' Mucho." There was traditional drum, cymbal and flute music. Dancers danced folk dances that grew frenzied as the music got raucous. Peddlers did a brisk trade in noodles and rice wine as well as binoculars for seeing the candidates from a great distance. People arrived early and sat on the ground, waiting for their candidate. They pressed close together, eating, laughing, waving their paper flags when the preliminary speakers extolled the candidate's virtues.

The candidates appeared on television and gave speeches to various associations. But the rallies were the heart of the campaign. They were celebrations of the new order. You could go to a rally and yell yourself hoarse. The police were not going to take you away or choke you with tear gas or knock on your door late at night. You could scream cruel things about the government. You could chant praises of the candidate you liked. You could do this in the company of hundreds of thousands of people who felt as you did. The crowds at the rallies reminded me of sailors on shore leave after months at sea. They couldn't wait to celebrate.

The government had not wanted this election. It fought hard to prevent it. During the spring it ordered thousands of its riot policemen and martial arts squads to clear the streets of all the people calling for an end to the military-backed government. The government did as Korean governments had always done, which was to respond to the demands by showing its muscle. Its spokesmen warned of the dire consequences of resistance. But the riot policemen, who'd always imposed order before, could not clear the streets of all the people turning against the government.

The demonstrations began in June, when the feared and hated president, Chun Doo Hwan, raised the hand of his designated successor at a party convention, thus anointing him. That night students occupied the Myongdong Cathedral in central Seoul, calling for free and open elections. Chun said this was impossible. The Olympics were a year away, he declared, and he would not allow the nation to suffer the instability of an election while it was preparing to host the world. For the next three weeks, after the national anthem played at six in the evening on public-address speakers, tens of thousands of people gathered at Myongdong and at the traffic rotaries, railway stations and municipal halls, where the students sat and chanted and punched their fists into the air.

The students threw rocks at the riot police. Men in blue suits and women in summer dresses—the growing middle class who the government insisted longed for stability—this time lined the sidewalks. They applauded the students. They chanted with them. Cab drivers honked their horns in support of the students. Old women walked up to the riot police and smacked their shields with their purses. Teams of riot policemen were outnumbered and overwhelmed by crowds who stripped them of their gear. The helmets, shields and gas masks were set on fire, as were tires and police buses. The air over the cities was filled with the white haze of tear gas and the billowing black smoke of burning rubber.

There was nervous talk that spring of a coup or martial law. But there was also a sense of abandon. Parents brought their children to the demonstrations and carried them on their shoulders. Couples walked together. People were angry, but they were excited too. They were beginning to see that they did not have to be afraid of their government anymore.

Peddlers sold swimming goggles and gauze masks to protect against the searing tear gas. Many still ran from the tear gas and the riot police. But the tear gas and the blows could not erase the exhilaration of standing in the middle of the street with ten or twenty or thirty thousand people and, in a single voice, telling the government, "Go."

For three weeks it seemed as if the government would take no more. Martial law seemed imminent. Morning would bring the tanks and the killing would surely begin. And then, when the opportunity for compromise vanished, when it seemed that the army would be sent in, the government surrendered. The man whose hand Chun had hoisted at the party convention, Roh Tae Woo, went on television and announced that the people had won. He would go to Chun Doo Hwan and ask him to give them their election.

Now four men were running for president and three of them were given a chance of winning. The government candidate was Roh Tae Woo, a former general instrumental in the 1979 coup that brought Chun to power. His chief opponents were Kim Dae Jung and Kim Young Sam, the longtime leaders of the opposition. The fourth candidate was a voice from the past, Kim Jong Pil, a former prime minister who in 1961 had engineered the coup that brought Park Chung Hee to power. He and Roh were reminders that there had never been a peaceful transfer of power in the forty-year history of the Republic of Korea.

This was not an election campaign built upon platforms or ideas. The candidates all spoke about the need to break from the harsh ways of the past. They spoke about the great things they envisioned for Korea, a nation they vowed to lead into the fraternity of important countries. No campaign is without its emotional content, but in this election feelings were paramount. People loved their chosen candidate. They loved him as much as they hated his opponents. The love for Kim Dae Jung and Kim Young Sam was especially strong because it represented an equal and opposite reaction to the loathing for the government. Roh Tae Woo, though the self-anointed hero of the spring, was still the candidate of stability and stability is, by definition, a hard quality to be passionate about.

The three strongest candidates each commanded 30 percent of the vote, with the balance going to Kim Jong Pil. That meant, of course, that if either Kim Dae Jung or Kim Young Sam dropped out of the race, the other would almost certainly win.

The Kims knew this, and promised the nation throughout the fall that only one of them would run. The sad thing was that people believed them. Kim Young Sam had waited a long time to become president of Korea, almost as long as Kim Dae Jung, who had run in the last election, in 1971, and narrowly lost to Park Chung Hee in balloting widely regarded as rigged. The following year Park had the constitution rewritten, ensuring himself the presidency for life. He was assassinated in 1979. Chun Doo Hwan seized power two months later.

Ambition alone would have made the idea of a single opposition candidate unlikely. But there was a further, greater obstacle, and that was anger. Kim Dae Jung and Kim Young Sam hated each other. This hatred had long ago spread to their admirers. All the love that people felt for either of the two Kims stood in equal measure to the animosity they felt for the other. Each man entered the other's home turf at his peril.

Each waited for the other to drop out of the race. On the sidelines stood Roh Tae Woo, who after years as a loyal and quiet deputy to Chun Doo Hwan began looking like a very clever man, calling for an election that, in the best democratic tradition, he could win by splitting the opposition. It would be the people, he wagered, who would return the government to power. And the government would be stronger than ever.

On the Sunday before the presidential election I went to Kim Dae Jung's rally in Seoul. It was a cold and sunny day. The rally was held in a field on the edge of the city. A million people were there, or maybe a million and a half. Kim Dae Jung's people insisted that three million had come. I stood at the base of the tall podium where Kim Dae Jung would speak and turned to see what he would see. The color green was visible only in the distance. Spread out wide and deep before the podium was a sea of people, people calling Kim Dae Jung's name. A man approached and asked how many people I thought I saw. I wrote down the number five hundred thousand. He shook his head, took my pen, added a zero and said, "Look at all the people."

They had arrived early to eat and drink and get a spot within a quarter mile of Kim Dae Jung, who was going to deliver them from the harshness of their lives. If Kim Young Sam was the candidate of those who wanted their changes incrementally, then Kim Dae Jung was the candidate of the disenfranchised who wanted a new world now. He was a fiery speaker who could keep a million people in thrall. Kim Young Sam, dapper but bland, seemed the safe choice, the opposition candidate whose victory was least likely to bring on a coup. He had long been a member of the National Assembly and though given few points for intellectual acuity, had still gained a reputation as a man the government could not buy. People were not afraid of Kim Young Sam, not as they were of Kim Dae Jung, whom the government for years had tried to brand a traitor, a Communist, a subversive whose name and face could not appear in the newspapers.

I climbed down from the bluff where the podium stood and began working my way through the crowd on the field. Though I could no longer see the crowd, I could feel it pressing against me. It was impossible to move on the ground, especially when Kim Dae Jung's motorcade arrived and thousands surged toward him. When the people saw Kim Dae Jung, they started chanting his name. They chanted as Kim Dae Jung slowly climbed the long stairway to the top of the podium and they cheered when he appeared high above them. Kim raised a thumb and beamed and listened to his name being called again and again.

There were empty soju bottles on the ground. There were the remains of crabs and clams and plates of steaming noodles. People waved Korean flags and yellow flags—flags the color of Kim's campaign. They jumped up and down. Pigeons flew into the clear blue sky and a man held up a sign reading KIM DAE JUNG—PRESIDENT OF THE WORLD. The crowd was in a frenzy that only Kim Dae Jung could quiet. All he had to do was begin speaking and the field fell silent.

"I can say to Chun Doo Hwan and Roh Tae Woo, 'Look at this and hear this sound,' " he said. "We are a free people. We are the owners of this country. We will show the world that for the first time in five thousand years we have begun a foundation for democracy in Korea."

He told them that even though a single opposition candidate would have been better than two, he could not "betray" their support. The people cheered. Then Kim Dae Jung told them that only deceit could rob them of their destiny, because only deceit—only a rigged election—could stop them.

Kim went on, reciting his litany of official abuse. And as those around me beamed and nodded, I began feeling uneasy. The crowd called out to Kim Dae Jung, telling him that they believed him, that he must win because only if he won could they win. And if he lost, then surely it was because the forces of darkness had once again conspired against them.

Wedged tight in this ebullient crowd, I thought of how quickly happiness could evaporate in Korea and how disappointment could turn the happiness to anger. The happiness had been building for months. It had been building since the first heady days in June. It had grown over the summer and fall. The election was two days away. It would complete the nation's redemption.

"My head is filled with plans for the future of Korea," said Kim Dae Jung. He spoke for an hour and the great crowd devoured his words. They pressed to be near him when he finished.

I had made my way to a van, hoping that I might be able to drive through the throng. Walking meant risking being crushed. I thought I was safe in the van. But people began to climb on the roof to see Kim. They enveloped the van. The ceiling and doors buckled. People pressed their noses to the windows and raised two fingers, for Kim Dae Jung's ballot number. They wanted me to raise two fingers too. They wanted me to smile with them. I smiled and nodded and prayed that the roof would not collapse.

I pried open the door and squeezed myself out of the van. Kim Dae Jung's truck had reached the street and I was swept along by the crowd that wanted to follow him into the center of Seoul. I walked alongside them, passing people who waved and others who turned their backs on Kim Dae Jung.

I remembered the November day when Kim Dae Jung came to Pusan, Kim Young Sam's town. A quarter of a million people came to a muddy field to hear him. That day too they followed his truck into town. Men with rough hands and heavy boots ran after the truck. They looked up at Kim Dae Jung with beatific eyes. They reached to touch the truck, to touch Kim Dae Jung, who looked down upon them and smiled a thin smile. It was raining. When they reached a traffic rotary, the truck stopped, halting traffic. Night had fallen and a spotlight was shone on Kim Dae Jung's broad face. The rain was coming harder. Kim took the microphone and the loudspeakers cracked and fizzled. He sang the national anthem. His people sang with him.

That night in Pusan a band of Kim Young Sam's supporters went to the hotel where Kim Dae Jung was staying. They threw rocks and bottles and started a fight. They did not want Kim Dae Jung in their town. When Kim Young Sam went to Kwangju, Kim Dae Jung's base, the crowd would not let him speak. They heckled him. They booed him and showered him with debris.

On election day I went to Kwangju. The day was sunny and crisp. Mist clung to the mountains and diffused the sunlight. The highway out of Seoul was all but deserted. The city gave way to the countryside, to barren fields, dried vines and frozen rice paddies. The countryside was empty and still. The silence was eerie after so much happy noise.

I stopped at a polling place in a rural elementary school. Outside boys played on the stone animals in the courtyard and an old woman squatted on the side of the road, waiting for someone to drive her home. A man was complaining that someone had voted with his name.

The line of voters stretched from the doorway. It ran along the dirty, wooden hallway to the voting room with its rusting stove in the middle of the floor. The voters stepped up to the flimsy booth, pulled aside the thin curtain, marked their paper ballots and tucked them in the ballot box. A poll watcher lowered a ruler into the ballot box slot to measure the depth of the ballots. An old woman folded her ballot over and over so that no one could see whom she voted for.

Election day was December 16. Winter began six days later.

The Morning After

O N the morning after the presidential election Kwangju tried to
explode but could not muster the will. There was talk of a
demonstration near the provincial capitol at noon, then of demonstration at five at the city hall, and then of a demonstration the next
day at the university. Students gathered in doorways downtown and
when the riot police decided too many had clustered, they fired tear
gas grenades. The students retreated to the alleys, but the "skeleton
police," the martial arts unit, did not bother giving chase.

The students briefly occupied a boulevard. Several hundred
formed a wall and blocked traffic with aluminum planters. The
students chanted, "Down with the military dictatorship," and threw
rocks at the riot police. The riot police fired more tear gas and the
students fled. They regrouped near a bridge. They saw an American
camera crew and stoned it because they had heard that the American
media had endorsed the results of the election.

Kwangju had cast nine out of every ten votes for Kim Dae Jung
and people could not believe that their candidate had lost because
an insufficient number of people voted for him. Someone was to
blame and it was not Kim Dae Jung. They blamed Kim Young Sam
for not allowing their man to fulfill his destiny. They blamed
the government for rigging the election—a charge widely made,
generally suspected, but ultimately unproved. They blamed the
Americans.

The night before, when the voting was almost done, people gathered outside the polling stations to make sure there was no tamper-
ing. I went to a polling station in a drafty warehouse. When the

voting ended, the student poll monitor watched the election officers seal the ballot boxes with vards of white tape. Outside, people prayed. When the door opened, they followed the ballot box as it was loaded onto a flatbed truck. They trotted alongside the truck all the way to the vote-counting office.

The people stood under the window of the counting office and when they did not see the lights turned on in each of the seven floors, they began screaming about fraud even though the counting was being done only on the seventh floor, and in the presence of television cameras and the poll watchers. The lights came on and the street was lighted. People waited outside in the cold until late in the evening, well past the announcement from the Japanese prime minister congratulating Roh Tae Woo on his victory.

A Western friend who knew Korea well once said that han in Kwangju was like a religion. No Korean city had suffered as Kwangju had suffered. And nowhere was the bitterness toward the government of Chun Doo Hwan greater. In Kwangju six months after he seized power, Chun showed the sort of ruler he would be.

In the months after Park Chung Hee's assassination there was talk of freedom of speech and even talk of a popular election of the next president. But weak men had followed Park and in December Chun decided that the moment was his. There were demonstrations against the new government that spring, demonstrations against martial law and the limitations of freedom. A hundred thousand people demonstrated in Seoul alone. There were not nearly as many in the streets of Kwangju, but that was where Chun sent his troops.

He ordered in three thousand paratroopers. For three days the paratroopers went on a rampage. They fixed their bayonets and fired into the crowds. Bodies were piled inside the bus terminal. Bodies were loaded onto trucks and carted away. Twenty girls were killed at Central High School. Troops chased two hundred students into the Catholic Center and killed one hundred of them. Eleven people were shot in front of a theater. A mother protesting the mocking of her daughter by the troops was shot dead, as was her child. A student was tied to a personnel carrier and dragged through the streets. Four cab drivers were shot for transporting students. The wounded were forced out of the hospitals.

People fought the soldiers. They threw rocks and Molotov cocktails and rolled burning oil drums. When they heard that the government-controlled television station was reporting that only one person had been killed, they tried burning the station down. Businessmen set fire to the government tax office. Public buses were commandeered. Rifles were seized. Soldiers were killed. The city hall was occupied. Students manned a machine gun on the roof of the Chonnam University Medical School. And the Twentieth Special Forces Unit was pulled off the Demilitarized Zone and sent to Kwangju.

A truce was attempted. A group of lawyers, academics and clergymen tried to mediate between the people and the army. The people would stop their fighting, they said, if the nominal head of state—there was still a president, but the power was Chun's—took responsibility for what was done, paid reparations to the families of the hundreds already killed and promised that there would be no reprisals. The talks were still going on when the Special Forces invaded Kwangju. No one is sure just how many hundreds of people died.

Chun had himself elected president. Dissident students were drafted into the army, where six conscripts mysteriously died—two by decapitation, three by gunshots and one by hanging. The government insisted the deaths were either accidents or suicides. Ten thousand were remanded to the twenty Samchong, or Three Purifications Reeducation Camps for the correction of "social evils"—a program at one point run by Park Seh Jik, who would later head the Seoul Olympic Organizing Committee. The sentences, imposed by military courts, ranged from a month to two years. The interned built 2,246 buildings for the army, laid 46 miles of underground telephone lines, paved 14 miles of roadway and somehow, along the way, six of the men were beaten to death, four were shot, thirteen died of "sudden external shock" and thirty-three of pneumonia, cirrhosis and colitis. The army released the figures years later with the explanation that there was no way of corroborating reports that many more had died because 39,789 records had been destroyed by the police in the interests of protecting the reputations of the accused.

The government blamed the uprising on Kim Dae Jung. He was tried and convicted of sedition. He might well have been executed if the American government had not intervened. As for the killings, the Americans said nothing. Chun went to Washington, D.C., where he was the first foreign head of state to meet with the new president, Ronald Reagan. And for each of the next seven years, on May 18, the people of Kwangju gathered at the cemetery where many of the known dead were buried—many more were never accounted for—and demanded that the government accept blame for what it did. Each year the demand was made and ignored. And each year the han in Kwangju grew deeper.

I went to Kwangju for the first time on the second Saturday of the June 1987 demonstrations. I traveled with three other journalists. The morning was warm and rainy and the highway was slick. We drove south, away from Seoul, passing army bases and police stations. We stopped first in Taejon, where a riot policeman had been killed the night before. A band of demonstrators had commandeered a bus, but the driver was blinded by tear gas and drove into the riot policeman.

At the university we met a missionary who had been in Korea for thirty years. He had seen the coups of 1961 and 1979 and the student demonstrations that toppled the first president, Syngman Rhee. He feared the worst, not necessarily because of reprisals for the policeman's death, but because the passions that provoked the fighting in the streets were not abating.

"If there's no martial law in twenty-four hours, there will be a coup in forty-eight hours," he said. "This can't go on much longer."

Then he said, "Don't stay here. Go to Kwangju. We hear that in Kwangju they're occupying the streets."

The sun broke through the mist over the mountains and shone on the villages along the way, on the fields and the flooded rice paddies. The countryside was green and dotted with old homes whose black tile roofs sagged. Farm wives carried bundles on their head. Men in broad-brimmed hats and pants rolled to the knee worked the fields with oxen. We passed an army base where a couple sat outside the cement walls and ate a picnic lunch. Armed guards with fixed bayonets stood watch at the gate. Jeeps and personnel carriers sped by. We turned as they passed, watching but not at all sure what we were looking for. Like everyone else, we wanted to know what the army would do. And like everyone else, we looked on in ignorance and fear.

* * *

The streets of Kwangju were not occupied, but they were crowded. We headed downtown, to the provincial capitol, where we'd heard the demonstrators were gathering. The killings of 1980 had taken place at the capitol.

Hundreds of riot police lined the sidewalks. They sat near the curb, helmets off, shields at their sides. They laughed and smoked and watched us pass. We turned off the main boulevard for the side streets.

The back streets were narrow, twisting and lined with shops and grilled-meat restaurants. From the main boulevard we could hear the chanting, which began with the end of the national anthem. After the chanting came the singing of patriotic songs and then the students' inevitable step across a line arbitrarily drawn by the commander of the riot police.

We heard the pop of the tear gas canisters. We pulled on our gas masks and helmets and ran along the sides of the buildings. The tear gas filled the street. People ran from the white clouds of gas and from the skeleton police who came running after them, tossing tear gas grenades. We ducked into a building. People stood in the doorway, coughing, crying, huddling close together. We ran upstairs, trying to find an open window so that we could see. But people had locked their doors, afraid that the skeleton police might storm the building.

The fighting quickly passed as the skeleton police chased the demonstrators toward the main streets. Even the students ran from the skeleton police. The skeleton police would force students onto their belly and kick them in the back until bones started cracking. They threw tear gas powder into the eyes of the students they caught. Then they shoved them onto "arrest buses," pulled the flimsy curtains and beat the students with their fists. No one knew who the skeleton police were or where they came from. There was talk that they were recruited from the prisons with the enticement of making money beating the children of the educated classes.

The street was spotted with the white dust of the tear gas. Women stood at the windows and poured out buckets of water to settle the dust. Restaurant owners hosed down the sidewalk. Soon their patrons returned, because when a demonstration passed the life of a street resumed as if nothing had happened. That fighting was taking place around the corner made no difference. It was time for dinner, or tea. If the tear gas filtered over, you dabbed your eyes, blew your nose and laughed at the soft foreigners who never ventured out without a gas mask.

The fighting moved to the street leading to the capitol. We slipped under the metal gate of an office building and hurried to the roof. In the distance, perhaps a mile away, we saw thousands massing to march on the capitol. Scattered at first, they closed ranks into a long column, growing longer and darker in the twilight. They sang "Morning Dew," the song of protest, the song of a man who wakes up in despair but, seeing the morning dew, takes heart and resolves to continue his fight. The singing was faint at first but grew louder as the marchers approached. It reminded me of descriptions of German infantrymen in World War I whose singing rose from forests and smoke and drifted across the battle lines, terrifying the enemy.

The riot police, in padded green uniforms and Darth Vader helmets, closed ranks, as did the skeleton police, who wore denim pants and coats, motorcycle helmets and thin, leather driving gloves with the knuckles left exposed. The students pulled Saran Wrap over their eyes and gauze masks over their face. Korean civilians were not allowed to own gas masks.

When the marchers closed within a hundred yards, the first salvos exploded. Some ran. The bolder students stood their ground. They ran at the riot police, kerosene bombs in hand. The bombs twisted and rolled in the air and almost always landed harmlessly at the policemen's feet.

The skeleton police, faceless in their gas masks, hurried along the back streets, trying to split the demonstrators' ranks. The students began breaking apart the sidewalks, making weapons. The riot police fired tear gas in rapid bursts.

For three hours they went at each other this way. Injuries were slight. There was no looting. There was no vandalism because this was not a riot. It was a demonstration, coordinated and controlled. A student pounded a bus stand. It was his drum and he was beating a rhythm for the chanting. The tear gas did not stop his drumming or the chanting. Not that night, and not the next.

Now, seven months later, I sat in a coffee shop with a man named Chae as he considered his alternatives. He did not want me to know his full name. He had critical things to say. Chae sat with his friends from the construction industry. He shoved his hands deep into his trench-coat pockets. "We're going to see what happens at the city hall," Chae said.

"What do you want to see done?" I asked.

"I want the election results to be annulled."

"Will you go out into the streets?"

"We don't have a definite plan yet."

"How long have you been sitting here?"

"Two hours. We've been sitting and talking about the results and how they are fabricated."

His friend, Yu, said, "I cannot yield to the results of the election. The KCIA is behind it. How, I'm not sure."

"Will you go out into the streets?"

"No, but we will not yield to the results."

"But how will you show that you will not yield?"

"I don't know how to show it. But they will feel this anger."

The anger, however, remained in the coffee shop, where the men sipped barley tea and slumped in their seats. More than anything the men were tired, as if they had been fighting with their wives all night and could not bear the idea of going home to resume the argument.

We walked along a downtown street and a man called after me, "We're going to cut off your balls and shove them in your mouth." Someone threw a rock. Later we stopped at the dissidents' office at the YWCA. When I mentioned what had happened on the street, a man who refused to shake my hand said that I deserved the threat and the rock because the foreign media had conspired with the government to deny Kim Dae Jung and the people of Korea their victory.

We went to see if the demonstrations were beginning elsewhere. Trying a shortcut, the driver headed along a back street. Men had gathered. A drunk emerged from the crowd. He saw our Western faces and threw himself on the car. He beat at the windshield with his fists. The others watched him do this. They surrounded the car.

They beat on the doors, hood and roof. They tried to smash the windows with their fists. The windows felt as if they would give. The driver tried easing away, but a man laid himself across the hood. The shouting and pounding grew louder and meaner and the men pushed their angry faces against the windows. The driver kept his foot on the accelerator. The man on the hood, sensing that the driver would not stop, finally slid off.

We sped away. My heart was pounding. My mouth was dry and my imagination raced with pictures of my face pulpy and bloody after a beating. I was still shaking when we got back to the hotel. We met an American cameraman who told us his crew had just been stoned.

That night, as I stood with the Western journalists in the hotel lobby, a mass of faces appeared in the plate-glass window. The faces were covered with thin gauze masks. The flat, empty eyes behind the masks were staring at us. An interpreter went to ask what they wanted. The hotel staff wanted no trouble. We worried that they might try storming the hotel. The interpreter was gone for five minutes. "They want to know whether you are all journalists," he said when he returned. "I told them you were tourists." Tourists, they decided, could stay. But they remained outside watching us until a squad of police cleared the sidewalk.

For weeks afterward I was haunted by the attack on the car on that narrow street. Three days before, when I was caught in the van at Kim Dae Jung's final rally, I felt as if I were being smothered under the weight of passion. I thought of the beaming faces pressed against the windshield.

The happy faces had turned to angry faces and I was once again being crushed by the force of unfettered emotion. Deep and profound disappointment had propelled the change. But so too had a self-fulfilling prophecy of bitterness, always imposed.

The Coffee-Shop Lady

I was weary of politics. I flew south to Pusan and began traveling north by bus. I had only driven through the countryside. I had never spent a night. From Pusan I went to the city of Taegu. In Taegu I heard about Koryang. There I met a woman whose han was not the nation's han, or a city's han. It was hers alone.

I went to Koryang to see the market, which I had heard from a woman in Taegu was like the markets of the past, even if there were no more dog- or cockfights. Koryang, she said, was her hometown, a country town where the farmers grew berries and melons and where you could fish in a pond. She spoke nostalgically about Koryang and so I assumed she had lived there. But her only attachment to Koryang were images of childhood visits to her grandmother's home, before the roads were paved. Her parents had left Koryang for Taegu, the city where she was born and where she worked as a hotel clerk on a twenty-four-hour shift every other day. "The town is not pretty," she said of Koryang. She went there only for family gatherings. The grown-ups played the same games they had played as children, then commiserated about the havoc on the nervous system caused by city life. No one, however, suggested moving back to Koryang, not even her grandmother, who had remained behind.

I arrived in Koryang the day before the market, a drizzly day. The bus from Taegu passed hamlets and rice fields that the elderly farmers plowed with oxen in the springtime. The rice fields were tucked in a long valley that ran alongside the mountain road to Koryang. Koryang began at the bus station and ended at the rice fields and in between were twenty thousand people and two main roads lined

39

with shops that sold the same goods as all the other shops along the roads. There were competing butchers, fishmongers, vegetable stands, fishing tackle shops and coffee shops. There were two funeral homes, one across from the other, filled with pine coffins adorned with red and white bunting. There were also two inns. No one could find the proprietor at the first, so I was sent to the second, where a young woman was sleeping behind the front desk. She rubbed her eyes, gave me a key, switched off the light and lay back down behind the counter.

Every fifth day was market day in Koryang and in the days between the markets the town drifted into repose. The quiet did not suit Koryang. Businessmen sat at desks in offices where no one came while their secretaries read the newspaper and listened to music on their Walkman. The farmers drove through town on tractors whose grinding engines broke the silence for the minute or two until they passed. Young men stood in doorways, arms folded, waiting. When they were tired of waiting, they went for a coffee at the shop where Chung Hee worked.

Chung Hee had been working in Koryang for a month, which was as long as she stayed in any town. She was thirty-eight years old, round in the face, and divorced. She had been in ten towns in two years and recalled nothing in particular about any of them. When she left a town she returned to Pusan, her home, and told her parents that she had been working in a factory, because working in a coffee shop was regarded as only a step above the streets. Chung Hee stayed home until she got word that a coffee shop in another town needed a new girl. New girls were always needed because after a month men got tired of seeing the same girls and wanted new ones to sit with and squeeze.

"The men say 'Can I touch you? Can I touch your breasts?' If I protest they say, 'Why are you here? Go home and take care of a baby,'" Chung Hee said.

Chung Hee's coffee shop was at the corner of the market streets. The market was all but empty except for the fishmonger's stand, where a customer poked her finger into the side of a fat squid as the old woman fishmonger worked her dentures around her mouth between reflections on the market days of the past, when people trusted each other and knew how to have fun. The window of Chung Hee's coffee shop was blacked over so that no one could peek inside.

There was a stove in the middle of the floor and its chimney ran along the ceiling, alongside the fruited vines of a plastic plant. Chung Hee sat on a brown velour love seat. She wore a green han-bok—a traditional woman's dress—and a white blouse and black high-heeled slippers. Her lips were brightly rouged and on one chubby finger was a heavy rhinestone ring. Her hair was rinsed brown, teased and pulled back from her face. Chung Hee smiled a coquettish smile and asked if I wanted to buy her a coffee.

Coffee was seventy-five cents a cup. Chung Hee sat with a guest until she finished her coffee and if that guest wanted her to stay, he bought her another. Sometimes she drank Coca-Cola. Chung Hee drank coffee from early in the morning until late at night but insisted that this did not hurt her stomach. She explained that she was the "madam" of the shop and therefore responsible for receipts. The other girls delivered coffee to the shops and offices along the street, but Chung Hee did not leave the coffee shop, not even to sleep.

"It's difficult to go out. I can't go out," said Chung Hee. "I'm in charge of the girls and must stay here. Many people come to see me." Sometimes, when the shop was quiet, Chung Hee rose from her love seat, opened the door and looked out onto the street as the tractors rumbled by. "When you use the word *madame* in French it means a noble woman," she said. "But in Korea it's the woman who runs the coffee shop. The image is very bad. My han is different from an ordinary housewife's."

Men came to the coffee shop in pairs and bought coffees for the girls. They did not talk to the girls. They chewed on match sticks and talked with each other about indigestion from eating in out-of-town restaurants, and the aches that required a doctor's attention. When the men got tired of talking they put their arms around the girls' shoulders and asked for a coffee on credit. Chung Hee kept a list of the coffees bought on credit. The men whispered in the girls' ears. The girls laughed and rose and led them to the booth in the back, where they petted in something close to privacy.

The television played, but nobody watched. The men without companions read their newspapers until there was no more reason to stay. The girls without customers picked themselves up, dragged their feet across the linoleum floor and dropped themselves on another love seat. The fish tank gurgled and steam rose from the kettle. "If the market is closed," Chung Hee said, "everything is like this."

* * *

Chung Hee opened the coffee shop at seven in the morning on market day because the farmers liked to get started early. The sun had burned away the morning mist. The farmers unloaded their cattle, anchored their hogs to heavy posts, lined up their piglets in rows and when there was money in their pockets from sales of bull semen, retired to the coffee shop. The market streets were jammed and loudest in the livestock stalls, where the pig farmers haggled and the dogs for sale barked and howled. The vegetable peddlers hawked cucumbers, garlic and cabbage, old men sold handfuls of seeds and a boy sold shoe inserts. "Have you ever had an ache in the heart or your bones or a serious cold or dizziness?" the herbal medicine seller bellowed as an old woman who'd just bought a mountain of medicines for these and more asked if he might throw in something for worms.

Chung Hee could not see that the sun was shining because the pale light in the coffee shop was artificial. She was weary. She did not care for the farmers any more than she cared for the businessmen with idle hours, or for the young men who came in with bursting libidos. The farmers liked to fondle, the businessmen talked to her as if she were an idiot—"What do you know about politics?"—and the young men talked down to her, even though she was their senior. Chung Hee had heard that in the cities young men used polite language with coffee-shop girls. But working in a city coffee shop was out of the question. She was too old to work in Seoul. She could not work in Pusan because that would humiliate her family. Chung Hee was resigned to making herself popular in the coffee shops of provincial towns.

"The most important thing is popularity. If I'm not popular, the owner will want me to leave," Chung Hee said. "So I have to sit next to the customers and ask them to buy me a coffee. I have to sell a lot. Everything depends on popularity and how much coffee I sell. If the owner says you have to leave because you're not popular, then you have to move around."

Chung Hee checked herself in the mirror and fixed her hair with a long-toothed comb. A customer rose and she followed him to the cash box, where she checked the numbers of coffees, colas and yogurt drinks and hoped that he would not ask for credit. Chung Hee could not say no when a man assured her that he would be back the next day to buy even more coffee and maybe even a dinner for her. The man would never buy her dinner and might not even pay for his coffees.

She wished she had someone to talk with. She wished she could meet "a nice guy" and get married and "have a nice life." The only decent man Chung Hee had met in Koryang was a booking agent for singers and comedians who did not play the cities. He was husky and a bit gruff and talked like a man who made promises about big things he could not deliver. Chung Hee recognized that this was not the man she was dreaming of, but he was pleasant enough company for a chat in the coffee shop, which was where they met. Still, it was hard to talk there on market day, when the farmers wanted to have their turn at sitting with the girls.

Market day was Chung Hee's last day in the coffee shop. Her month was over, but she could not leave Koryang until she collected all the money for coffees bought on credit. With the closing of the market the town sank back into its slumber. And it was not until I saw what Koryang could be on market day that I realized how much the town felt like a shell. The farmers had packed and left, as had the rice sellers, the vegetable peddlers and all the customers who crowded the benches of the lunch stands, backs bent over steaming bowls of noodles and grilled beef. In the absence of the market the monotony of Koryang's two- and three-story shops and homes became especially noticeable. So too did the way the old women squatted when they stopped to gossip, and the particular sound bicycle tires made when they rode along empty roads.

I went to the coffee shop to find Chung Hee. The other girls said she was gone but that I might find her at the inn where she had moved now that she did not have to live at the coffee shop anymore.

Chung Hee was no longer wearing her work clothes. She wore red and black harum pants and a silky blouse. She sat on the floor of her small room, smoking cigarettes with her friend the booking agent. The double bed, covered in a frilly comforter, filled the room. The wallpaper was faded and torn. The sun shone through the gauzy curtains and "That's Incredible," in dubbed Korean, played on the television. Chung Hee reached for the notebook of coffee debts she kept and calculated that she was still owed over a thousand dollars, part of which went to the man who booked her in the coffee shop. I asked Chung Hee how it was possible that in just one month of selling seventy-five-cent cups of coffee, cola and yogurt drink she could be owed so much. Chung Hee reminded me that she had worked fifteen hours a day for thirty days without a break.

Chung Hee thought that most of the debts would be easy to collect but that there would be the inevitable nasty scene at the civil servant's office when the man would refuse to pay her and she would have to yell at him in front of everyone. The man would yell, "Why are you coming to my office?" and Chung Hee would yell still more, just as she would with the young men whose rude talk she had had to endure for a month. Chung Hee could not bear being spoken to the way the young men spoke to her.

The booking agent listened to Chung Hee and decided to inject an empathetic voice. He talked for her. He pulled on the skin of his hands and offered opinions about the need for an association for coffee-shop girls, the loneliness of their life, the crude manners of customers and the interminable hours the girls had to work without complaint. "As a human being it's hard to find someone who is nice and kind," he said. "But sometimes it is possible."

The booking agent smiled at Chung Hee and she gave him a punch in the shoulder, which was meant to show casual affection. He continued. "The women should be pretty and should make the customers comfortable," he said.

"Of course she must be pretty," said Chung Hee. "But she must also be skillful at conversation. Then the customers will buy coffee. She must be diligent in keeping the conversation going. I want to be serious but the customers don't like that."

Chung Hee stubbed out another cigarette in an ashtray overflowing with butts. She assumed she would have to spend another week in Koryang before she could collect all her money. When all the money that could be collected was in her hands, Chung Hee would go home, to her parents. Chung Hee said that she could work in a factory, but the hours were just as bad and the money was not as good. Factory work would remain the lie that made it possible for Chung Hee to keep coming home.

For a week Chung Hee would have the company of the booking agent. She could even sleep late and go to the public bath. She could spend part of her day outside, in the sunshine, passing dimly lighted shops, silent offices and worn and sagging cement homes, passing grandmothers and infants and the occasional face of a man who would make believe he did not know her.

Panmunjom at Christmas

*A*T Camp Boniface, which sat in the Demilitarized Zone, little cotton tufts were stuck in the shrubbery so that the place might have the feel of Christmas. There was no snow on the ground at Panmunjom. The air was cold and the sun was bright and in the Sanctuary Club "Silver Bells" played on the loudspeakers.

"Two days to merry Christmas," said the soldier at the bar to Mr. Kim, the bartender. "You know what that means? Twenty days and I'm home with my wife."

I had come to Panmunjom to see the border. I came on the tour bus. The woman in the booking office told me that I could not wear dungarees to Panmunjom. And no sneakers, either.

"Why not?" I asked. And she replied cryptically, "The black North Korean propaganda."

You were not to wave at the North Korean guards at Panmunjom because the waves might be photographed and represented as hostile gestures. You could not point. It was best to keep some distance from the North Korean guards because they were known to put nails in the soles of their boots and impale the feet of unsuspecting tourists.

"Since you've joined the tour you have to see, because seeing is believing about this North Korean aggression," the tour guide told us.

We drove north from Seoul. And as we passed under concrete walls as thick as houses—"No pictures of the anti-tank walls!"—and sentries whose heads snapped from side to side as vehicles passed before them, the tour guide told us about the dams. The North Koreans had dammed a river just north of the border. The South called this dam the Dam of Aggression. The South had deduced that the North would wait until the water behind the dam was high and then explode the dam, sending the water cascading over the border and into Seoul, thirty-five miles away.

"We have to do something to fight this," he said, barking into the microphone. The tour guide did not speak so much as preach. He was a thin bespectacled man with a disheveled look but a passionate delivery. "We dug our own dam, the Peace Dam," he said. "Our dam will stop the water and push the water back to the North Korean side. There have been 99,952 cases of hostile acts from North Korea."

A convoy of jeeps and camouflaged trucks sped past us, the loud grind of their engines cresting and then disappearing as they headed south, toward Seoul. "We can still say we are in a state of war," said the guide, who admonished us to keep our hands in our pockets at the border.

First he took us to the Third Tunnel of Aggression. We had passed Munsan, the last town before the border. The homes were scattered now, just a few in an occasional thin band of buildings alongside the highway. The countryside was flat and empty and on a frozen rice field boys played baseball. The railroad tracks that once ran north now ended at Munsan. The tracks stopped at a squat barrier screened from the road by sculpted shrubbery.

We slowly crossed the narrow, wooden bridge over the Imjin River and drove past the sentries, barbed wire and sandbags that marked the gate to the Demilitarized Zone. There, in a briefing room at the mouth of the Third Tunnel of Aggression, the guide stood before a broad map of the border and told us how this tunnel, like the two previously discovered "tunnels of aggression," were part of North Korea's grand plan for conquest: They would burrow under the border; they would surface in the South; their long-feared invasion would begin well past the first lines of defense.

But the South had foiled the North, or at least delayed this plan: It had discovered three tunnels, the third after smoke—presumably from explosives detonated underground—began rising from the earth on the southern side of the border. The South dug for three months before the third tunnel was discovered. But the nation was still not safe; there were rumors of another fifteen or twenty tunnels under the border. The guide told us that that was what people who knew something of the North and its tunneling plans had said after they'd defected to the West. And if we doubted him, if we did not believe that the tunnel had indeed been dug from north to south, we had only to look at the drill marks on the tunnel wall. There were yellow splotches painted on some of the drill marks, to illuminate the view for the doubters.

The Third Tunnel of Aggression was perhaps a quarter mile deep and its walls were black and wet. At one end of the now-truncated tunnel stood sentries, young and grim. They manned a single machine gun aimed at a section already walled off and filled with poison gas. Still, the sentries took turns maintaining their vigil, should the North Korean army manage to pass through the gas and the thick wall. I left them to their mission and walked back along the dark, arching tunnel, from north to south.

Naked bulbs hung from the ceiling and water dripped onto the stone floor. No one was in front of me and for a moment I felt alone. And in that moment, freed from the haranguing of the guide but nonetheless fueled by his catechism of vigilance against treachery, I imagined the tunnel filled with a hundred thousand armed and angry men racing underground toward Seoul.

They ran in the dark, but because the tunnel was wide and high, they did not have to bow. They could race into the South with heads high, running in the name of the Great Leader, Kim Il Sung, or if the Great Leader's time on earth had expired, in the name of his son and designated heir, the Dear Leader and Great Teacher of Journalists, Kim Jong Il. They could finish the work begun with the invasion of the south in 1950 but stymied first at the gates of Pusan by the American general Walton Walker, whose troops managed to hold onto the last bit of the South, and then by Douglas MacArthur's counterattack, which began with the unexpected landing at Inchon. They could carry on with the task of conquest that resumed—though fell short once again—in the second invasion, in the winter of 1951, an offensive that ended without victory or defeat at the thirty-eighth parallel. No longer would they have to be satisfied with merely blowing up four members of the South Korean cabinet, as happened in Rangoon in 1983, or destroying a Korean Air jet over the Andaman Sea and killing 115 people, as had happened only a few weeks before. Now they could unify the nation without need of negotiation.

But the tunnel ahead of me was empty. I turned and saw the

yellow paint on the walls, just as the guide had described. I did not doubt that the North was capable of a plan to dig and conquer. But my belief had little to do with the short course in North-South relations I had been receiving during the morning, a course that, not surprisingly, made no mention of the perpetuation of the Korean War well into 1953 because Syngman Rhee, who then ruled the South and wanted the North, would not sign a peace treaty. Both sides had taken turns inflicting cruelties upon the other; and while I knew what the North had done when they entered Seoul—mass roundups and executions—and had seen too much evidence of the lunacy, the sometimes deadly lunacy that pervaded the thinking of North Korea's rulers, I could not help but recoil at this none-too-subtle attempt at indoctrination thinly disguised as a tour.

Perhaps the North had dug this tunnel and twenty more. And perhaps a tunneler, digging this short section alone and heading in the opposite direction, from south to north, had simply turned around periodically and cut a few well-placed marks in the other direction so that visitors might see what he wanted them to see. If the tunnel was sealed and filled with gas, why was a sentry on guard with a single machine gun? Was he supposed to stop the first wave of the North Korean army by himself? Or was he just there for us to note, armed and resolute against the enemy from the north, the enemy who spoke his language, whose mothers prepared the same foods as his mother and who might even be related through one of the large clans like Kim or Lee or Choi?

I believed the North capable of mad acts. I believed the North was to be watched. But that was not enough, not for the guide and the people who had told him what to say. We were being made to believe all the way—to see as they saw that there was one good Korea and another, though its brother, forever cloaked in black. It was all too much like a bad science-fiction movie—identical twins separated at birth, one brought up in decency, the other in darkness. The virtue of the good one stood in inverse proportion to the wickedness of its twin.

I climbed back to the surface and emerged squinting into the sunlight at the mouth of the tunnel. Sentimental music played over a loudspeaker. Birds sailed overhead. But the birds did not sing here; they squawked. At Panmunjom, amidst the accusations of treachery, evidence of planned invasions and warnings that came at a scream, it was easy to forget that the border, the thirty-eighth parallel, represented the nation's great collective bitterness—the han of being hopelessly split in two.

On the television in the Sanctuary Club, Brigham Young was playing Virginia in the All-American Bowl. It was halftime. There was Mogen David 20/20 and Boone's Farm wine in the liquor cabinet. There were Planters peanuts, Pringle's potato chips and beef jerky for snacks. In the television room four young American soldiers watched a spaghetti western and waited for their pizza.

"Where's my pizza?" said one who was testy, glum and tired of waiting. "I told him I was in the TV room."

The soldiers sat slumped in their chairs as if they were trying to sleep.

"There's a game on tonight," said one soldier, reminding the others that there was something to which they could look forward. It was quiet in the Sanctuary Club and the soldiers' company was limited to one another. The club might have been a bowling-alley lounge in Manville, New Jersey, or Billings, Montana, or Shreveport, Louisiana. The lights were dim, the video game was Ms. Pac Man, paper bells hung from the acoustic ceiling and in one corner a soldier told his buddy about a girl who might be coming up for the weekend.

Outside, and a few hundred yards away, the members of the American rapid deployment force waited. They could be on the border, armed and ready for combat, in sixty seconds, ninety at the most. They were skilled in various forms of killing. But now, in the chill of the early afternoon of yet another uneventful day, they tossed a football. When the North Koreans came, they would be the first men in their path. Thus far the North Koreans only threatened to come. But as long as they threatened, the rapid deployment force and the young men in the Sanctuary Club and the other forty-three thousand American troops behind them would continue maintaining their edge through drill, emboldening slogans—IN FRONT OF THEM ALL—and all manner of nonlethal competition. And as they did, the two Koreas stood on either side of them, holding fast to their respective and seemingly intractable hatreds.

The briefing corporal spoke in the monotone of a man who'd memorized a script that was not supposed to vary. He told us the story of the flagpoles. We would see two sets of flagpoles at the border, one on either side. The North Koreans built a tall flagpole, so the South Koreans built one even taller. The North Koreans erected one that was taller still. It was five hundred feet tall. The two Koreas also took turns hanging the larger flag from their flagpoles-cum-towers. First the North had the bigger flag, then the South. Now the North had a flag so big that it barely moved. It weighed six hundred pounds, the briefer said (how did he know that?), too heavy to flap in anything less than a gale.

The two sides also took turns broadcasting propaganda at each other from large loudspeakers. Each had its own border village. The South called its village Freedom Village and populated it with people who, because of the precarious nature of life on the border, were exempt from paying taxes. At harvest time the American soldiers helped the farmers in the fields. Photographs were taken of their arduous labor. The North Korean village was called Kaesong, which was its original name, hundreds of years old. But the South called Kaesong Propaganda Village and insisted that while there were new buildings in the village, there were no people in them.

"Who gets to come here from North Korea?" asked someone in our group.

"Members of the U.S. Communist party. One of the biggest Communist parties in the world," the corporal replied, perhaps forgetting those of the People's Republic of China, the Soviet Union and India.

"How often are there incidents here?" asked another and the corporal told the story of the attack on American soldiers by North Korean troops in 1976. The Americans were tending a tree close to the North Korean side. The North Koreans killed two of the Americans with axes.

"When was the last attack on tourists?" asked yet another, and the corporal told us that had not happened.

"Are there any shootings across the border?"

"Off and on. Usually not by U.S. soldiers."

"Is there any fraternization with the North Koreans?"

"We're not allowed to talk with them."

When the briefing was done and the corporal had warned us once again not to wave or point at the North Korean soldiers, he took us to the border.

* * *

The North Korean soldiers stood on their observation platform and looked at us through binoculars. I stared back, expecting to see an unfamiliar species. They wore green greatcoats and green cossack hats. They looked cold.

The corporal brought us into the negotiation room, a tin-roofed hut that straddled the Korean peninsula's dividing line. Four microphones hung over the center table, so that each side could listen to what the other side's visitors said when they were alone in the room. The table was situated so that it sat in equal parts in both Koreas. A strand of microphone wires ran across the table, splitting it in half, following the path of the seventeen-inch concrete slab that ran through the Demilitarized Zone, dividing the peninsula. The corporal invited us to walk around the table and as we did he told us, "You are now stepping into Communist North Korea." We could, for a dollar, buy certificates written in bold calligraphy attesting to the fact that at this date and at this time we did, indeed, cross the border into the enemy state. As I slipped around the edge of the broad table, I looked at the window, at the concrete dividing line. There was soft ground on either side of the concrete. On the North Korean side were boot prints of a certain pattern and on the southern side boot prints of another. Neither set of prints appeared on the other side.

A squad of American troops assembled at the base of the observation deck, turned north and assumed a defiant pose. We climbed to the top of the pagoda-shaped deck. We huddled close together, taking turns taking glimpses through the binoculars at the North Koreans observing us.

It's at moments such as these, when nothing happens but your imagination suggests what could, that you note every occurrence and seek significance in each. One of our group, forgetting the repeated admonitions about pointing, did so just the same. And I, reacting upon an instinct that until this day did not exist, told him to get his hand down. In retrospect, all that might have happened was a picture taken by a North Korean soldier would, at the next futile meeting at Panmunjom, be passed across the table, from north to south, as evidence of the sort of nasty people whom the South brought to Panmunjom. But I wasn't thinking of that. I just remembered that it was a bad thing to point here. And at that moment I didn't remember why.

Then, on our way from one observation point to another, I looked at the North Korean soldiers and saw one of them raise and lower his hand. He did it surreptitiously, or so it seemed. But I was sure I saw a definite raising followed by an equally definite lowering. Was it a wave and was he waving to me? Was it a brief gesture of friendship? Was he thinking of defecting? What sort of person was he? I replayed his wave over and over as the North Korean soldiers hurried to their jeep to follow us. And as I recalled the soldier's hand rising and falling, I wondered whether, to counter the chill, he just needed to flap a bit.

The North Korean soldiers followed our bus to the lookout at the edge of Panmunjom and waited on their side as we scanned the bleak terrain. There were no trees in Panmunjom, no barriers or obstacles or hindrances to the view. The flat ground gave way to hills and, in the distance, mountains. Mountains covered the peninsula on both sides of the border, mountains with craggy peaks that made the harsh landscape meaner still.

The wind whipped across the wide expanse and, in the fading sunlight, the browns and flat greens of the hills turned pale and lifeless. I looked from side to side and as I did, I lost sight of the border. I saw no barbed wire, no wall, no thin concrete slab, only a desolate valley.

Martial music came from North Korea. But the music, though powerful at its source, dissipated in the cold air and Panmunjom was all but silent.

The Strongest Man under Heaven

*A*T the gateway to the Hyundai shipyard the helmeted guard asked me to state my business. I had come to Ulsan, to the shipyard, to see Yi Man Gi, the Strongest Man under Heaven. The gateway was walled and heavily guarded. It looked like the entrance to a prison. The guard pointed to a waiting room and told me to sit for a while.

Yi Man Gi did not work on the ships. He was a wrestler. His sport was ssirum and ssirum is Korea's sport. It is a form of wrestling five hundred years old. Yi wrestled for the Hyundai team.

I was in a car when I first heard of Yi Man Gi. We were listening to a ssirum tournament on the radio. The contest was between Yi Man Gi and the giant Yi Bun Gul, who was almost but not quite as good. I asked my companion whom he wanted to win. He did not hesitate. He said, "Yi Man Gi." I asked him why. And in an answer that suggested that ssirum represented more than sport alone he replied, "Because he's manly."

Korean men had their poses, their "manly" poses, all of which were meant to suggest a hardy gender. Tough men did not just put cigarettes in their mouth. They stuck them between their teeth, locked their jaw, curled their lips in a snarl and left the unlighted cigarette sitting there for a while, occasionally working it around their teeth. Men slurped their noodles and their coffee. They walked with a swagger, bellies out, shoulders back, feet splayed. They were physical with each other. They held hands. They touched each other's arms when they talked. They laughed with their mouths wide open. They acted out the ritual of manliness for each other and for the women around them, so that the women might know how strong they were.

The strong young men who became ssirum wrestlers were especially adept at this ritual. They had thick shoulders and heavy legs and there was no premium placed upon bulk, as there is in Japanese sumo. Ssirum wrestlers were powerful and quick and the best of them, the Strongest Man under Heaven, was Yi Man Gi, who, at the age of twenty-five, had certain clear and unequivocal opinions on what it meant to be a man.

The team bus came to bring me to Yi Man Gi. We drove into the shipyard, past the long back end of a tanker in progress, the tall cranes and steel ship sections as big as ranch houses. We drove for half a mile, until we reached the white plastic tent where the wrestlers practiced.

The ssirum ring was covered only in the cold weather. On warm days the wrestlers practiced out-of-doors so that the shipyard workers could watch after work. The workers sat in the stone bleachers of the amphitheater that surrounded the ring as the wrestlers threw each other around on the dirt. Hyundai had one of the nation's five professional teams. It was regarded as a corporate morale booster: When the wrestlers did well, it was said, the workers were proud and production went up.

The ring was wide, perhaps thirty feet across. The inside of the tent was cold for the morning practice—there was afternoon drilling too—and the only warmth was close to the heaters that sat by the door, where the coaches stood and talked about the bar they had been to the night before. One of the older men drank bottled ginseng extract. (Korean men swore it could restore the strength sapped by beer and rice wine.) Inside the tent the air was laced with the overly sweet smell of muscle balm, the universal smell of training rooms.

The space heaters were of no help to the thirty wrestlers. They peeled off their sweat suits and paired off along the outside of the ring. They wore only their gym shorts. The door flew open and the cold air blew in. The wind whipped and banged against the tent walls. The wrestlers did not seem to notice or care. They joked and talked and loosened their muscles until it was time to wrestle.

The dirt in the ring was thick and the wrestlers sank in it up to their ankles. When the fighting was fierce, the loose dirt flew. The bottoms of the wrestlers' feet were brown from the dirt and the backs of their right thighs were red and bruised. Ssirum wrestlers wore sashes around their waists and right thighs. The sashes were broad sheets of fabric rolled tight and tied in a thick knot.

They held each other by the sashes when they wrestled. They faced off and grabbed onto the sashes, bending forward at the waist like two rams about to butt horns. The wrestlers worked their hands under the sashes, changing their grip until it was tight and sure. They rested their chins on each other's back, tugging and adjusting their grip like arm wrestlers. And when they were ready, they pulled hard.

They pulled each other in at the waist and up at the leg, locking each other in a tight embrace. They rose on a single leg, trying to lift the other off the ground. They wrapped their sash-wrapped leg around the other man's calf. The winner was the man left standing.

It was a deceptively simple game. There were many throws and many holds and a lot to know about leverage. But more complex still was the interplay between opponents. "When we wrestle, we have our shirts off and we can feel each other's skin," said Yi Man Gi. "We feel a strong jong for our opponent."

Yi Man Gi was stocky and handsome. His face was wide and his jaw square. His shoulders and chest were thick with muscle. His smile was quick and his manner engaging. He was a relentless flirt.

Ssirum had been a professional sport for only seven years. There had been wrestling in the countryside for centuries and, more recently, wrestling in college too. But since the wrestlers starting fighting for money, Yi Man Gi had won more tournaments than anyone else. There were tournaments about the country, often in the provincial cities, where ten thousand people might attend. Twice a year, however, the wrestlers gathered to fight for the title of Strongest Man under Heaven. Unlike the other contests, which were divided by weight classifications—each named for one of the peninsula's famous mountains—the Strongest Man under Heaven was open to all comers. The Strongest Man under Heaven contest was aired on the television and radio. Twenty thousand people filled the arena. And the man the nation saw win the title again and again was Yi Man Gi.

He was a star. He appeared on advertising posters and sang on television variety shows. Though he lived in Ulsan at the Hyundai dormitory with the rest of the team, he was often traveling to Seoul, to meet with television and advertising executives. He did not care for all the travel, especially with all the flights into Ulsan, where the air over the mountains was always turbulent.

"I don't like the way you're pulling his leg at all," the coach, Hwang Jyung Soo, bellowed at Yi Man Gi. "If you sense the slightest weakness in his leg, just pull."

Yi Man Gi pulled, but his weight was poorly placed. He slipped and fell. Hwang was not happy with his best wrestler. Yi could not do anything right. His feet were in the wrong place and he had forgotten everything about leverage. "What are you doing?" Hwang screamed. Yi spat on his hands and rubbed them together. He placed his hands on his hips and accepted the abuse. Hwang screamed, "Where should your body be?"

I waited a while until Hwang was calm and then I asked about ssirum's appeal.

"There used to be women ssirum wrestlers, but now it's only men," he said. "People call it a manly sport. Look around. Most of the wrestlers are better looking than the average man. Their faces are rounder and better shaped." Hwang went into a lengthy and confusing explanation about how these better-shaped faces were the result of the time the wrestlers spent bent over with the blood rushing to the face. Ssirum wrestlers, he said, were fit and strong and in the best of health. "Ssirum," he said, "brings out the best in a man."

Hwang had cauliflower ears and meaty hands. His voice was gruff. He looked across the ring at Yi Man Gi and yelled to him that if he kept wrestling so badly he would not be the Strongest Man under Heaven much longer. "Why did you stand there and give him a chance?" he screamed. Yi Man Gi bent down, grabbed his lesser opponent's sash, tightened his grip, gritted his teeth and with the blood flowing quickly to his face, pulled the other man close before throwing him to the ground.

Yi Man Gi ran his juniors through their paces. The coach had criticized only him; Yi, in turn, criticized his juniors, in keeping with the strict, feudal hierarchy of the gym, in which seniors deferred to coaches and juniors to their seniors. The wrestlers gathered in a circle and bowed, first to each other and then to their coaches. Yi Man Gi pulled on some clothes and suggested sashimi for lunch.

We drove through the sorry town, a place made sorrier by the reminders of the picturesque place it had once been. The city was a village not long ago and was supported primarily by fishing. Now Ulsan was a company town and once you passed the lone auto-parts store on the highway in from the airport, you saw enterprises identified by a single name, Hyundai. Stretching along the highway and extending to the horizon was a sea of industrial gray that comprised the factories where Hyundai forged the steel and built the machinery it sold around the world. The company belonged primarily to the family of Chung Ju Yung, a refugee from North Korea who at age seventy-four still descended from his office for the annual company outing and took on his newest workers in bouts of ssirum.

Yi drove past rows of squat shops and the ubiquitous pale green housing blocks. The sun was bright and in the midday glare the town looked flat and dusty. We drove through the city center, toward the water, and stopped at a restaurant by a cove, the lone pleasant view in town. There was a small beach at the shore. Green hills rose up behind the sand. There were sailboats on the water.

"What are you wearing so much makeup for?" Yi asked the smiling waitress as he walked through the rickety restaurant door. "You look like you're in a horror movie."

The waitress kept smiling and so did Yi Man Gi as he walked to a room in the back overlooking the sea. He sat by the window on the heated floor and ordered the fish and a bottle of soju. The room, with walls papered in pink and gray, was shabby and unadorned, but the sunlight made it feel brighter. Yi lighted a cigarette. He asked my interpreter, Bae Yu Chung, where she was from and smiled when Yu Chung said that she was from Kyongsang Province. Yi, too, was from Kyongsang, a province, he said, where men were men and women understood this, a province where men did not bother with the petty flatteries that Seoul men performed for their women, such as lighting their cigarettes.

"If a Kyongsang man's girlfriend asks him to light her cigarette, that's it; it's over," said Yi Man Gi, who did not like the idea of women smoking in public. Yu Chung rolled her eyes. Yi Man Gi grinned at her. Their speech fell into a spirited Kyongsang dialect, filled with throat-clearing, expectorant exclamations. Yi bullied playfully. Yu Chung, who once punched me on the subway for making faces at a child, held her own.

As they bantered, I thought about what Yi had said about the jong he felt for the men he fought. It was the second time I'd heard a Korean athlete talk about this bond. The first person who spoke of it to me was Yi Bun Gul, Yi Man Gi's greatest opponent.

Where Yi Man Gi was broad and appealing, Yi Bun Gul was towering and frightening. His face was long and dour. As a child Yi Bun Gul was the bully who beat up classmates for their lunch. Now he administered the occasional slap in the face to an underling remiss in attitude or performance. That was his responsibility as a senior member of his team. Yi Bun Gul was sitting with one of his juniors when we met and I asked the younger man, Kim Song U, whether these smacks from Yi Bun Gul upset him. He explained that they were to be expected, especially when he was lazy. "Because this is a contact sport," he said, "we have a kinship with each other."

"Friendship is a bond between school friends, childhood friends," Yi Bun Gul said in his deep voice. "But for people in ssirum, jong is much stronger. We're like brothers, except that our blood is not mixed."

"There is no distance between us," said Kim, who knew that Yi Bun Gul cared about him.

So too did Yi Man Gi. When their bodies met in the ssirum ring, he understood that Yi Bun Gul felt as close to him as he did to Yi Bun Gul. They were brothers, in ssirum and in the greater fraternal order of the Korean Man.

Now, as he waited for his lunch, Yi Man Gi rubbed his thick hands over his face and explained why ssirum was a mirror of Korea, or rather the Korea that men had built for themselves.

"We're not individuals," he said. "We're in contact with other people. We care for each other. Of course there's jong between men and women. But the friendship between men is very strong. It's immeasurable. I don't know about the American women, but the Korean women understand how men are in this society. They understand the important roles men play."

Yi Man Gi did not shrink from the company of women. But on Saturday nights, after a week of practice, he sought the company of men. He was known about town and was welcomed in restaurants and drinking places. On Sundays he played golf with his friends. And in all their time together, no matter how late the hour or how addled their brains, they maintained the strict lines of seniority in speech and behavior. This demarcation in status, however, did not weaken their bond. Instead, it heightened their sense of mutual responsibility. When Yi was a boy, his parents told him that a true man was one who understood his responsibilities.

Women, it seemed to him, lived in a different world, one where they had to fend for themselves. Younger women disappointed him because they were not like the women of his mother's generation, who had worked so hard, caring for husbands, children and aging in-laws. "Korean women are strong, that's true," he said. "They had to do so much. They had to be strong. From the outside it seems that men are strong because they have strong muscles. But in Korea women are like reeds that blow in the wind. They lean with the wind. When something too stiff is hit by the wind, it will break."

Yi lighted a cigarette. He pinched the cigarette between his thumb and forefinger and held it cupped in his hand, so that the smoke rose into his palm. "I guess ordinary men would picture me as an ideal Korean man," he said. "I'm very energetic. I fight with a lot of speed and vigor. That must look manly to the viewers. Korean men like things black and white, right or wrong. I'm that way too, so they can relate to me."

I asked about his marriage prospects and with the appropriate degree of humility and a disingenuous grin he replied, "Who'd want to marry a big, fat guy like me?" His fiancée, he later admitted, was in New York, studying for her graduate degree. I asked whether he thought life in the West might somehow compromise her in his eyes, make her less adaptable to the world as he saw it. He simply raised a beefy hand, to display all that was necessary for ensuring harmony and obedience at home.

We plowed through lunch and when Yi saw that I favored the grilled fish, he called to the waitress and insisted that I have more. He drank more of his soju. He devoured more fish. He turned to Yu Chung and told her that he could teach her husband a thing or two about treating a woman right. This made Yu Chung laugh. Women, said Yi Man Gi, did not suffer the way men suffered, even though it was often said that women's han was much the worse.

"When a woman has han," he began, waxing poetic, "it is like the frost in May. But when a man has han, the mountains tremble."

Yu Chung, looking ill, shook her head.

Yi Man Gi believed that it was men, not women, who understood the concept of loyalty. It was men, not women, who were dependable. "Women," he said, "are not faithful anymore."

"You sound like you've had a painful experience," said Yu Chung.

And Yi Man Gi lowered his head, looked away and nodded slowly.

We did not speak about his encounter with heartbreak. We talked about unimportant things for a while. But soon we returned to the question of the gulf between the sexes.

"Men might look strong," said Yi Man Gi. "But inside they're lonely. I like to depend on other people. But in extreme circumstances a woman has the power to overcome by herself."

Lunch was done and Yi Man Gi finished his soju and his cigarette. A second waitress came in to clear our table. She wore no makeup. She wore jeans, a flannel shirt and did her work without pleasure.

Yi did not tease her about her appearance. Instead he insisted upon interrogating her.

"Who's stronger," he asked. "Men or women?"

The waitress ignored him. She stacked the bowls and glasses.

"Really, c'mon," he said. "Men are stronger, right?"

The waitress wiped the table clear. She gathered the dirty dishes and bowls of unfinished kimchi in her arms. She bent over the table, raised her eyes to the Strongest Man under Heaven and with a look of sublime indifference replied, "If you say so."

Diary from the Greenhill Textile Company

S AMMI had met a young man she liked. She wondered whether he liked her. She thought about him a lot and got angry with herself when she fantasized about marrying him. She hardly knew the young man.

What remained of Sammi's diary began: *"As I was leaving the street, roses were dying. It was nice when the roses were blooming. Somehow I feel empty. Could it be because I compared them to a person? People are the same. Even after showing burning love, they separate with the pretext of some problem. I look forward to the ideal and set sail with hope and dream."*

Sammi had a mother whom she loved and pitied, and an older brother whom she did not like. Her brother drank. Her mother's face had become so drawn that, to Sammi, the flesh seemed to have withered away.

"I am sick of life, struggling for my livelihood. I want to die. But I have someone I love. My words tremble every time I talk to him. My steps shake. I feel like falling. I don't like this. Why do I love him when I dislike men? I don't understand myself. There is quiet music. The time for myself. Friends are out. My time. In a way, a romantic feeling. But only for a while. . . . I daze at the ceiling. I want to be closer to him, but he seems to be distancing himself."

Sammi worked in the Greenhill Textile Company, a factory upstairs from a poolroom and across from a church in the Seoul suburb of

Anyang. One hundred thirty people worked in the factory. They worked from 8:30 in the morning until 7:30 at night, and longer if it was a busy season. They made about three hundred dollars a month. In the busy seasons they worked seven days a week. Usually they worked six. They had two holidays a month. The owner had been issued citations for illegally operating a factory in a residential neighborhood and for keeping a dormitory in his factory. The owner was not a rich man, although in the summer, when the factory was hot, he did put in an air conditioner. He gave his employees thirty minutes for lunch. They could eat on the roof, where there was a snack bar.

"Older sisters tell me that one is more funny about appearance when one is in love. I am not like that. I want to be pure. Love is pure."

The Greenhill Textile Company made sweaters for export to Japan and France. The factory was a long room, maybe a hundred feet long. Along the windows were rows of sewing machines and next to the sewing machines was the cutting area. At the end of the day the cuttings were piled in a heap on the stairway and the gate was locked from the outside. Most everyone went home except for the thirty women who lived at the factory. They were all young women, unmarried, from the countryside. They slept in a dormitory that adjoined the factory.

The women had to be in at 11:00 at night, because that was when the gate was locked. Young men got drunk and loitered outside the factory. That was the reason given for locking the gate, to protect the women.

"I write as if I am walking in the silence of dawn.

"I look at the sky lying on the green grass as my pillow. I feel as if I have wings that are open wide. What will the sky look like? Clouds will be floating about and I will be there transforming myself as time passes by. But at times I will live in silence.

"It is a sleepless night for some reason. My thoughts are free of thinking about someone.

"Let me forget. Even when I try to forget all, your face emerges again."

* * *

The women slept three to a room. The cinder-block walls were covered with pink and white wallpaper. The women had collapsible closets to store their clothes, and shelves for their photo albums, magazines, cassette tapes and letters. The rooms were small and had no windows. The only window was in the bathroom and that is where most of their bodies were found on the morning after the fire.

"What can I do so that there will be a chance to meet him again?
"I am curious. As usual I am setting out for a walk.
"Today is 'eat-out' day. He will be there too. I talked to a friend over the telephone.
"Why am I thinking about him as my marriage partner?
"Does he like me?"

Sammi's diary was lost in the debris. It lay somewhere among the scorched posts, the soot-black sewing machines, the cinder blocks and the heap of burned cloth in the stairwell next to the gate. The long room stank of rotting cloth. The floor was covered in deep puddles from the water used to put out the fire. The firemen could not reach the women in time to save them.

Twenty-two women died and Sammi was one of them. She died, as she and the others had lived, in anonymity. For a few days after the fire the newspaper editorials called for better working conditions for the young men and women upon whom the nation's economic might was built, those who did not work for the big companies, which were safe and clean, but in the small factories that existed beyond regulation and safety standards.

"As I wished, we went on a date today. I felt my daily load of fatigue melting away.
"When I talk to him, I don't realize how the time flies.
"What he tells me in conversations about everyday life is amusing. It seems like everyday living is fun. Perhaps I am thinking about him as my partner for good. I hope he is thinking the same."

The factory was cleared of the victims' belongings and Sammi's diary was found. No one was sure what Sammi's real name was, or where she came from or how old she was or what she looked like. All they knew was that a section of a diary by a woman whose nickname was Sammi was found, that it began on June 21, 1987, and ended on an unknown date, presumably several weeks later.

Whoever wrote the diary did so during the same spring Korea was engulfed in the protest movement that set in motion the great changes in the nation's life. But Sammi did not write in her diary about politics or tear gas or Chun Doo Hwan or the fear of martial law. She wrote about being confused and wanting her confusion to be over.

"It is an irritating day. It was hot with the air conditioner off. It was dreadful having to work.

"I will endure this moment and overcome."

The families of the victims came to Anyang for a group memorial service and to negotiate their compensation with the owner. The families got angry with the money they were offered and marched through the streets of Anyang in protest when their price was not met. The police arrested the factory owner. The windows of the Greenhill Textile Company were boarded over and soon people stopped talking about the women who died.

"I've seen him again.

"I feel a stronger attachment as I meet him again and again. Is it because I like him?

"But he will soon be in the army. At most we have about eight days to be together.

"It's a shame. Why does time pass so quickly? I want to capture the time. I want to stop it. But my ability doesn't reach that far.

"What am I to do?

"My love, do you feel the same?"

I went to the Greenhill Textile Company two days after the fire. The windows were not yet boarded up and the room was lighted by filtered sunlight. I walked up to the third floor, past the poolroom and the church. In the doorway of the factory were cinder blocks and a freezer, for ice cream. Chang Wan Kil was in the long room sifting through the rubble. Chang was the night watchman. He picked up photographs of handsome young stars, clipped from magazines, and snapshots taken of the women. There was one of a young woman surrounded by red flowers and another of a woman at what might have been a picnic. Chang picked up some of the letters from the wet floor. One was a letter from a man in the army.

"It is a little sad and lonely on this Sunday.

"After spending the entire day stuck at the dorm, wrestling with the TV, why is it I cannot sleep at night?

"What is the source of my coldness and contempt? I haven't replied to your three letters.

"I dislike our encounter. I hate the environment that draws us together and that makes me like you.

"Why?

"I feel that we got close too easily and got to know everything about each other in such a short time.

"This just proves that we are young. I think about you at work pathetically. I hate myself.

"When I liked you, it probably was because I was taken with your image of diligence and responsibility. Your aura was attractive to an immature eye.

"But why am I thinking that I am wrong now? I don't know what is what. I don't want to think about anything except my work."

Chang took me up to the roof, where the women ate their dinner. He was fond of the women who lived at the factory. Chang had had his own business, but the business failed and he took the job as the watchman. He was fifty-nine years old and said that this was the hardest job he ever had because of his responsibility to the women. He said his favorite was Yoon Young Sook, who had graduated from high school this year and wanted to go to college. Chang said that she studied hard. When he talked about her, he began to cry.

Chang said that the women sometimes complained about the hours they worked. They worked until they married and then they left to have children. He said that the owner was a good man, a kind man, who gave the women meals and cakes.

The snack bar was gone from the roof. I walked to the edge and looked down at the street, crowded with traffic. Across the street, on the road to Seoul, were new apartment blocks, a wall of pale green buildings. All of Korea was beginning to look like Anyang, a town like so many other towns, without character but with its apartment blocks, crowded streets and people working well into the night. The towns looked the same and so it was sometimes easy to mistakenly conclude that the people's lives, too, were the same.

"When I think of the future I wonder what kind of person I will become.

"Will I endure and live through the dangerous life well?

"The word death *is always on my mind. I envy my friends. I envy my friends who sleep in peace.*

"What is it I am thinking of?

"Future."

At a center where young women like those from the Greenhill Textile Company can live in safety, I met a woman who asked to be called Miss Kim. She was twenty-two years old and worked in an electronics factory testing television screens. It was midafternoon and she had just woken up. Miss Kim rubbed her eyes and said that she had begun work the night before at 8:30 and finished twelve hours later. "Work itself is not difficult," she said. "The only hard part is that I get sleepy."

Sometimes her eyes hurt, especially after a long shift. A long shift might last eighteen hours. But this work, she explained, was better than the work she had done before, at a fabric factory where it was hot and dusty. Miss Kim came from the countryside. As her older brothers and sisters had, she left her parents' home the day after graduating from high school. She stayed with her brother and, through a friend, found a job.

"I heard through the older girls that I would work hard all day but I could earn lots of money," she said. "I thought I'd save more money, but my savings plan was unrealistic. I was going to send a third to my mother and save the rest for my dowry."

Miss Kim made $5.50 a day but could make more by working overtime. She usually worked twelve hours a day. She had three days off a month but would have to work if she was needed. Sometimes she went on outings with her friends if her day off fell between two overnight shifts.

"Do you enjoy living in the city?" I asked.

"No, I want to go home," Miss Kim said. "There is no green here. I was disappointed in city people. They have bad values. They are egotistic. They get things done for themselves first. I'm worried that I might be one of those people now. I've tried but I'm becoming like that."

"When I think of the future, I get a terrible headache.

"What will it be when a dewdrop tear swells in your large eye as if it will flow over? Look up at the sky and stare at the alley he left. You walk away never looking back, with your shoulders drooping. I hope, perhaps, you will look back.

"But he who promised left me taking a leave of great pain. Breaking my heart. Without a promise to return in the future.

"But my heart waits because I love.

"If this is love, I detest love.

"I will burn it off."

The fire at the Greenhill Textile Company began in the stairwell, where the cloth was piled at the end of the day. The owner of the poolroom said that flames were shooting up high between the first and second floors and that he sounded the alarm. The owner of the poolroom also said that he heard an argument outside the second floor exit at two in the morning. Others said they noticed several young men having a fight outside the factory at about the same time. But these were just stories. The police did not know what caused the fire. They reported, however, that the factory, like a kindergarten, movie house and church in the neighborhood did not have fire-fighting equipment. The factory did not have an emergency exit, only a window that led to the church.

The people who had worked at the Greenhill Textile Company and who were able to go home after work began looking for new jobs.

"My heart is aching. It is aching very much.

"I hate everyone.

"I hate older brother, Mom, older sister, all those who abandoned me in this environment.

"I will live always despising them. They think that I will live comfortably, but I am always chased by something.

"Everyone is not adapting well. I too am adapting only on the outside, but inside I always feel empty.

"Sad and lonely and empty room.

"Someday I will not be young."

SPRING

*K*OREA'S spring feels like a reward. Back streets, narrow and steep and, in winter, caked with ice, are once again passable. Spent charcoal no longer piles up in the alleys and the wind does not howl between the tall buildings.

Before the rainy season the air feels light and dry. The sky is clear. There are outings to riverbanks and forests in the countryside, which begin half an hour from Seoul. Farmers leading bullocks plow the rice paddies for the seedlings. After the planting the flooded paddies shimmer in the sun.

In the spring Korea loses its harshness. On Sunday afternoons families stroll in Seoul's Pagoda Park, Secret Garden and Kyongbok Palace, where the kings lived. The last king's two daughters still live on the palace grounds. They are never seen. They live in a modest wooden house, a house tucked among the trees. They are vestiges of the royal family that deeded the country to the Japanese in 1910. The princesses, it is said, wish only to be left alone.

The families do not pause in front of their home. It is as if the princesses did not exist. Instead, the families stop to look at the royal car and royal carriage. They stop to read the many plaques describing the destruction of the buildings on the palace grounds by the Japanese in the invasion of 1592 and the murder of the Korean queen Min by the Japanese in 1895. Then they stop at the snack bar, where the owner has packed away his space heater and begun serving ice cream.

Sunday is family day. And in the spring of 1988 families could stroll near the grounds of the Blue House, the presidential palace.

The Blue House grounds were closed to them for years. But now the government wanted to be seen as an accessible government and people were invited to stroll up to the grim-faced guards in front of the Blue House, though they could not take photographs. The National Assembly election was approaching. The government was learning the art of courting voters.

In the spring of 1988 Seoul Land, an amusement park modeled after Disneyland, opened on the outskirts of the capital. It featured Tomorrow Land, Fantasy Land and Western Land. Tomorrow Land had a ride on a UFO.

Two men with long hair and tanned faces arrived in Seoul and announced that they were North Korean defectors. People did not believe them, not with the long hair and tattoos forbidden in North Korea, and not with their odd tale of having swum the frozen Tumen River into China in December. The government gave defectors gold and houses. But these men didn't even know the North Korean dialect.

The nation's first AIDS victim, a seaman from Pusan, was forced from his home and then from the hospital. Doctors did not want to treat him. His wife also contracted the virus and their children were sent to live with relatives. Bars and brothels in Pusan began losing business.

The remains of two bears were found with their bellies slit open and their paws cut off. The bear livers and paws could fetch thirty thousand dollars on the herbal medicine market.

China and the Soviet Union announced they were opening trade offices in Seoul after the Olympics.

Five hundred new publishing companies opened.

Forty-six political prisoners were released.

The government changed its classification of the 1980 Kwangju uprising from "riot" to "democratic movement."

Chun Doo Hwan's younger brother was indicted for embezzling hundreds of thousands of dollars from the rural development institute he headed when his brother was president. People wondered how far Roh Tae Woo's government would investigate the abuses of Chun's rule, whether he would use the case against the younger Chun to show that he had broken with the past. Chun Doo Hwan apologized on his brother's behalf and resigned his honorary chairmanship of the ruling party and his position as leader of the Advisory

Council of Elder Statesmen. His younger brother was taken into custody. He was led through an angry crowd in handcuffs. A man in the crowd reached out and slapped his face because, he said, the younger Chun "did not look repentant." The younger Chun bore a striking resemblance to his brother. The arrest came three weeks before the National Assembly election.

The warm weather brought the beginning of the campaign. The campaign brought the rocks, iron pipes and kerosene bombs. The animosity of the presidential campaign had not abated.

There was only one arrest for vote buying during the National Assembly election campaign, which was surprising, considering how widely cash and gifts were distributed. The arrested government-party assemblyman had been foolish enough to have 3,754 envelopes, each stuffed with twenty thousand won—or roughly twenty-five dollars—delivered to a Seoul post office in plain view of a group of opposition supporters, who then staged a sit-in at the post office to prevent the police from seizing the envelopes and perhaps destroying the evidence.

Towels and soap were distributed in the poorer neighborhoods. When a group of opposition supporters in Pusan saw thirty boxes of soap being loaded into a truck belonging to the government party's candidate, they commandeered the truck and parked it outside their candidate's office as evidence of what was termed a gift offensive. Twenty emissaries from the government party's candidate attacked the office, beat up the opposition candidate's men, and destroyed a car and two vans. Firebombs were thrown at campaign offices and at lecterns where candidates were speaking. Candidates hired body-guards. When a band of government-party boosters attacked a smaller group of opposition men, the opposition people attacked the government-party office with rocks and firebombs.

All of it seemed a painful and expensive exercise to no purpose. The government seemed all but assured of victory, with the two main opposition factions still blaming each other for Roh Tae Woo's victory in December. This victory would set the government on a course of sustained rule. It had won the open presidential election and now it would win the assembly. That the president could no longer dissolve the assembly did not matter (the constitutional changes enacted after the June 1987 demonstrations denied the president that power): The assembly would remain his rubber stamp.

The opposition would remain fractious and removed from power. But this time, for the first time, it would be the people, and not the military, who would seal the government's claim to power.

The National Assembly was the legislative equivalent of the blue suits and civilian titles the nation's succession of generals had used to create the illusion of leaders of a democratic nation—functioning like the high-minded names the military-backed government parties had given themselves: Park Chung Hee's Democratic Republican party and Chun Doo Hwan's Democratic Justice party.

The assembly had its opposition members. And while they could vote against the government and, if they were bold enough, speak against the government, they could not stop the government from doing what it wanted to do. The assembly was housed in a giant white and green block far from the center of Seoul. Its size and remote locale spoke volumes about the legislative body's role in the nation's life: The assembly's building looked commanding, but the institution was as hollow as the inside of its great white dome.

Although the opposition had scored well in recent assembly elections—especially in the cities—it remained in the minority, a fractured minority with the respective opposition camps seemingly incapable of unity on any score other than their opposition to the government.

The approach of the election brought none of the euphoria of the presidential campaign but, rather, a sense of resignation, a feeling that the revolution of rising expectations that began the year before was all but over. The opposition leaders, Kim Young Sam and Kim Dae Jung, now seemed like old vaudevillians performing long after vaudeville had died.

The impending fall seemed especially profound for Kim Dae Jung, who had always sought the moral high ground for himself. Kim Young Sam was a pleasant man whose office reminded me of a big-city ward heeler's, with an anteroom filled with hangers-on reading newspapers and waiting to go for lunch. But Kim Dae Jung had worked hard at seeming like something other than a politician. He spoke of sacrifice, suffering, the refusal to compromise and the importance of moral purity. Moral qualities were the idealized qualities for leadership in Korea and morality could be displayed by suffering for a purpose. Kim Dae Jung reminded everyone through his somber bearing and angry rhetoric of his personal han—his being kidnapped

by Park Chung Hee's KCIA agents in Japan in 1975, his arrest after
the Kwangju killings, his solitary confinement, his rigged trial and
death sentence, his exile to America.

In the year after his return from America—but before the events
of 1987 began unfolding—Kim Dae Jung had played the role of the
statesman wronged by cruel men. In his years spent in and out of
house arrest Kim would invite foreign correspondents to his home—
he was banned from any political activity until June of 1987, although he continued operating behind the scenes—and offer as gifts
his own hand-written platitudes about democracy and the people. So
potent was the force of Kim Dae Jung's suffering that Kim Young
Sam went on a twenty-three-day hunger strike to show that he too
had suffered for the people. Kim Dae Jung was so adept at creating
an aura of high moral standing that during the presidential campaign
people believed he might even yield to Kim Young Sam so that his
rival could defeat Roh Tae Woo. But Kim Dae Jung was also a man
with a desire, a politician's desire, and that desire was to be president.

Now the Kims were spoken of with a weariness reserved for a
relative who has overstayed his welcome. People speculated that one
consolation of the government party's victory would be the chance
to make the opposition parties true parties with platforms, beliefs
and a choice of leaders, and not vehicles for two men's grand ambi-
tions. So widespread was the antagonism to the opposition that it
was easy to forget that for all the anger with Kim Dae Jung and Kim
Young Sam there was still considerable hatred for the government,
and that that hatred combined with the loyalty that remained for the
Kims in their home provinces could make the opposition a force for
checking the government's power.

In a sense nothing had changed since December, except now the
contest was not a zero-sum game. The unlikely combination of the
two Kims and the conservative opposition party of Kim Jong Pil—
who had a score to settle with the present government for forcing
him out of power in 1979—could still lose as separate entities while
at the same time eclipsing the government party in assembly seats.
But no one expected that, not with the seeming disintegration of the
opposition and the government's new-found wisdom in public relations. The cause that began in the streets in June was lost. The
government would be stronger than ever.

I headed south, to Pusan. I did not want to be in the capital to witness more handwringing and accusations, or listen to more talk from the grinning government spokesmen about the wise voice of the people.

On the morning after the National Assembly elections, however, Kim Dae Jung was smiling. The government-party chairman resigned in disgrace. Roh Tae Woo said he would humbly accept the election results.

The split was roughly the same as it was in December. The government had indeed won the most assembly seats. But it did not win as many as the opposition parties had together.

Kim Young Sam, whose party finished second to Kim Dae Jung's, was relegated to the role of leader of the second, and not the leading, opposition party. He remained secluded for a few days before beginning to display any pleasure. He emerged into a new order—an order without precedent in the nation's history—in which he, Kim Dae Jung and Kim Jong Pil had only to agree on making life difficult for the government. And that is just what they began to do.

The opposition, with its new and unexpected power, called for a meeting with the government party to discuss committee chairmanships. The opposition wanted hearings to investigate corruption under Chun Doo Hwan. The opposition wanted a parliamentary investigation of the Kwangju killings. The opposition hinted that it might well force Roh to make good his campaign offer to hold a midterm referendum on his rule.

The word *share* entered the political vocabulary. Politicians, some gleefully, others mournfully, began searching for ways to define it. The word seemed new, but only because it had been out of use for so long that people had forgotten that it was part of their heritage. Sharing implied the balance between ruler and ruled that Confucius had spoken of thousands of years before. Korea had embraced Confucianism, or rather the elements of the philosophy that were most useful. It took five thousand years and the seemingly banal exercise of a legislative election to establish in fact a principle so long ignored.

Confucius's disciple Mencius was once asked "What is the standard of a ruler?"

He replied, "The mandate of heaven."

"What is that?"

"The voices of the people."

In the heady weeks after the National Assembly election, when the despair of the campaign gave way to a sense that change was coming—that so much once again seemed possible—I instead chose to look back. I sought out the Confucianists. I knew what had gone wrong in the recent past for Korea. But I knew little about what had once been the nation's promise, and how that promise had been turned to ash—and the ash to han—a long time ago.

The Mandate of Heaven

*F*IFTY men, middle-aged and elderly, attended the rites for Confucius. They greeted one another with smiles and handshakes. The men were descendants of the yangban class, the class of scholars. Their ancestors were the elite of feudal Korea; they had enjoyed the honors and benefits that Confucian philosophy accorded the learned. The men gathered to honor Confucius twice a month, on the first and the fifteenth days of the Chinese calendar.

Most wore somber business suits and a few came in traditional clothing—baggy pants drawn in at the ankles, silky white tunics and long, flowing coats that tied in big bows high across the chest. Those whose turn it was to officiate at the rites wore white or blue robes and tall, stiff, brimless black hats that tied tight under their chins. At ten in the morning they formed a line and walked in silence across a courtyard to the shrine on the campus of the Sung Kyun Kwan University.

The university had moved to its present location in Seoul in 1398, roughly a thousand years after its founding. It was established in the second year of the rule of King Sosurim of the Koguryo dynasty, in the year 372. Sung Kyun Kwan was moved and renamed several times as dynasties fell and were replaced by new dynasties. Now the university was spread across a modern campus, near an entertainment district lined with coffee shops and inexpensive restaurants where students from many universities jammed the narrow side streets on Saturday nights.

The shrine to Confucius was wide and built of fading red wood. It stood in a compound of similar buildings that had comprised the

Confucian academy when only the scholarly class studied the teachings of Confucius. The compound sat on the edge of the new campus, separated from the noisy street and the modern buildings by a gray stone wall. The men assembled under the sloping tile roof of a wooden shelter, slipped off their shoes, placed their coats in a pile under a thick, leafy tree and assembled in neat rows on straw matting. The leaders of the rites climbed the stone steps to the wide doorway and kneeled before the dim entrance to the shrine.

Inside was a simple altar: a high, wide wooden chair, empty but for a wooden tablet upon which was written the characters of Confucius's name. The chair was surrounded by smaller chairs, each of which bore a tablet with the name of one of Confucius's followers. The shrine was arranged like a classroom.

The descendants of the scholarly class listened to the brief prayer and then dropped to their knees. They placed their palms on the ground and bowed their heads. Incense was burned. An elderly man who arrived five minutes after the prayer began stood outside the wall and berated himself gently for having missed the rites.

Before the rites began, one of the elders approached and told me that he had been to China and visited Confucius's birthplace. There was a shrine there and several men to attend it. But the twice-monthly service was no longer conducted. Though this saddened him, it also reinforced his belief that only in Korea were rites for Confucius still performed as they should be.

The Confucian elders were the priests of tradition. They believed that the best future of the nation lay in resurrecting the virtues of the past, just as Confucius had believed that the best future for China lay, in part, in principles that had made for the glorious times that preceded his time, when rulers were wise and good men who understood the importance of humanity.

Confucius said, "If a ruler is upright, all will go well without orders. But if he himself is not upright, even though he gives orders they will not be obeyed."

It was the latter that spoke of Korea. This distressed the Confucianists. "If you look back at our history, there was never a king who lived up to Confucius's expectation of a good king," Choi Jeun Duk, the vice-president and dean of Confucian studies at Sung Kyun Kwan, told me. "You should not rule with law but with virtue and the people will obey with their hearts. But that was never realized."

A virtuous ruler would enjoy the mandate of heaven, a vague and endlessly pursued qualification that granted him the right to unquestioned rule so long as he was benevolent. For centuries before and after Confucius—who did not invent the concept but built upon it—rulers sought this mandate, manufacturing various qualities to show that they indeed possessed it and were therefore entitled to be obeyed. Though the modern rulers of Korea had shed their military ranks and uniforms and assumed the pose of popularly elected civilian leaders, the mandate of heaven eluded them.

People did not always obey and did not give them their heart. Confucius had spoken of "reciprocity" between ruler and ruled and this essential point was lost upon the men who ruled Korea and wanted to be obeyed by people to whom they did not feel obliged to extend the slightest humanity.

The two-thirds of the nation that voted against Roh Tae Woo in the presidential election believed that the logical culmination of the campaign that began in June of 1987 would be the ascension of a leader who enjoyed this mandate. But because they were divided on who the ruler should be, Roh became their president with a plurality that did not represent a mandate of any sort, let alone one of heaven.

Still, he would lead and he vowed to at least practice some forms of benevolence. But people did not seem pleased or convinced. And so, with the coming of spring the nation found a way to secure for itself the benevolence its rulers never bothered to extend. Confucius had not spoken of parliamentary elections as a way to achieve the mandate of heaven.

While I was devouring all this talk of the tidy confluence of politics and principle, Professor Choi was getting bored. Politics, as such, did not interest him, despite all that Confucius had said about the proper behavior of rulers. "His ideas are not limited to leaders and leadership," said Professor Choi. The professor was concerned about family values and the ruin of Confucianism, a set of beliefs he regarded as a religion, despite the Western critics who saw it as no more than a philosophy. "Anything can be called a religion if it solves the questions of life," said the professor, who believed Confucianism accomplished this and wanted more Koreans to believe it too.

The professor sat in his large and drafty office in the middle of a long corridor of a large and drafty building. (Korean universities, historically without money for such extras as heating, are so cold in the winter that students wear jackets and long underwear to class.) Behind him hung a long scroll painting of Confucius. The professor wore a blue suit and long, gray sideburns. Despite the twice-monthly rites performed at the university and the major rites performed twice a year to honor the spirit of Confucius, he worried about the absence of Confucian ritual in Korean society, most especially the absence of the rites performed for the spirits of ancestors—rites that bound each generation to the preceding generation so that the past was never far removed.

Professor Choi did not shrink from attaching blame: He pointed to the Christians, who now claimed one in every five Koreans. Christians filled both the ten-thousand-seat Yoido Full Gospel Church and the small evangelical congregations founded by charismatic leaders of varying degrees of legitimacy. So ubiquitous were these storefront churches that their red neon crosses dominated the nighttime view of Seoul from above. Christianity, banned for centuries by Korea's kings, had made many converts in the late nineteenth and early twentieth centuries, in good measure because of the Western political ideas they brought with them, ideas that proved popular in a nation that had passed quickly from feudal to colonial rule. Ministers and Christian associations were in the vanguard of resistance to the Japanese colonial government. This, however, did not much matter to Professor Choi.

"To tell you the truth, a lot of us Confucianists voted for Roh Tae Woo in the presidential election," he said. "The two Kims were too Christian."

He continued in this bitter vein. "There has been sixteen hundred years of Confucian influence in Korea. Confucius's analects have been our spiritual pillar," he said. "The way the Christians went about spreading their religion did away with traditional ideas. They didn't want to compromise. The Christians who died in the past did not die because they were martyrs but because they refused to worship their ancestors."

They died because they had failed to perform their duties. Confucius envisioned a harmonious world in which each man and woman understood the duties inherent in his and her relationships: the relationships between ruler and subject, father and son, husband and wife, elder brother and younger brother, and between friends. Yet, said Professor Choi, "it's true that over time these principles have undergone a lot of distortion."

The distortion generally came in a downward direction—in the arrogance of rulers, in the bullying of husbands, in the superior airs older brothers assumed with younger brothers. The Confucianists believed, as Confucius's disciple Mencius had taught, that man was an inherently good being who came into life as a sheet of white paper, unsullied. Corruption was learned behavior. "We're trying to go back to the original state of man, which is good," said Professor Choi. There were 231 Confucian academies across the nation and Sung Kyun Kwan was the greatest. At each of these schools the ideas of duty and responsibility were disseminated.

And yet the message did not always take. Younger people were expected to bow in the presence of their elders, children in the presence of their parents and wives in the presence of their husbands. But often only half of the responsibilities were being fulfilled. Now relationships were questioned and strained. Children went away from the cities leaving parents behind. Parents threatened to disinherit children who did not marry according to their wishes. People who once desired only stability had turned against the government. When Confucius was asked by a student, "Is there any one word that can serve as a principle for the conduct of life," he replied, "Perhaps the word *reciprocity.*"

In its absence there could be no harmony, which is why the Confucianists turned to the past—to see how harmony might be achieved. "Yes, it's part of our Confucian tradition to constantly reflect upon our past," the professor said. "Some say that Confucianists want to go back to the feudal system. I disagree. Confucianism looks back at the past not because we want to embrace the past but to learn from it."

To learn from the past meant to honor it and celebrate it. Food was provided for the spirits of ancestors. An oversized chair was provided for the teacher, Confucius, and twice a month the Confucianists gathered to bow low before it.

This was their duty. The Confucianists wanted all Koreans, both weak and powerful, to know their duties. But only the weak, the restive weak, seemed aware.

The Apocalypse and the End of Han

*C*HAE Hyung Woo, who was twenty-four years old and had been a believer in the faith of Cheungsando for eight months, knelt before a blackboard and, with diagrams and mathematical equations, explained how the earth was going to shift on its axis and place Korea at the center of the world. He took an empty juice container, punched a pen through it and demonstrated the realignment that was coming with the apocalypse.

"When will the apocalypse come?" I asked and Chae and the other five members of the Cheungsando circle of Yonsei University laughed.

"The most we can say is that it is not far away," said Bae Byung Cheol, a believer for over a year and the group's senior member. "We don't reveal the date because it will cause a panic and people will give up and wait. All I can say is that the date is near."

"Most will perish in natural disasters," said Chae. "I can point to the spread of disease."

"The spread of AIDS is a sign from God of what will happen in the future," Bae said.

"But just as the center of the storm is quiet, so too will the center of this new axis be untouched," Chae said of a line that will extend northward from a point in southern Argentina to Korea. "After the apocalypse the Korean people, with the mandate of heaven, will go out and save foreign people if we can get there in time."

"And how will this saving be done?" I asked.

Again the members of the circle laughed. "Top secret," said Jung Young Jae, once a student radical and a new believer.

Chae said, "I can summarize Cheungsando like this: We are the doctors of the earth. If the patient refuses to accept the medicine, he cannot survive. Only when they embrace our method can they survive."

"It's not as if we own the world," said Jung. "We will lead the world."

The circle met every day for study and chanting in a cramped room in the student union annex. At the far end of the room was an altar to Cheungsan, who will bring salvation. The altar was covered with red felt topped with white paper. There were fresh roses on the altar, as well as an incense burner and a brass candelabra. It was raining and the room felt dank and oppressive. A heavy white curtain drooped over the window, covering rusting bars. The members of the circle sat on the linoleum floor as Chae, first with a plastic-covered display and then on a blackboard, explained how the apocalypse will herald the dawn of Korea's ascent.

He said, "In any society there is a group in control and by the same token there's a nation that acts out the will of God and that nation, to us, is Korea. The ultimate goal of Cheungsando is saving the human race."

Like its followers at Yonsei and other campuses, Cheungsando was new, at least when compared with Buddhism, which came from China in the fourth century, and shamanism, which preceded Buddhism by a thousand years. Cheungsando was an early-twentieth-century adaptation of a mid-eighteenth-century religion called Tonghak, or Eastern Learning. Tonghak was to be not only the salvation for the nation's peasantry—its founder was a fallen nobleman—but the means of halting the spread of Western thinking, especially Catholicism, which had won many Korean converts. Tonghak's founder, Choe Che-U, was arrested and beheaded in 1864 for misleading the people and fomenting social discord.

Thirty years later his followers, seeking both a posthumous pardon for him and a halt, this time, to the spread of Japanese commercial influence, began demonstrating across the nation. The government responded with force and the demonstrations became a rebellion. The king, desperate, turned to the Chinese, to whom the nation had paid tribute for centuries. The Japanese, anxious to preserve their position, entered the fray and the Sino-Japanese War ensued. Tonghak all but vanished. It was not until the formal annex-

ation of Korea by Japan that nationalists, seeking a religious foundation for their cause, returned to Tonghak, which envisioned an ideal
world where the dignity of mankind was paramount and man and
God became one. Cheungsando was one of the faiths that emerged.
Today it claimed a million followers, many of them young.

Chae asked me, "What books on Cheungsando have you read?"
I replied that I had not read any books but that I had read articles
and spoken with a professor about the faith. Chae wanted to know
the name of this professor because the professor might have spoken
unsympathetically about Cheungsando, as did many nonbelievers.
(The professor, a Christian, dismissed the articles of faith. But he was
struck by its popularity among his students.)

Chae explained why my conversation with the professor, or most
any academic who was not a believer, might distort my view of
Cheungsando. "We've heard that our history was five thousand
years old," he said, citing the date generally regarded as the begin-
nings of the Korean people. "Most Korean history was based on our
thinking of Korea as subservient to other nations. But in Cheungsando we've discovered that our history is nine thousand years old.
Cheungsando is part of an effort to enlighten people about our lost
history. We also have a movement that transcends religion—the
Movement for the Great Nation."

Chae wrote down complicated formulas that made his explanation
seem more a proof in theoretical physics than the basis of belief. He
scribbled out the equation for cosmic years—each, he said, equalled
129,600 standard years—and explained that the spring of a cosmic
year had ended and the world was well along in summer. Soon the
fall would come, and with it the apocalypse. "We believe there will
be a new season and a new Korea and only the good people will
remain."

He spoke in a loud voice, sure and resolute. He did not waver in
reciting his catechism. And as he spoke, the others sat in silence,
commenting only to underscore a point. Scattered on the floor were
the books they studied, the books of proofs and evidence and history, which, they believed, they had been denied all their lives.

I listened as they offered me a short course on faith—the standard
introduction, Chae said, was three hours long—and fought the urge
to dismiss them. It was not the faith that moved me. It was the need,
the need to erase the han of Korea's history.

* * *

Among the books the believers produced was a volume called the *Handangogi.* It was one of the pillars of Korean history and was a difficult tract to decipher. But recently the task had been accomplished by an amateur historian named Kim Tae Yong, who had spent ten years on a story version. I had met Kim Tae Yong in his office at the *Korea Times,* where he edited special advertising inserts. He was thin and drawn and the collar of his white shirt was yellow and frayed.

"I'm not a historian," Kim said. "But I want to explain to you why I wrote such a story. Ask me why."

So I did.

"We don't know the true history of Korea," he said. "There are historians in Korea who were educated by the Japanese imperialists. People do not have ways of getting in touch with the true Korean history. Up to now we were educated to believe that we were brought up in a Chinese-based culture. But Chinese culture is five thousand years old and ours is ten thousand years old. The Chinese were influenced by our culture, even the Chinese written characters."

As Kim spoke, a man at the next desk looked up and smiled. Kim told of the federation of twelve counties 9,185 years ago that comprised the first "Korean federation" and of the origins of the Korean people in Mesopotamia. He said, "Those people are the ancestors of the Korean people."

I asked Kim how he researched his book. He became tentative. He had read many issues of a magazine called *Freedom,* he said, and collected documents from the magazine's library. He went to secondhand bookstores and collected books. He read perhaps four hundred books, he said, and shared his research with a circle of friends who, like him, were "nationalistic historians." The circle gathered once or twice a month to discuss new findings.

"The original thinking about the Korean people was demolished and went underground," he said. "Our rulers submitted to the Chinese rulers and we have not recovered from that influence yet."

Kim had been a soldier in the North Korean army during the Korean War. He was captured by the South Koreans. He spent most of the war as a prisoner. When the war ended, he remained in the South and did not see his family again. He was alone. "I felt a sadness at being a nobody," he said. "I asked myself, 'How did Korea become such an insignificant country?' That's how I started to study history."

* * *

It was the professor who had dismissed Cheungsando who told me how disappointed he was when he returned home after visiting the great monuments of China and was struck by how small Korea's monuments looked in comparison.

The nation was dotted with monuments to epochs grand and tragic, and the greatest of these monuments was Kyongju. Kyongju was a small city in the southeast that had been a capital thirteen hundred years ago. It was not the capital of Korea because there was no Korea then but, rather, three warring states. Kyongju was the capital of the kingdom of Silla, which today is Kyongsang and Kangwon provinces. Silla fought with Paekche—now Cholla Province—and Koguryo, which covers part of what is now North Korea. Of the three, Silla was the greatest and, ultimately, the strongest. It conquered Paekche and then part of Koguryo, so that by the eighth century the peninsula was reduced to two states—Silla and a new kingdom, Parhae. A single Korean nation—encompassing today's North and South—did not come into being until the fourteenth century. It lasted until 1945 and in its final thirty-five years was reduced to the status of a Japanese colony.

Still, it is Kyongju that Korean students learn of and where they are taken on class trips, which resemble pilgrimages. The city's primary attraction is the burial mounds of the Silla kings. The Korean countryside is filled with burial mounds, small round hills several feet high, often set in pairs. But the burial mounds of Kyongju are the size of two-story buildings. They rise from the flat earth in gentle arcs. Devoid of angles and hard edges, they do not punch at the sky as do the pyramids but instead sit perched upon the earth, fat and wide. They are covered with grass. They are so smooth that their majesty is lost when the view is cluttered. But all of Kyongju is cluttered, cluttered with the residue of monument building.

I went to Kyongju with a Korean friend who reminisced about his first trip to the city, when he was in school. He was taught all about what the capital had been and the grandeur of Silla civilization, with its poets, temples and stone pagodas. (Kyongju was then a country town without paved roads and with few buildings, so that the burial mounds dominated the horizon.) What he liked best about the Kyongju of his youth was the feeling of being transported.

But now, he said, Kyongju was different. The roads were paved. The downtown was crowded, dusty and noisy with motorcycle and tour-bus traffic. The wooden homes of the noble class sat next to restaurants that tried to replicate the traditional architecture, like the roofs of service stations and phone booths in America's recreated historic villages. Kyongju had a museum and gift shops and, on the outskirts of town, a new resort with golf, tennis, a kiddie land called Dotoruk World and pleasure boats shaped like giant swans.

Kyongju had been left alone until 1971, when Park Chung Hee decided that the city could be of use. Park drafted a plan. He wrote to his subordinates, "The old city of Kyongju must be redeveloped to show the feeling of beauty, grandeur, luster, sophistication and far-reachingness." Park set down a primer on development, as if he were instructing children. He reminded his subordinates that the new Kyongju would need a plan, wide roads and plenty of parking, as well as reconstruction of the historic sites. Cement was used where the wood was old.

Not everyone in Kyongju liked Park's idea, but Park was in charge and people did what he wanted. "Most of the plans were absurd," said Oh Pyong Ok, who was then a journalist and now worked in the Kyongju tourist center. Oh had opposed the plans in his articles. "But Park Chung Hee was too strong," he said. "He controlled everything. No one listened to me. Park wanted to make Kyongju an international tourist city."

Oh slipped off a shoe, lit a cigarette and reflected on a protest movement that went nowhere: "Park wrote, 'Make it an international tourist city and we can make a lot of foreign currency and develop our national culture.' He thought there were a lot of historic relics here and he wanted to make the best use of them. One organization tried to pressure the government to keep the old Kyongju. But we had no way to protest. We lost the pure image of old Korea. Everything has been modernized, even in an old city like Kyongju. Park Chung Hee wanted to make Korea grand—big and strong."

His comment reminded me of something a Korean friend had said of Park. He suggested that Park's particular han was a combination of his being a physically small man and the president of a small nation. Park struck my friend as a ruler intent on making Korea great, so that he could feel he was the president of an important place. Kyongju would be the monument to a Korea that could glory in its past.

* * *

I returned to the burial mounds. In the central park that contained several mounds—mounds dwarfed in scale by a vast, concrete plaza—visiting high-school boys from Seoul played guitars and eyed the girls. On the far side of this park, away from the ranks of tourist buses, was a second park bordered by a barbed-wire fence. The fence had a hole in it and that was how Im So Hee and her two friends from school got in.

Today was a vacation day. It was warm and sunny and the girls wanted to sit outside instead of at home watching television. They pulled on blades of grass as the wind blew gently through the trees and talked about the Kyongju they had read about in school.

Im said, "Even though I live here, when I read about Kyongju in the history books and read how grand it was, I was disappointed. I expected something grand and good."

"The scale is not as important as the spirit," said Chae Yun Chong. "But in the old days there must have been something great here. But after time it was tarnished and destroyed. There is no palace, even though this was the capital city. There are no reminders. I also expected something great."

"Like the Eiffel Tower?" asked a friend.

"Yes."

"Like Pudak Temple?" asked another, referring to the famous temple nearby.

"No," Chae said. "That's not great. That's just a temple."

I asked the members of the Cheungsando circle about doubting their faith. Chae Hyung Woo said he had not yet experienced doubts. "I worry about what will happen to a lot of people when the apocalypse comes," he said. "That bothers me at night."

Jung Young Jae had been a Christian. His father was a minister and Jung was keeping his new faith a secret from his parents. His doubts were about Christianity. As he grew older, he said, he came to believe that each nation had a faith that belonged to that nation alone. Christianity could not be that faith for Korea, but Cheungsando could. "I believe that Cheungsando is the only way of showing the particularness of the Korean people," he said. "And of saving the world."

On the gray wall of the meeting room was a map of both Koreas, with a blue line that ran parallel to the border. The line showed the path that the believers would follow in a few weeks, on the faith's three-day trip across the width of South Korea "for the resurrection of the national spirit." Chae said that many people had shown interest in this trip. "We have four thousand years of history lost to us," he said. "We want to make people aware of this. That is our chief purpose."

In the meantime the message of Cheungsando was spread by young men and women who stood on street corners distributing literature and answering questions. There were lectures. The last lecture at Yonsei, Chae said, attracted three hundred people. There were four Cheungsando shrines in Seoul and the members of the Yonsei circle went to the shrines to pray twice a week with other believers.

The newest member of their circle was Sung Mi Kyung, who was the only woman. She was twenty-one and demure in a white blouse buttoned to her neck. I asked how she saw herself in the world before she discovered Cheungsando.

"I was suffering from anxiety," she said. "I was very nervous because Korea was a small country and divided and there was a constant threat of war."

She spoke of the way many of her generation reacted to the world beyond Korea, those who were convinced Korea's problems lay with the presence of foreigners and if the foreigners left, the nation could be one again and the world would treat Koreans with dignity.

"A lot of people cry out, 'Yankee, go home!'" she said. "But I always felt that the responsibility of how we are treated falls on us. We have to face up to this so that others will respect us. I have only been a member for a month. I was caught up studying for exams. Now I feel that I need to study more, to know about Cheungsando."

In Seok's Courtship

IN Seok's parents wanted him married and he did not know how much longer he could keep them at bay. In Seok was not opposed to marriage as a concept, only to the idea that he marry because it was time to marry and that he quickly find an acceptable woman. The suitability of this woman would, of course, be determined by In Seok's father, who had already rejected the woman In Seok wanted.

In Seok and I were traveling north by bus from Pusan toward the countryside and Kyongju. The bus station was on the outskirts of town and that was fortunate because the traffic in Pusan was reputed to be the worst in this country where traffic was always bad. No one had expected so many people to own their own cars and the roads could not accommodate them, especially in Pusan, where if the highways were jammed—and they often were—the only alternative was the alleys, where the paving was old and uncertain.

In Seok, who was twenty-eight, had been back in Seoul for less than a year. His parents were not entirely pleased. In Seok had left home for a company job in Seoul. He had gone to college in Pusan, not to one of the famous universities in Seoul, but he had found a job with the sort of cachet and promising future that weighed heavily in the mind of Korean fathers seeking sons-in-law. But In Seok hated this job, hated having to stay late in the office because he could not leave before his superior, hated the drudgery of his paper-shuffling assignment. In Seok wanted to see the world. Although he had never left Korea, his English was fluent. So In Seok, much to his parents' chagrin, returned to their home and began looking for work that might interest him. In the meantime he worked as a per-diem interpreter. When I called, he was just finishing interpreting in court for an American serviceman accused of theft.

I had met In Seok during the June demonstrations. On a Sunday night in their midst we walked along a wide boulevard in downtown Pusan following thousands of people as they marched toward the district police station. Just before they reached the station, the riot police launched a tear-gas attack and before I could get my gas mask on, I collapsed in the street choking. In Seok grabbed me by the collar and dragged me away as the skeleton police attacked the crowd, kicking and punching. Tear gas did not bother In Seok.

"You may think I am a mild-mannered person," he said and, indeed, with his wide face and gentle smile, I did. "But I was in the special unit of the riot police for my military service. I fired the pepper pots—the rapid-fire cannon. In our training we had to go into a room filled with tear gas without a gas mask, do calisthenics and sing."

I offered a gas mask to In Seok, but he said he did not need it. His fortitude only heightened my amazement and humiliation at the sight of Koreans in the face of tear gas. They coughed. They gagged. They dabbed at their eyes. But they took it. My lungs felt as if they were being hollowed out with sandpaper. Koreans liked the tear gas no more than I did. I choked and collapsed. They endured, blew their noses and even helped a prostrate foreigner to his feet.

The bus station was crowded with soldiers, families and old men who spent the day sitting in the waiting area smoking cigarettes and making their points by jabbing each other with their canes. The bus was full—it was a holiday weekend—and In Seok and I were pressed close together in our seats. Pusan's gray rows of shops, high rise apartments and warrens of old homes gave way to the rice fields and mountains. The land was green and the sun was bright and In Seok talked eagerly about a new international airline opening in Seoul. He had applied for a job. In Seok thought the work might involve overseas travel. He was also working on Spanish.

But that was the dream, a dream pricked and deflated every time his parents presented him with the name of a new girl to marry. In Seok had already had thirteen arranged meetings and rejected, or been rejected by, each of the girls. In Seok had known whom he wanted to marry. She was his girlfriend in college and now she was gone. In Seok's father did not approve of her because her father had died. This death, sad as it was, had lowered her value as a prospective addition to In Seok's family; in a land devoted to filial piety a fatherless family was a family of diminished worth. Their boy could do better. Their boy could command a family intact, with a father to whom his father could talk.

There was also the matter of her weight. The girl, In Seok's father decided, was too thin. He reasoned that her thinness bespoke physical weakness, which meant, in turn, that she would be unable to assume the responsibilities of the eldest son's wife. These responsibilities involved cooking, caring for her husband's parents when they got old and supervising the wives of his younger brothers. In Seok's father decided that this girlfriend would not be up to the task.

"What did you do?" I asked.

"I resisted," said In Seok.

"And then what did you do?"

"Then I became resigned."

In Seok could have continued resisting, refusing to obey his father's command. But he could not ignore his father's warning—that should he disobey, In Seok need not bother coming to him for an apartment loan when he married. In Seok explained to me that this had happened to many of his friends. They had plans and ideas and were then told by their parents that any attempt to realize their dreams would mean the end of financial assistance. The amount needed for an apartment down payment was too great for a young couple. A young man needed his parents, who were pleased to offer loans with strings attached to their resigned and obedient children.

In Seok told me about a friend who was engaged to marry a woman he loved but was then told by his mother that the marriage was out of the question because her fortune-teller thought the union inauspicious. The wedding hall had already been booked and the guests invited. So the young man's parents replaced his bride with another.

"What did your friend do?" I asked.

"He resisted," said In Seok.

I asked In Seok what happened next and he said that the wedding went ahead as planned and that his friend showed no despair in marrying the replacement. Nor did In Seok seem terribly upset telling his story, which made me think that perhaps the days of his resistance were numbered. Resignation, now registered in In Seok's soft voice, could not be far off.

A bus of revelers passed. The men were in the aisles singing into a microphone and drinking. In Seok thought that they likely were returning from a company outing and engaging in the mandatory drinking. You could not simply smile and put up a hand and say, "Thanks, but no," when the soju bottle was passed your way. You took it and drank and then drank some more and then laughed very loud and sang into the microphone. There was no point in resisting, In Seok said. The last time he tried resisting the offer of the soju bottle, a friend grabbed him by the collar and screamed at him for not having fun. In Seok did not like to drink, but that did not matter to his friend. They were out and the workday was done and it was time to have fun. "What's wrong with you?" barked In Seok's friend as he pushed the bottle on him. In Seok was already suspect because he had quit his job, resisted his parents and did not smoke. After a while, he said, it was just easier to take the bottle, just as it was easier to marry the girl your parents wanted you to marry.

Still, In Seok was holding out. So too was his younger brother, who was in the army. In Seok's brother had a girlfriend and she was a stewardess. In the eyes of conservative parents like In Seok's this made her little better than a street walker. But In Seok's brother wanted her and would not relent. In Seok did not know how long his brother would resist before he dropped his girlfriend.

The pressure was too great. One morning at breakfast In Seok's mother served him ground antler horns. The horns were an herbal cure for impotence. In Seok's mother was concerned that there might be a physiological explanation for her son's refusal to marry any of the girls to whom he'd been introduced. There was no point in In Seok trying to explain to her that he had wanted someone else.

The bus sped along the rural highway, passing cars going too slowly. We passed farm villages where the roads were not paved and the elderly farmers worked the fields with bullocks. There were wild-cherry blossoms in the mountains. But in the bright sun the mountains looked hard and craggy. In Seok looked out the window. He smiled and shook his head. His father knew the most famous matchmaker in Pusan. A wife would be found, an acceptable wife, obedient and durable.

"I've seen tons of people like that," Shin Hye Yong told me. Mrs. Shin had been in the matchmaking trade for thirty years and had introduced six thousand couples. Mrs. Shin, who operated out of a dingy office in downtown Seoul, was above all a realist. Romance was all well and good for Westerners but was inapplicable in Korea, where the interests of the family and child were bonded together by the "stickiness" of jong.

Romantic notions, however, had been muddying the thinking of the young people and Mrs. Shin recognized that she would have to accommodate their needs. Parents continued accompanying their children to the initial meetings she arranged. But now the parents were expected to leave after the introductory chitchat, so that their children might have the chance to get acquainted without adult supervision. This represented a significant departure from meetings of the not-so-distant past, when children sat with their heads bowed while their parents took turns extolling the educational background and wealth of their family.

"Family was all that mattered," Mrs. Shin said. "But now there is a conflict between parents and children. Parents still want to know about lineage. But the mood among young people is that love is all that matters."

At times Mrs. Shin worried about a future in which love became the dominant consideration in courtship—"I'm afraid we'll soon be just like the United States. Young people will meet someone on the street and say, 'I love you,' and get married. It's not that it's bad. It's just that we have different habits." The different habits eased Mrs. Shin's fretting, especially when she reminded herself how Korean parents reared their children.

"A child's happiness is connected with his family's happiness," she said. "Our life is a web that we spin. We don't teach our children to be independent. Korean young people don't have the ability to cut away from the web of the family."

Few parents still imposed a union upon their children. But Mrs. Shin could not envision a time when a Korean parent would allow a child to choose a spouse without familial consideration. The child, if disappointed by his parents' intervention, might resist parental pressure, hoping they might surrender. Or the child could do as his parents wished and nurse the han he felt toward them for forcing him to marry a woman he did not want.

When I saw In Seok again, he had moved to Seoul to work not for the new airline—his father did not think the aviation industry, with its emphasis on travel, a seemly line of work—but for a consumer electronics firm. He hoped that in a few years he might at last be able to go abroad.

In Seok worked from 8:30 in the morning until 8:30 at night six days a week and then returned, alone, to the apartment his father had helped him rent in the fashionable Yoido section of town. In Seok's father had given him a considerable sum of money and with it he bought a television and some furniture and when his friends from work needed money, he lent it to them. In Seok did not want his friends to think he was the spoiled son of a wealthy man, but he also did not want to risk losing their friendship by failing to extend credit. In Seok also invested in the stock market.

The money for the apartment and the television and the stock market made it all the more difficult for In Seok to refuse his parents when they insisted he come to Pusan on his days off and meet girls. The trip, by train, took five hours and In Seok made the trip on alternate Sundays.

He and his mother went together to hotel coffee shops, where they met the matchmaker, who introduced them to yet another mother and daughter for In Seok and his mother to scrutinize. First the matchmaker left, and then the mothers and In Seok and the young woman had two hours to talk before In Seok had to be at his next meeting. Sometimes he had three meetings on a Sunday. By the time we saw each other again, In Seok had had thirty-two meetings. In Seok returned to his parents' home at the end of these meetings and his mother asked, "Yes or no?"

And each time In Seok replied, "I don't know."

"You don't know?" screamed his mother, whose patience had all but evaporated.

In Seok had developed a strategy for having women he did not like reject him, so that he did not have to incur the wrath of his mother when he rejected them. If In Seok did not like a woman he affected boorish manners. He picked up his water glass by curling his fingers around the far side of the glass, puckered his lips, leaned over the table, brought his mouth to the glass and slurped. When the young woman asked his hobby—hobbies was the second topic of conversation, after school and before income potential—In Seok replied, "Playing go-stop,"—a card game played by men who slurped their water and spat a lot.

In Seok had met a medical student among the thirty-two women.

When his mother heard that the woman might be a doctor, she offered to build her a clinic. In Seok's parents were desperate, but they were not fools. They knew that In Seok was resisting them and they would not tolerate his resistance much longer. A few weeks before we met, his mother and father sat him down and for four hours berated him for his selfishness. His mother told him that she was tired of cooking and cleaning and wanted a daughter-in-law to move into the house and do the housework for her. She reminded him that his brother could not marry until In Seok married and that his bride had to be at least twenty-seven years old because his brother's new and acceptable girlfriend—the stewardess he loved had been dropped—was twenty-six and could not be ordered about by a woman her junior.

"Think of your family," said In Seok's mother. His father joined in, reminding In Seok that his business was not going well and he could sorely use the influx of cash that would come from friends and customers who came to buy as a congratulatory gesture for the marriage of his son. Besides, said In Seok's father, the time had come to make some changes in the family business and if word got out that his financial situation was questionable, the family's options in selecting a bride might be limited.

In Seok listened and listened and could take no more. He blurted out the words, "All right. I'll get married."

"Do you promise?" his parents asked.

"Yes, I promise," said In Seok.

"I felt as if I were strangling myself," he said when he told me of his concession to his parents. He put his hands to his throat. In Seok's father told him that the meetings would now stop and he was free to choose a bride by himself. Implicit in this statement of freedom, however, was the warning that In Seok marry someone other than the woman he had always wanted to marry.

In Seok had seen her last two years ago. Her family was moving to America and In Seok flew with her from Pusan to Seoul to say good-bye. Her mother wanted In Seok as a son-in-law so badly that she offered to take him with them. But In Seok knew he could not do that to his family. He saw her off and then took the train back to Pusan. It was a hot day and the train was full and In Seok had to stand for five hours.

"This is her picture," In Seok said. He opened his wallet and took out a snapshot of a young woman with freckles and bangs. She was smiling. They were on an outing at the beach. In Seok pointed to the windbreaker she wore and said, "That's my jacket." He looked at the picture again. He had last heard from her a year ago, when she wrote a letter telling him that he was free to marry anyone he wished.

"My parents say, 'You can't live on love.' But I don't want comfort. I want romance. I've had a girlfriend. I know what love is. I don't believe in love at first sight. How can I know if I love someone in a two-hour conversation? My friends say I'm resisting my parents and maybe it's true."

He thought of his distant girlfriend. "When I hear that she marries, then I'll get married," In Seok said and returned her picture to his wallet.

Fathers and Sons

NO one can be buried in Yongdong-mal anymore. Too many people came to the village, found the setting propitious and wanted to bury their father there. The mountains into which the village was tucked faced the sunrise. For five thousand years the people of the Korean peninsula believed that when the dead faced the sun, good fortune came to those who buried them. Yongdong-mal could not accommodate all the sons who wanted to bury their father in the mountains facing the sunrise. So the village elders decided that no one, not even those who lived in Yongdong-mal, could be buried in their village.

But sons in their middle years still came to the village looking for suitable grave sites. They took the bus from Kyongju, got off at the closest stop and walked the final mile or so, past the wide, flat stretch of barren land where excavating machines where digging up the earth. The visitors passed under the railroad bridge and followed the narrow road, past the rice fields, toward the mountains.

Yongdong-mal sat at the foot of the mountains and some of its homes were built in the wedges of the foothills. The fifteenth-century Confucian scholar Yi On Chok, who pioneered a philosophy of the nature of behavior in the universe, had lived in Yongdong-mal and there was a plaque in the village attesting to this and to the presence of three historic treasures, twelve important folklore materials and three provincial cultural properties.

Important families once lived in Yongdong-mal, families of the yangban class. Because so many fine examples of yangban homes remained in the village, the government had decided they could not be leveled and replaced, as so often happened, with the squat concrete buildings that symbolized progress toward a new Korea. The stone and mud homes were to remain as they were, so that people could come and see what a yangban village looked like, with its series of compounds, each walled off from one another and all set at an appropriate distance from the homes of the lower classes, who tilled the yangban fields. But all that remained of the yangban in Yong-dong-mal were their homes and the descendants of those who worked for them.

"Many people come to see the old houses," said Yi Won Tae. "They want to see the old way of life. When they were young, they must have heard from their grandfathers and grandmothers about this village. They also come to bury, if their father has died. It is good luck for the children if their father is buried in a good place. But now no one is buried here."

Yi, who was seventy-nine years old, sat on a flattened corrugated box on the side of a dirt road drinking soju with a friend whose name he could not recall.

"Song Jin Yong," said his friend, who was eighty-four and helped himself to another gulp of soju and a few cornflakes from the little bag they shared. They took turns buying the bottles of soju and when the bottles were finished, they argued about whose turn it was to buy the next one. Both men wore the clothing that old men still wore—baggy, silky, pale blue pants and jackets; white, deep-necked shirts—but which their sons wore only on holidays. It was a sunny day and the men wore straw hats with the brims turned up. They had patchy, stubbly beards and their hands were gnarled.

Song Jin Yong smiled a toothless grin and slipped back into his reverie as Yi Won Tae smoked his cigarette and talked about the strains on filial piety. For centuries sons did not leave their fathers, not even in death. There were grave sites to be tended and spirits to be fed. But now neither duty nor jong stopped the sons from leaving, not if they wanted to share in the nation's ascent. In less than a generation the population had moved from the countryside to the cities, most especially to Seoul. The future was not on the farms, as it had been for thousands of years, but in the factories.

"My grandfather died thirty years ago and my father died twenty-eight years ago," said Yi Won Tae. "I couldn't leave. I couldn't think of living in the city. My grandfather and father ordered me to stay in the village. Even though they died, I couldn't break their order."

Yi had four sons. Three had left Yongdong-mal. He regretted not teaching them more of what he knew about rice farming, because then they might have had a reason to stay. But even that knowledge, he admitted, would not have kept them from leaving. Only his fourth son remained in the village.

The rice fields still cut through the center of Yongdong-mal. The village rose up on either side of the fields, along dirt paths that twisted around the hillsides. The compounds—a wooden house with mulberry-paper windows, perhaps a barn and patchy garden—grew broader and grander farther uphill. One house, which had belonged to a prominent family, had ninety-nine rooms, but no one lived there anymore. The house looked down on the flooded rice fields, which shimmered in the harsh sunlight. The fields ran to the edge of the village and then beyond, spreading themselves across the flat landscape. They stretched east, toward the sun, toward the railroad tracks, where the train to the city passed.

It was noon and in a compound across from the leafy tree where Yi sat and drank, Kim Suk Chan was serving her husband's lunch. She and her husband, Chung Man Gi, were both fifty-five years old. Chung Man Gi had gone to the rice field at five, which was an hour later than he went when there was planting to be done. The couple had three sons. "I want my sons to go to the city," said Chung Man Gi. "I can't afford their education. It's better to get a salary in the city than to be a farmer."

"We wanted to live in Pusan," said his wife. "But we didn't have the money."

"Even if we had the money we're still used to the fresh air," Chung said. "We'd be afraid to live in the city."

"If we had the money," said his wife, "we'd like to live in the city."

Chung Man Gi finished his rice. His wife, her brief introspection over, resumed ladling the sauce she made. She squatted on the brown, dusty earth beside three rows of pots for pickling cabbage. Her husband rose and looked out on the rice fields, where he would work until seven and where he would work the next day and the next, without a day off. He stood before his house, which was the sort of house that the government had ordered remodeled in the

1970s because it had a thatched roof and thatched roofs were regarded as a vestige of the past.

Chung fiddled with the leg of his baggy brown trousers. The wind picked up and whipped through his gray hair. His face was brown from the sun and the deep lines were especially pronounced when he grimaced. "Nobody wants to live here," he said.

The work was too hard for the young men. The pay was not good and the prospects of marriage dim. Young women did not want to stay in the farm towns and marry into a farm family because that would mean a lifetime in service to the family. Farm parents sent their daughters to the cities, where they could make money working in factories and meet young men with possibilities. There was no one for the farm men to marry.

The Home Problem Information Bureau of Korea, which was the important-sounding title a Seoul matchmaker gave her agency, decided in 1982 to promote marriages between city girls and country boys. The first meeting attracted seventy men and women and a hundred reporters. No marriages came of the meeting. The matchmaker contacted some of the larger Korean companies and got them to donate gifts that the girls might bring to the farm families as a form of dowry. Samsung donated fourteen-inch televisions and Kumsong donated washing machines. The washing machines, however, were not popular with the farm families because they used up too much water. The electronic dowries were a substitute for the agency's original dowry, which was ten piglets. The piglets were given under the condition that when they began breeding, five piglets be returned to the agency so that they could be given to new couples. But only three or four couples bothered paying the piglet interest on their dowries.

The Home Problem Information Bureau of Korea got itself designated a nonprofit agency. It held village matchmaking parties. It had brought together two hundred couples in eight years. But countryside matchmaking was a money loser and the agency was finding it impossible to divest itself of the program. The owner of the Home Problem Information Bureau of Korea had to sell her cars and two houses to cover the cost of the program. The city girls did not want the farm boys. And the farm boys were leaving home.

* * *

"I miss my sons," said Yi Won Tae. "But how can I pull them to me? They left for the city to fill their stomach." His sons visited him four or five times a year, if they could get away. Two of his sons lived in Seoul and the third lived in another city, but which city he could not recall. Yi's sons always rushed to leave as soon as they came to see him. Only on the traditional family gatherings of the New Year and the thanksgiving holiday of Chusok did they stay a night or two.

"They come in the morning and have to return in the evening," Yi said of the visits, which sounded like similar visits to hometowns I had heard of, visits made in blue suits and rented cars so that parents might be fooled into thinking that a son who had gone off to the city in search of a wealthy man's life but instead found a life serving the meals or washing the plates or delivering the orders of wealthy men had nonetheless returned in what might have been his own car and wearing the suit he pretended to wear at the office.

"I don't know what they do," Yi said of his sons. "They're very busy."

His fourth son remained busy caring for his father or, rather, making sure that his wife cared for his father. In the warm months Yi could sit outside, but when it was cold he did not like to leave the house. "In winter I look for a warm room and stay inside the room," Yi said. He sipped his soju and smiled at his friend. "I drink with my friend. That's what I do now."

He poured a cup of soju for his friend, and then another when the first disappeared. Yi said, "Now, even though my son wants to leave for the city, he can't because he has to take care of me."

His daughter-in-law fed him. His son accompanied him to the distant hill, where Yi had buried his father and grandfather, when it was still possible for sons to bury their father in Yongdong-mal.

There, before their tombs, Yi dropped to his knees. He bowed his head to the ground, rose and bowed low again, offering a silent prayer to his father and his grandfather, who, even in death, kept him close by.

Senior Year and Mother

SENIOR year was over and Shin Hye Ra could sleep as much and as late as she wanted. Not that this made a difference to Hye Ra, who was used to four hours of sleep preceded by periodic visits from her mother, bearing coffee, reminding her that while she dozed, someone else was studying. Now Hye Ra woke up late and lazed around the house and called her friends. Sometimes they went shopping. Hye Ra was eighteen years old and this was the first real vacation that she had ever had, if you did not count her freshman and sophomore years of high school, which were merely difficult. Disposable time was a commodity that unsettled Hye Ra. She said, "Now I've got all the time in the world and I don't know what to do with it."

College would soon begin, but that would just be more of the same. College meant time—to breathe, to go to coffee shops with boys, to talk about the boys with her girlfriends and to study only when the mood struck. College was nothing like junior high school or high school. And nothing in high school was like senior year, when college entrance examinations loomed almost as large as the spectre of Mom by the bedroom door pleading, begging you to keep your eyes open for another hour or two.

This is how Hye Ra lived during her senior year: She woke at 6:30, was in school at 7:30 for an hour of study hall before homeroom. After homeroom came math; after math, English; after English, gym; after gym, Korean Literature II; after Lit II, lunch; after lunch, home economics; after home economics, biology. After biology the class cleaned their homeroom. Then they had another hour in study hall.

104

They had to study in study hall because the teachers checked on them to make sure they weren't talking and fooling around the way they did in class when overcome by the need for purposelessness.

The class broke for dinner at 5:30 and was back in study hall from 6:30 to 10:00. When Hye Ra got home her mother would say, "Welcome home. Now go and study." Sometimes her mother asked about her day and if Hye Ra told her that her day was hard, her mother said, "You've done well. It must be rough. Have a little patience. It will be over soon."

Now it was over and Hye Ra was going to college, even though college had not much mattered to her. Hye Ra's mother told her that it was important for her to go to college—"My parents always said, 'You're going to college for your own good.' " But on the eve of enrollment the only significance to a college degree that Hye Ra could discern was the possibility of marrying a boy from a better family.

College had become an important qualification for a woman, even if her degree did not assure her of a job upon graduation. The government's economic planning board reported that in the past dozen years the percentage of parents who wanted their sons to attend college had risen from 56 to 85, while the percentage who wanted their infinitely less employable daughters to get a degree had more than doubled. Seven out of ten parents wanted to see their daughters in college even though half the nation's college graduates could not find work when they graduated.

There were periodic calls in the newspaper editorials for parents to think of commercial high school for their children, so that Korea might produce a work force skilled in various technologies. That, however, was a practical consideration that held no weight when compared with the status of a college degree. Confucius valued education above all things, most especially commerce. For centuries the educated classes studied his teachings. That they could and did put them at a social advantage—which corresponded with the economic advantage in being of the landed gentry. Confucius also spoke of nations ruled by scholar-kings. And while no one would confuse the nation's modern rulers with scholars, many of its bureaucrats, especially its economic planners, returned from the United States with doctorates from MIT, Harvard or Stanford. A diploma, however, signified more than knowledge acquired; it was a certificate of class. People of the better classes went to college and children from the most humble classes could gain social mobility by admission to the better schools. The top qualifier in the past year's Seoul National University entrance exam was the son of a Pusan cleaning woman.

No one really expected college students to study. They had studied hard enough and long enough in high school, especially when they were trying to get into college during their senior year. Senior year was a time of stomachaches and mysterious muscle ailments, of headaches and sore, red eyes. Hye Ra's homeroom teacher told the class of a student who was wheeled into her college entrance exam on a stretcher, her arm hooked to an intravenous unit. Students killed themselves during senior year, students like the eighteen-year-old girl in Cholla Province who poisoned herself because she was ranked only twenty-third in her class of sixty while her brother and sisters were ranked first or second in theirs.

Hye Ra explained that it was easy to get weak and sick during senior year because breakfast was a meal often skipped in the interests of rushing off to school and study hall. Doctors were practiced at diagnosing any number of gastrointestinal ailments as psychosomatic manifestations of the emotional pain of senior year. Senior year was a time when, more than any other, a boy or girl needed Mother, or so Mother told them at two o'clock in the morning, when all they wanted was to go to sleep.

It was on nights such as those that Hye Ra, indifferent as she was about higher education, recognized why she was enduring the agony of senior year. She was doing it for her mom.

I met Hye Ra and her sister and two of their friends in a coffee shop at a gaudy shopping center, where they had come to spend the afternoon. Hye Ra was short and her face was round. Her hair was spiky with styling mousse. Hye Ra's sister, So Yong, was twenty-three and a college graduate, as were the others in their group. Their senior year was five years past. But as Hye Ra told me about what hers had been like, they nodded and smiled and began to remember the hours and pain and sufferings of their mothers. It was hard to relax around Mother during senior year. It was hard to feel free because she was always close by. Jong, after all, is not about freedom.

Hye Ra said, "When I looked at my mother, I saw that she was going through the hardship with me. She'd wake up earlier than me to make my boxed lunch."

"Mothers suffer more than we do," said Yoo Eun Jung.

"We did the studying, but our mothers did the worrying," said So Yong. "Whether she was home or out, she was always worrying about us. We are indebted to our moms."

But Bae Yumi was not comfortable with the debt. "My mom did so many things for us, for me," she said. "I saw my mom worrying. Sometimes I was very thankful. But seeing her toil like that upset my conscience. Every time I was drowsy and wanted to sleep, I'd think of my mom. I couldn't sleep. I wasn't free because of my mother's kindness."

So Yong smiled. I asked the women whether they ever wished they could have told their mother to set them free, to stop worrying about them, to stop bringing meals to their room and snacks to the library.

"Many times," said Eun Jung.

"I know what my mom was going through," said Hye Ra, "and how difficult it was for her. But it's also a burden. You sort of rebel against her kindness. I'd say, 'Just leave me alone.' But that made her sad."

The others laughed. I asked Hye Ra what her mother said when she tried to rebuff her.

"She said, 'If I could trust you with this burden, I would. But I can't. You can't do it alone. You need your mother's support with this.' I couldn't respond because I knew she was right. You can't do it without your mother."

Mothers could be hard as well as soft and persuasive. Fathers could be hard too, but they were not always home to administer the rod when it was deemed necessary. Beatings were common. The Korea Child Protection Agency reported that all but 3 percent of Korean children it surveyed were beaten. Most were beaten by their mothers. The children told the researchers that they were beaten at home mostly because they fought with their siblings. The second most common reason, they said, was not studying enough.

When they went to school, their teachers slapped them. I remembered looking down on the roof of a girls' high school in Seoul during what I had thought was a physical-education drill but which I soon saw was punishment. The girls were set in rows and ordered to put their hands on their heads. The male teacher stood on a podium, surveying the girls. Then he ordered them to begin deep knee bends. The girls bobbed up and down and as they tired, their hands slipped from their head. Their shoulders sagged and heads bowed. They bent at the waist instead of the knee. The teacher walked between their ranks and, using the sharp end of his loose-leaf binder, smacked them on their head when they faltered. The girls did their deep knee bends for fifteen minutes and then stood at attention. The teacher spoke to them. And then he ordered them to start the deep knee bends again.

At home mothers had much to battle. There were new temptations along with the pressures, temptations like glue and amphetamines that joined the older temptations of beer and rice wine. The drug use and drinking were not limited to the rising number of juvenile delinquents. Good children sniffed glue and popped uppers. They sniffed glue when they were upset—one university researcher reported—and popped pills when they had to stay awake.

The coffee Mother brought kept you awake just so long. If you were sleeping four hours, there was someone else sleeping three. Hye Ra, with her 2:30-to-6:30 sleep schedule, considered herself among the late sleepers. But now the pressure was off, and Hye Ra, like her sister before her, could look forward first to some idle time and then, if she chose, to a world never seen when all that mattered was learning the facts necessary for admission to college.

"In my freshman year I wasn't really thinking too much about myself and the world," said Eun Jung.

"I didn't experience new ideas before college," said Yumi. "But then I met with so many possibilities and ideas and lives I didn't know existed. I didn't work hard at academics." Instead she met people from backgrounds far more humble than her own. She joined the student movement and took part in demonstrations against the government.

Eun Jung, who had studied music and wanted to teach the piano said, "Until college all that mattered was playing the piano. But I learned more about music in college. I saw there were different dimensions, especially in how to teach the piano. It was so new to me. I also became aware of myself. I asked myself why I had come to college. Was it to marry someone who society said was respectable? I didn't think that was the case."

So Yong, too, had studied the piano. She wanted to teach children how to play. In college So Yong learned about herself and about music, but she also learned about a relationship forged during senior year but made apparent only when the agony was finished. In the rarefied atmosphere of college So Yong discovered her mother.

"In high school we have duties to perform for each other," she explained. "But after all that's over, the relationship with your mother changes. You become a friend to her. We go shopping together. She talks about things with me."

Other pressures applied by mothers could not be far off—the pressures to marry and have children, preferably sons. But those demands felt very far away for Hye Ra, who was not quite used to the fact that she did not have to be concerned with anything for a while.

Hye Ra had enrolled in the college education department. She thought she might like to be a teacher. She was sure that her four years of college would fly by. But now, in the empty days before school, Hye Ra sometimes found that when she was at home with nothing to do, she was seized by the impulse to pick up a book and study.

Her mother, however, no longer stood by the bedroom door. Her mother left her alone. Hye Ra rested her hand on her chin when she spoke. She smiled and let herself relax. She had succeeded. She had made her mother happy.

The Law and Park Chong Ki

*P*ARK Chong Ki had come to Seoul to see his family but would leave the next day to attend the memorial service for a young man who two years before killed himself in protest against the government. The young man's family had asked Park to attend. Each month families who had lost a son or daughter to death or prison called Park and asked him to come to their services. "Of course," he said, "I cannot attend all of them."

Besides the memorial services and funerals there were comforting gatherings of parents whose children, like Park's son Chong Chol, were gone. "When I'm at home," he said, "I can never talk about Chong Chol. When I look at my wife or daughter, it is too painful. Other mothers of sons who died say the same thing. When they sit home alone they cannot bear it."

It had been eighteen months since Park was summoned to Seoul by the police and told that if he had Chong Chol's body cremated immediately, he would receive a settlement of twenty-five thousand dollars. Park, a janitor for the Pusan City Water Department, did as he was told; in the fearful place Korea was before the spring of 1987, this was the wise thing to do. Park put the money in the bank—where it remained, untouched—and went alone to the Han River to scatter his son's ashes. The river's name bears no relation to the bitterness that would consume Park Chong Ki during his painful education in justice and truth in the Republic of Korea.

In the winter of 1987 Park Chong Ki, however, was not yet one to dispute the government's first version of his son's death—that he had died of shock during questioning about the whereabouts of a student activist. Others did. But Park received the chief of the National Police Agency at his bread box of a home above the Chonghak Water Pumping Station. His surviving children stayed away from home and his wife took to her bed. Park accepted the police chief's apology, as well as his admonition that he lessen his grief through hard work.

The visit came a week after the government announced its second version of Park Chong Chol's death, an announcement that coincided with the arrest for his killing of a lieutenant and sergeant assigned to the police Anti-Communism Bureau. The arrests came only after the doctor who performed the autopsy mentioned to a Korean journalist that Park Chong Chol, then a junior at Seoul National University, had died not of shock but of a windpipe broken over the side of a bathtub.

Still, it would take one hundred days before Park Chong Ki's questions about the government's versions of his son's death were transformed into the han that would turn him into a very angry man.

I had not seen Park Chong Ki since the morning his son's killers were convicted and sentenced. That was in early July, several days after Roh Tae Woo had gone on television and announced that the demonstrators had won and that he would try to convince Chun Doo Hwan that the nation be allowed to choose the next president. Still, the government, as was its practice, packed the courtroom with shills and police, so that protesters could not find a seat in the gallery.

The courtroom was long and wide and paneled in dark wood. It was a gloomy room, poorly lighted and threadbare. The protesters lined the walls and screamed at the shills to give up their seats. Park Chong Ki found a seat near the front. The judges took their places on the bench. The side door opened and the policemen accused of killing his Chong Chol were hurried in. The men and women in the gallery screamed, "Kill the murderers."

Park Chong Ki rose from his seat and threw himself at the wall of policemen. He tried prying them out of his way and his short arms and small hands flailed at the air. The accused, small men with frightened eyes, cowered, covering their face with manacled hands. The gallery bellowed for their heads. The accused tried to make themselves smaller still.

The three judges found the policemen guilty. They sentenced

them to three to fifteen years in prison. The light sentences enraged the gallery even more and the judges fled the courtroom. Park Chong Ki leapt from his seat and rushed at the killers. The women in the front beat the policemen with their handbags as the killers were spirited from the room. Park tried to find them but could not see over the wall of police. He fought like a man caught in rapids. In the end he slumped in his chair, his shirt torn open, his face sagging.

Now, in a gray suit and white shirt, he slipped off a shoe and tucked his foot under his thigh as he finished his lunch of beef-rib stew. His eldest son's wife had given birth to a son one hundred days before and his wife now had a new child to dote upon. The family had moved from Pusan to an apartment in Seoul. The apartment was on an alley so steep and narrow that a car could not pass. It was a long climb from the main road to the building, a climb made worse in the winter when the pavement was covered with ice.

The alley was dark, as was the building, where the outdoor lights were kept on timers to save electricity. The apartment was small and the first time I went there, the family was gathered in the living room admiring the baby. There were no reminders of Chong Chol in the room, no photographs or keepsakes. His mother held her new grandson until she could not bear the pain in her joints. Her sore hands were wrapped in gauze.

Park Chong Ki had not joined his family in Seoul. He remained in Pusan, not yet ready to leave his home. He was visiting on the weekend we met. We talked about his grandson and his other children a while longer. Then we talked about Chong Chol.

"Chong Chol was very bright when he was young," he said. "When he was five years old I wanted to send him to kindergarten, but the teachers said he didn't need it, that I should send him straight to school. He was at the top of his class for six years, or sometimes second. The teachers loved him, mainly because he was the youngest. In high school he became rather serious and had serious discussions with teachers."

He had won admission to Seoul National University, a matter of great pride for the family of a janitor. Prominent businessmen and government bureaucrats graduated from Seoul National, even though college was not necessarily a time to study. Teachers complained that students did not care about their studies. University, for the less than politically motived was the chance to go to the billiard parlor or magazine shop with friends, or meet on dates in coffee shops. It was also the time for those involved in anti-government politics to participate to the exclusion of almost everything else.

Chong Chol studied linguistics and his grades began slipping. This concerned his father, who heard that he was talking about politics with his brother and sister. "Through my daughter we told him, 'If you have to be interested in politics, please wait until you finish college,' " said Park Chong Ki.

Chong Chol, however, did not wait. He made friends with people in the student movement trying to oust the military-backed government. He was arrested three times for taking part in demonstrations. He was sentenced to two years in prison, but the sentence was suspended. He was living in a student boarding house and it was there, early on the morning of January 12, 1987, that officers of the police Anti-Communism Bureau came to take him in for the seemingly benign business of questioning him for allegedly lending money to and providing a place to sleep for a dissident student still at large.

On the forty-ninth day after Park Chong Chol's death, a date when, according to Buddhist philosophy, the spirit ceases its wandering, Park Chong Ki and his wife and daughter attended a midnight memorial service for Chong Chol. Later that day the government deployed fifty thousand riot police across the country to block similar memorials. Forty opposition leaders, including Kim Dae Jung and Kim Young Sam, were placed under house arrest. The government vowed to maintain its vigilance against "impure elements" seeking to exploit the death of Park Chong Chol.

The memorial services had begun on the campuses shortly after Park Chong Chol's death. Park Chong Ki's wife and daughter attempted to attend the services. But Park remained fearful of trouble. He asked that his son's death not be used in a way that might cause controversy. The memorial services were quiet at first and the government had little trouble blocking those whom it did not want attending. The Christian Broadcasting radio station tried airing a program on torture. The transmission was somehow interrupted and replaced by musical selections.

But now the families of the policemen held for the killing were talking of payments made to secure the policemen's cooperation in not implicating their superiors. Winter turned to spring and the solemn, bespectacled face of Park Chong Chol began appearing on banners and posters. The government could not seem to stop the services and rallies and calls for an honest accounting of what took place on the morning of January 12 in the Anti-Communism Bureau of the National Police Headquarters.

It was not until his son's death that Park Chong Ki, an apolitical man, learned how many parents had experienced what he and his wife had experienced, how their children, their once obedient children—"He was a good boy, never once gave us trouble"—began talking of and acting upon anger for official injustices that their parents had once found it easier to overlook.

Beyond the obvious manifestations of abuse—the torture, the tear gas, the beatings in the streets—was the law itself, an institution ostensibly written into the constitution to protect the rights of individuals but which in reality represented yet another club for the government to wield against those it regarded as a threat.

The idea of a "right," after all, had no place in the nation's history. The "right" to do what you wanted extended only to those with the power to get what they wanted. The law was not the arbiter of right and wrong. It was something to impose if you had the power, to fear if you were powerless and to avoid if you had the connections to get you off for offenses other than political ones.

There was no consistency in applying the law, no essential principle, nor could there be in a nation whose overarching philosophy was not a striving for, but a reaction against—in South Korea's case, anti-communism. The prefix contained the operative letters, because *anti* was at the heart of the law. The law was anti-dissent and anti-labor and anti-anyone who held an opinion other than the opinions the government deemed acceptable. As a result the judges and prosecutors appointed by the government prosecuted those whom the government wanted in prison and overlooked the charges against its friends.

The flaunting of the law did not stop at the government. People ignored the law, in good measure because there was no tradition for respecting it. The individual's attitude toward the law became, as a Western friend who'd lived in Korea for thirty years put it, "The law does not apply to me."

The law, however, did apply to those who made their opposition to the government public. There were laws for just such people, laws written so loosely that dissidents ran the risk of arrest and what in the Korean courts meant almost certain conviction. You could, for instance, violate the much-feared National Security Law by joining an organization that either advocated the overthrow of the government, or, in the government's view, "disturbed the state." Leaders of such organizations could be sentenced to death. You could get seven years in prison for "praising, encouraging or siding with an anti-state organization" or for "defaming" the state in front of foreigners. Taking part in a demonstration that advanced the cause of "a banned party" or one "greatly feared to cause social unrest" meant seven years for the leaders, five years for those who helped with leaflets and advance work and three years for the participants.

You could go to jail without ever having had the chance to defend yourself in a trial. The law stipulated that the police could arrest you without a warrant and hold you for forty-eight hours—seventy-two hours if there was no judge around—if you were judged as a "flagrant violator" who had just committed a crime. A summary court—with a district judge presiding—could sentence you to up to twenty-nine days in prison. You could appeal, which meant a court trial, which meant that you waited for that trial in your cell. Those sentenced to ten days often accepted their punishment and counted themselves among the fortunate. The least fortunate were those accused of violating the National Security Law, because they could be held without a warrant for up to fifty days.

When the government's critics, both domestic and foreign, pointed out that these laws were used only to keep dissidents in prison, the government spokesmen pointed north, to the enemy above the thirty-eighth parallel, as a reminder of what lay in wait if the government lagged in its vigilance against "impure elements."

Yet the curious thing about this official contempt for the rule of law was the pains the government took to make itself appear to be the law's true defender. Though the government had the muscle to do as it pleased, it still held public trials, investigated occasional acts of official abuse and leapt to its own defense when such foreign monitors as Asia Watch and Amnesty International criticized it for using the law to quash human rights.

If it were not so arbitrarily cruel, the government could have almost seemed pathetic in its attempt to convince the many doubters at home and abroad of its legitimacy. Its striving for acceptance stood in direct proportion to its willingness to use the law to bludgeon those under its sway who insisted that it had no right to rule. The government was caught between its own wishful thinking and its own authoritarian inclinations. It gave its laws names that suggested it had only the interests of the nation at heart, and then used those laws to protect its own interests.

The government allowed trials but packed the courtrooms with shills. It allowed the friends of its victims into the courtrooms, allowed them to hurl invective and eggs at the government's agents and then made sure that those agents were sentenced to the minimal terms or given suspended sentences. The government wanted to look good and thought that by looking good, people would believe it really was. When that didn't work, the government was forced to turn to the law, to make sure things did not get out of hand.

The result of this system of selective and arbitrary jurisprudence was cases such as that of Ahn Sang Ku, who edited a Korean-language newspaper in West Germany and was arrested on charges of being part of a student "spy ring." From the time of his arrest in September 1985 through the end of his trial—at which he was not present—his family and lawyer did not see him. Three months after his arrest he died in prison. The authorities reported that he killed himself, which also is what they said several months later, in June 1986, when the body of Shin Ho Soo, a twenty-four-year-old Inchon gas company employee, was found partly clothed and badly beaten in a cave in Cholla Province. Shin was reportedly taken from his home by three men who claimed to be policemen but were believed to be from the Inchon police Anti-Communism Bureau. Suicide was also listed as the cause of death of Woo Chong Won, whose body was found beside the railroad tracks. Woo, believed to be involved in a student organization, had been in hiding.

Kang Hon Kan and Chang Yi Ki were in the army when they died. Kang, a member of the opposition New Korea Democratic party, criticized army political indoctrination and was sentenced to three days in detention. Shortly afterward he was rushed to the hospital, where, three hours later, he died. The opposition party claimed that his chest and arms were bruised and several fingers broken. Chang also made critical comments about politics and the army. He was beaten and then turned over to the police. His family did not see his body before it was cremated.

"I didn't know about deception and lying by the government. I didn't think about it," said Park Chong Ki. "I was surprised at how many good people, good young people, had been sacrificed."

By the one hundredth day after Park Chong Chol's death—the day when the formal mourning period ends—his father was seeking the assistance of the Korea Bar Association in filing suit against the government. Five lawyers were assigned to his case. Park said that now he wanted to know "the truth."

The government had created several versions of the truth and each time discovered that fissures developed in its respective versions. First there was the shock story—a ludicrous yarn; Park was reputed to have died of shock when the interrogating officer banged his hand against a table. Then there was the version of the killing by the two policemen who insisted that Park was not tortured—this despite the discovery on Park's fingers of burns of the sort that result from electric shock and a blood clot in his lung, a clot that the police attributed to a childhood bout of pneumonia. By the time the five men accused of the killing went on trial, the prime minister, the Home Minister and the national police chief had been fired.

The arrests of three additional policemen came after the wife of the imprisoned lieutenant admitted that she had received thirty-five thousand dollars from the National Police Headquarters and fifteen thousand dollars from the Anti-Communism Bureau's investigation division and was also shown a bankbook by the deputy director of the National Police Headquarters: one hundred thousand dollars had been deposited in her husband's name, funds that would be made available "when the incident is smoothly completed." The five had initially agreed to let the lieutenant—the senior officer present at Park's killing—and the sergeant—the youngest—take the blame in anticipation of securing sentence reductions for them.

The accused reenacted the crime for the prosecution. A prison guard played the role of Park Chong Chol. The men performed the reenactment calmly. They showed how they had tied Park's hands behind his back because he had been writhing too much when they lowered him into the bathtub the first time. The lieutenant had ordered Park to put his head in the water, but Park refused and one of the sergeants had to get in the tub to force Park's head under.

Park was lifted by the legs. His neck was held against the side of the tub. His head was forced under the water for two minutes. The lieutenant said he was "astonished" that Park could not be revived after his head was held under water for two minutes. The men waited half an hour before calling a doctor.

At the trial the five defendants took turns accusing one another of being the one who actually did the killing. One said that he was in another room questioning someone else and another said that he had only held Park's legs. Fifteen blood clots were found in Park's body and in his groin were stab marks of the sort made with a pen.

"Let me see the men who killed my son," Park's mother called out in the courtroom. The spectators threw eggs and milk cartons at the defendants, who offered written apologies to the Park family.

This spring three university students killed themselves. Two set themselves on fire and the third cut open his belly and jumped from a roof. They were given martyrs' funerals. Thousands, dressed in mourning white, marched behind the coffins through the streets of Seoul. Park Chong Ki, who now used many of the same words and rhetorical phrases that the dissidents used, did not begrudge the public its vicarious grief. But while he understood the need to use the deaths as evidence of the cruelty that had been imposed upon the nation, he also recognized that it was still the families who wailed at the grave side.

Everyone wanted a piece of these families. Student organizations and opposition politicians invited them to join them on the platform during their rallies, so that people might associate their causes with those of the survivors of the victims of the state. In June of 1987 politicians made the pilgrimage to the bedside of Lee Han Yol, who was hit in the head with a tear-gas canister and lapsed into a coma from which he did not emerge. The politicians extended their hands in sympathy to Lee's parents. Even the woman whose company manufactured tear gas later visited Lee's parents to beg forgiveness and to promise that even though the sale of tear gas had helped make her the single biggest individual taxpayer in the nation, she was halting production—a step that came at some inconvenience to the government. She was its chief supplier.

The families were instruments for displaying outrage as well as sincerity, although sometimes, caught up in their grieving, they did not seem to understand this.

On the first anniversary of their son's death, Park Chong Chol's parents went to Sariam Temple in Pusan for a memorial service. Park Chong Ki bowed his head and held his hands together in prayer, while his wife held a handkerchief to her eyes. The service was also attended by the press, for whom the Park Chong Chol story remained very much alive. On the anniversary of Park's death the prosecutor's office announced that it was reopening its investigation. And later that week Kang Min Chang, the former director general of the National Police Headquarters, was arrested for having ordered the attending physician to falsify Park's death certificate.

Kang was arrested just after midnight. He was also charged with official neglect of duty. Conviction could bring ten years in prison. Kang denied the charges. But the physician, Hwang Juk Jun, produced his diary and showed the prosecutors the entries in which he detailed twice being "persuaded" by Kang to list the cause of death as shock. Hwang did as he was told, and then told a reporter the true nature of Park's death.

Fifty-six days after his arrest Kang was convicted. The courtroom was packed with a hundred uniformed police and plainclothesmen. Kang bowed his head and the judges admonished him for not ordering his subordinates to conduct an honest inquest. The prosecutor asked the court for an eighteen-month prison sentence. But Kang was sentenced instead to eight months in prison and the suspension of his civil rights.

The prison term was suspended and Kang was set free. The court decided that Kang would not have to go to jail because he had worked hard to maintain "public order" and had fought against communism.

Park Chong Ki returned to Pusan. He joined in a suit with sixty other people, including Lee Han Yol's parents and survivors of the Kwangju killings, seeking reparations from the government for their losses. Just before I saw him, Park and his wife tried to attend a National Assembly Home Affairs Committee hearing on human rights abuses but were blocked from entering the committee room. The hearing came a year and a day after Park had received the chief of the National Police Agency in his home and accepted his apology and advice for coping with Chong Chol's death.

Park continued answering the calls from grieving parents and solicitous politicians. He attended funerals and memorials and rallies. People needed him.

~~~~~ *SUMMER*

SUMMER in Korea feels like a season without end. The skies clear after the rainy season. But the air still spreads itself flat, heavy and moist over the land. The air is still. For weeks on end it feels as if it does not move.

Summer is a time of white short-sleeved shirts sweated through after heavy-legged, short-winded climbs up the underground walkways beneath Seoul. It is a season for undershirts and boxer shorts after work, a season of folding hand fans, cold barley tea, lotus and hibiscus blossoms and incense to keep the mosquitoes away.

Korea makes no allowance for the heat. There are production quotas to meet. In the factories the fans are switched on and in the offices the occasional air conditioner. Jackets come off, but ties stay knotted to the throat. The pace never slackens. By mid-August the temperature in Seoul rose to ninety-nine degrees. Stores were running out of fans and in the marketplaces ten dollars was tacked onto the list prices.

In the summer of 1988 fifty-four teachers at Pusan National University's College of Arts threatened to resign unless students started treating them respectfully. Students occupied the dean's office for six days, demanding that "incompetent" professors be fired.

A woman jilted by her lover was arrested for kidnapping and murdering his three-year-old son.

Four men ransacked the office of a dissident group, after raping the woman and beating the man who'd been working and sleeping there.

A cabinet minister and the ruling-party chairman called for a constitutional amendment giving the president the power to dissolve the National Assembly.

In the months since the assembly election that brought the opposition to power, the parties of Kim Dae Jung, Kim Young Sam and Kim Jong Pil were driving the government to distraction.

One assembly committee wanted to subpoena Chun Doo Hwan and Roh Tae Woo to testify about voting fraud during the presidential election. Another committee wanted to subpoena Chun to testify about his role in the Kwangju killings. Yet another committee was investigating how Chun and his family had managed to make themselves very wealthy during his presidency. The committee members wanted to inspect the elaborate tombs Chun built for his parents and the provincial governors' mansions built and furnished so that Chun would have appropriately grand places to stay when he toured the country. There were rumors of Chun real estate holdings in New York and Australia. The opposition demanded a thousand documents relating to abuse during Chun's rule. The ruling party subpoenaed eighty-seven documents that it hoped would show that Chun Doo Hwan was an innocent man. Kim Dae Jung wanted to retrieve all the money and use it to retire the nation's $6 billion farm debt. But the estimates for Chun's holdings were closer to $20 million.

The government was unable to stop the investigations. Besides, it was preoccupied. With the coming of the Olympics there remained one nagging and potentially explosive question—North Korea. Nobody knew what the North would do, whether it would attend, whether it would try to sabotage the Games. Seoul was beginning to have the feel of an armed camp. Soldiers armed with assault rifles patrolled the airport and sports venues. Wanted posters for members of the Japanese Red Army—the terrorists responsible for the Lod Airport massacre in Israel and now believed to be working for North Korea—appeared at immigration offices. Anti-terrorist commandos practiced breaking into hotel rooms from windows to rescue hostages, parachuting into the Olympic Stadium and descending, face-first, from the stadium roof, holding onto a rope with one hand while firing a pistol with the other.

While the black-clad commandos drilled, the two Koreas talked about talking. They had been haggling for over a year about co-hosting the Games. South Korea offered a few events for Pyong-yang—events like Ping-Pong and archery. North Korea wanted half of all the events. They met periodically with the International Olympic Committee in Switzerland. They agreed on nothing. Now, with the Games scheduled to begin in mid-September—it would have been cruel asking athletes to compete in the summer heat—the South offered to talk again, this time at Panmunjom. The meeting would be the first between government ministers in three years.

At the border the representatives from the South crossed over into North Korea. Journalists were warned before they crossed over that South Korean security men could not protect them on the other side of the border. The representatives, meanwhile, smiled and shook hands across a wide conference table. They talked about signing a nonaggression pact, and about a single, Korean team that would march together into the stadium under a new flag and singing a new anthem. The South invited the North to send its athletes to Seoul. The North still wanted to play co-host. The South said it was too late.

Then the yelling started, the insults and the table pounding. The North wanted all the members of the South's National Assembly to come to Pyongyang with their aides and fifty or so other people for a grand intra-Korean gathering. The South said that sending what would be a thousand people to North Korea would be too unwieldy. They suggested a smaller number. But the North wanted everyone.

"Have you ever heard of such a joint conference in the history of the world?" asked a South Korean delegate.

"Why do you compare us with the foreigners?" snapped a North Korean. "We are Korean."

The North Korean representative insisted that his side had cars and hotel rooms to transport everyone to Pyongyang.

"We have plenty of cars too," retorted his counterpart from the South.

On the first day the North Koreans served beer, dried fish, juice, water, peanuts and pound cake. The day was oppressive and the air-conditioning broke down. Reporters dozed in their chairs. The South Koreans would not drink the North Korean beer for fear of poisoning.

On the second day the North Koreans crossed over into South Korea. The South Koreans provided box lunches, an open bar and complimentary packets of 88 cigarettes, a new Olympic-year brand. The air-conditioning was turned up high.

They met for the final time in the North. The North served the same snacks and turned the air-conditioning up higher still.

The talks broke off with each side blaming the other for their failure. In truth they had never started. Each side took its turn saying what it had to say and dismissing the other's reply. The South Koreans said they would wait for the North Koreans to initiate another meeting. The North Koreans said they would wait for the South. The commandos continued their drilling and all passengers flying to Seoul had their carry-on baggage checked twice—the second time in the entrance ramp—to make sure bombs were not passed to them in the waiting area or duty-free shops.

The government turned its attention to the Games and implored the nation to join in the grand national mobilization. It was impossible not to know how much time was left before the opening ceremonies because there were digital clocks on buildings and billboards and intersections counting down the days. Each day the government issued new calls for diligence and determination. The opposition parties agreed to wait until after the Games before pushing on with their investigations. It was deemed politically unwise to sully the Games with political discord.

The government, temporarily free from having to explain itself in the National Assembly, began admonishing construction crews to stop all excavation work so that they would not pollute the air with debris. Street sweepers stopped using brooms because the brooms made the air too dusty. Twenty new vacuum trucks cleaned the streets. Cab drivers were warned that failure to pick up foreigners—a common practice—would mean suspension of their license. Cabbies with dirty cabs were fined seventy dollars.

Riot policemen stopped using tear gas because the gas might choke the foreign guests. They were to use truncheons and electric prods on those demonstrators who dared assemble in the designated "peace zones." The National Assembly had declared that the Olympic venues, the roads near them, the roads leading to them, the roads leading to the airports and all the land for two kilometers in either direction were closed to demonstrations.

At the Olympic Village 2,560 eight-ton trucks delivered 2,660,000 items for the 14,000 athletes, among them 15,000 boxes of tissues, 14,000 rolls of toilet paper, 75,000 towels—30,000 a day, with 45,000 in reserve—20 tons of rice, 136 tons of meat, 300 tons of vegetables, 1 million eggs, 25 varieties of bread and 40 sorts of condiments.

Restaurant toilets were inspected to make sure they flushed. People were admonished not to spit or smoke when the foreigners arrived, this despite the national mania for smoking and the proclivity for public expectoration. The Religious Advisory Council to the Olympic Organizing Committee began a "civil drive" for traffic order. And the twenty-six thousand Olympic volunteers were drilled on guiding irate people to their seats without losing their temper and never straying more than three feet from their post—too many were drifting to get a better view of the pre-Olympic sports events.

The dancers for the opening ceremonies were ordered to practice in long sleeves because the organizers did not want their arms tanned by the sun.

Dog-meat restaurants were shut down because foreigners would not understand that dogs were considered a delicacy. Street vendors were ordered out of the markets and alleys for the duration of the Games so that the city would not seem a poor place filled with peddlers.

Twenty-five hundred members of the Korean Housewives Association were enlisted to clean up the athletes' rooms and make their beds.

Olympic fever was not so much infectious as it was judicious to catch. "The Olympics has been a religion since 1981," a Korean friend said, citing the year Seoul was awarded the Games. "Anyone against it is labeled an infidel."

Yet only the government sounded passionate about the Games. The coming of the Olympics did not bring great excitement or joy, only more work and enthusiastic calls by the government and the newspapers to make the Games a spectacle the likes of which the world had never seen. The Olympics would be Korea's moment before the world. Korea had never had such a moment before and nothing could go wrong. Then the Olympic flame arrived from Athens. It was to be carried by runners from Pusan to Seoul. But on its first leg of the journey the flame flickered out. The organizers declared that it would not happen again.

The drive for perfection—the need to prove that Korea was capable of hosting the great event—rendered the preparation and anticipation a joyless exercise. When I mentioned to an official of the

Olympic Organizing Committee that there appeared to be little room for the Korean people to enjoy themselves, he told me that the Korean people were playing the role of host and in Korea a host is too busy making sure his guest is happy to have any time for himself. Yet these weary hosts were well aware that it took the coming of the guests to dredge the Han River, to get the dust out of the air, to clean the streets. It was not being done for them. It was being done in the hope that they would be well thought of by visitors who would come for a few weeks and perhaps never return. I met many Koreans who wanted Seoul to look its best for the foreigners, who believed that the Games were a way for Korea to impress the world. But they were removed from the Games.

The world's perception of Korea may have been important in Korea's perception of itself—"You see, we are not an insignificant country anymore." But it did not go to the heart of the pain Koreans felt about who they were. The bitterness, the han, was Korean in its inception. Foreigners may have triggered or exacerbated it. But they could not resolve it, not for all the kind things they might say about how good Seoul looked during the Games and how well everything worked. Han was not going to be overcome with a smile and an approving nod from outsiders, especially when those outsiders were approving of a Korea that was being told to present itself as something that it was not.

Despite all the parades in traditional costume and the recitals celebrating thousands of years of Korean civilization, the preparation felt false. It sanitized the country. The joy—and frustration—of being in Korea was in the endless display of the edges and seams. But Korea was being made over into a serene and pristine place where people did not lose their temper, did not spit, did not push, did not eat dog meat.

One morning, walking through a subway underpass, I started chatting with a young man who worked in a bank. We talked about the Olympic preparations, the stickers of Hodori—the Olympic mascot tiger—in all the shop windows, the breathless television coverage of the arrival of the delegations from Chad and Bhutan, the endless demands for the nation to check its reflection in the mirror and make sure that no hair was out of place. "I ask myself," he said, " 'Why can't we just be ourselves?' "

The Games began on September 17. By then the hot days were

over. The Korea the world saw those first few days of the Seoul Olympics was an efficient place where security men smiled, where volunteers tried their best to speak English, where no one seemed to talk very much about politics, where the streets were free of litter and spittle and tear gas. By the time the Games began, the ferment of the summer—the last of the demonstrations, the freeing of political prisoners, the cursing at the American soldiers, the hopeless talks between North and South—had not so much ended as it had been shut away until the guests departed.

Liberation Day

ON Liberation Day the students tried to march to Panmunjom. The government told them they could not, just as it warned the students in June, when they tried and failed the first time. One hundred and thirty thousand riot policemen were put on full alert. One thousand students were arrested in the days before the march.

The students planned to march and drive from Pusan to Seoul, enlisting the support of the populace along the way. Forty students at Chungnam University in Taejon wanted their school to give them a bus and money for the trip. When the dean of students refused—school funds, he explained, could not be spent on "unauthorized" activities—the students, armed with pipes and sticks, smashed windows, chairs, tables and a clock in the president's office, which they occupied for half an hour.

The trip north to meet with students from Kim Il Sung University invited little but tear gas and rocks and people did not pay the students much attention. A three-day weekend was approaching and people were leaving the cities for the countryside. The students and riot police remained in the cities. The police were posted outside subway entrances and at rail stations, checking identification cards so that students could not congregate.

The students tried holding rallies. They fought with the police in Kwangju and Pusan, where they attacked police boxes and burned police buses. In Seoul they fought outside Myongdong Cathedral, where they had often sought refuge. But when the students began throwing kerosene bombs, a priest came to tell them that if they were going to fight, they could not stay. At night the shopping streets near the cathedral were jammed with young men and women shopping at the Ralph Lauren and Yves Saint Laurent boutiques and stopping for coffee and Baskin-Robbins ice cream. There was one deserted place in all of Myongdong and that was the cathedral plaza, where the only people about were the riot police and a young man singing folk songs.

There were even rallies against the students. The protesters were said to be residents of the working-class neighborhood near Yonsei University who were tired of the tear gas. The demonstrators, whoever they were, threw rocks at the students, who retired to the campus to review the timetable for their march to the border.

On the morning of August 15, Liberation Day, the anniversary of the day in 1945 when Koreans, much to their surprise, woke to discover that their ruler was defeated (the Japanese had made sure they knew nothing of how badly the war was going for them), three thousand students sat and listened to speakers exhort them to march north and bring the nation together again. Outside, holding steel pipes and wooden sticks, sat a thin band of young men. And across the avenue, in front of the school, sat hundreds of riot policemen, drinking milk and eating sweet rolls.

Tear gas still lingered in the air near the gate, a residue of the demonstration the day before. I walked onto the campus, past the medical team's table outside the university hospital—piled with gauze, Mercurochrome, saline solution—and stood in the back of the rows of students who sat on the ground listening to the succession of speakers.

It was as if it were happening in a vacuum. The speakers, some old, most young, went on and on and their voices barely carried past the avenue. The streets of the nearby neighborhood had been cleared, but that was hardly necessary. It was a holiday and shops were closed. No one was there to listen.

The morning dragged on and in the course of the four hours of speeches a young woman carrying a suitcase stepped under the gray concrete Yonsei gate, crossed the avenue, slipped between the ranks of the riot police and headed away from school. Just as this day would mark the end of the students' disappointing 1988 spring offensive, a spring in which fewer and fewer people listened to what the students told them, so too did it mark the end of Christine

Armstrong's sobering return home. No one had listened to Christine, either.

Christine was nineteen years old and a student in Ventura College, in Ventura, California. Christine was the name her adoptive parents gave her when she was thirteen years old and had left her mother's home for a new life in America. Her two sisters remained at home, a home without a father. Christine learned English. She learned to dress like other girls in Ventura, in baggy pants and tank tops. She learned about makeup and nail polish and getting a tan. When Christine's sisters saw her in her new clothes they said, "Get a haircut. Stop dressing the way you dress. Start looking like a lady."

"They looked at me and said, 'My God,'" Christine said. "We used to think alike. Now we get into arguments."

Christine did not make friends during her six weeks at Yonsei. Boys did not ask her out even though Christine was an attractive woman. Christine's natural mother welcomed her back, but her sisters warned her that she would have problems. They told her, "If you want to come back and get along with people, you have to go along with what they say." But America had ruined Christine, at least for making friends and dating on campus. Christine questioned. She was, by her own admission, not a political person. But she did not like accepting what people told her just because they expected her to listen.

"They think that just because I went to school in America I've got all these imperialistic ideas," she said. "I argued back, but it was always one against five or ten."

Each summer people like Christine came back to a Korea left long ago, often because their parents had decided that the future was elsewhere. The children of these parents, raised to speak English and think as Americans, returned to Korea to hear their parents denigrated for having left the fatherland. The children were told by the children of those who had remained behind that they were politically naive, hopelessly bourgeois and in all ways lacking in what it took to be a true Korean. They couldn't even speak the language of their people.

Christine could. But that did not matter, not to those who found the differences between them appalling, who saw in her the ruin wrought by the West. Christine may have been born a Korean. But she was no longer pure, not like those with whom she disagreed and whose modest dress she did not emulate. She stood on a street corner, near a phalanx of riot police, and said, "I was really happy at first. I was born and raised here. But the way they treated me was like a foreigner. Friendship means understanding each other."

The sound of the student speakers was barely audible where Christine stood. She was not listening. She was leaving. "I like all the excitement. But it's a small country and it's giving me a headache."

Christine expected to discover many things when she came home. She did not anticipate intolerance. Then she met her peers.

I saw my first radical students in the window of the United States Information Service building in 1985. They had stormed into the building in the early afternoon and were demanding that the United States apologize for its role in the Kwangju killings. The government threatened to storm the building. The students threatened to kill themselves. They held the building for four days before surrendering. They marched out, fists in the air, chanting songs of protest. I thought them terribly brave.

I still did. But I also thought them arrogant, insular and imbued with an overweening capacity for self-righteousness, which made them no different, in certain ways, from most anyone between the ages of eighteen and twenty-one. Tradition, however, set them apart. What the students of France, Japan and America had done at various points in the 1960s Korean students had been doing for centuries. They were the self-proclaimed—and generally acknowledged—"conscience of the nation," a role they had assumed five hundred years before, when students of the Confucian academies regularly brought petitions before the government. Then as now the idea was achieving a purer state. To that end they risked imprisonment, torture, even death—thousands were killed in the 1919 protests against the Japanese; scores died in the 1960 demonstrations that brought down the government of Syngman Rhee.

The most dedicated among them seemed on a quest for martyrdom. They invited arrest. They punched and kicked at the riot police. They braved the tear gas, protected by flimsy masks even though they could have used the gas masks captured from the riot police. (The gear was piled in the corridor of the Yonsei student center, on a floor stained with paint and ink, the signature of generations of protest-banner painters.) They wanted their sacrifice displayed prominently. They wanted their views accepted without question—as Christine Armstrong had learned—and as a result there was no conversation in Korea quite as numbing as one with a student leader.

While the recitation of respective party lines was familiar in Korea—the line changed only with the party, the idea of imparting "the word" was fairly constant—it reached a new level of tedium with the students. You did not have a conversation. You entered the student-organization headquarters and stood by the door until you caught the attention of someone at a typewriter or phone. You offered a card and explained your purpose.

If you were deemed acceptable and granted an audience with the designated spokesperson, you were invited to sit among the clutter of cigarette butts, leaflets and assorted papers that generally ended up in piles on the floor. You asked a question and then listened. There was little need for a second question, in part because the often-windy first answer was intended to be all-inclusive and in part because there was no intention on the part of the speaker to answer what you asked anyway. He or she had a message. It was recited. To seek amplification or to question an element or the logic was to commit the offense of asking "a foolish question." "That is a foolish question," you were told or, "That is an imperialist question," or "... divisionist question," the latter reserved for those who broached the possibility that the two adversarial philosophies governing North and South Korea made it difficult, if not impossible, to envision a united nation. If the Americans leave, we can unite the country, the students said. And that was that. The departure of the Americans would begin to make the han go away.

Further interrogatories put you firmly in the imperialist camp. Inquisitiveness was not a virtue. The proper affiliation was paramount. If you were not a friend, then you were an enemy. To explain yourself away as a curious bystander was to admit to ad hoc status in the enemy camp. Why would a friend ask imperialist or divisionist or foolish questions? A friend would not. So surely you were an enemy.

Which led to a discourse on dependency theory. And then to one on the American conspiracy to support the military dictatorship in its aiding and abetting the killings at Kwangju. Dependency theory, a philosophy left over from the 1960s, was better suited for the banana republics of South America: The United States (any other large capitalist state would do) exploited Third World economies for its own purposes, keeping them dependent upon sales to the wealthy state in order to keep themselves afloat. (The argument broke down in the face of the ten-billion-dollar trade deficit with the United States and the emergence of Hyundai, Daewoo and Samsung. Some still argued, however, that despite its wealth, Korea continued to be dependent upon the United States as a buyer, albeit for a higher line of goods.)

The idea may have been dated, but one could hardly blame the students for that. For a generation the government had maintained a monopoly not only on power but on ideas. Ideas that did not support the ideas of the government were banned ideas. (The ideas of the government, in a distilled form, were these: The government may be stern, but it has only the interests of its flock at heart; the United States is a friend; Communists are enemies; North Korea is the greatest enemy of all; Koreans love their friends and hate their enemies and those who do not do enough of either are not friends of the state; woe betide enemies of the state.) People went to prison for thinking or reading about banned ideas, if they could get their hands on the reading material in the first place. As late as June 1987 the government had banned over six hundred books; within a year scores were deemed no longer "dangerous." The result of the book ban was not a surge of interest in reading, say, *Chun Doo Hwan: Man of Destiny*. ("The rest is history," concludes the flimsy volume as the central character, whose childhood nickname was Spotty, goes off to seize power.) Rather, it was a hardening of ideas on the left, an equal and opposite reaction to the right-wing blather the government shoved down the nation's throat.

The dissemination of the "wrong" ideas was conducted in study groups that incoming freshmen joined. Their instructors were upperclassmen who filled their young and eager minds—these were the best survivors of the rigors of college entrance exams—with the same catechism that they had had cemented into their brains in their first year on campus. The groups were small and not a place for discussion. Elders spoke; juniors listened. And when those juniors returned home for holidays, they were able to recite what they had learned to parents whose ignorance they'd perhaps never quite noticed before, parents who survived the Japanese and the war and the hungry years of the 1950s but were woefully ignorant and in need of instruction in the victimization of the Korean people by the forces of global imperialism.

The first time I sat and talked with a group of student leaders, they were still residing in a place in my brain reserved for fond memories of 1960s America. I had been to Korean student coffee shops with guitars on the wall and Simon and Garfunkel on the record player, and to student tea houses with mulberry-paper walls and hand-worked pottery where young patrons sipped ginseng tea in an atmosphere that was meant to approximate the nation's unsullied past. My meeting with the student leaders, however, disabused me of my more innocent notions. We met, through the arrangement of an intermediary with friends in the student movement, in the offices of a group disposed favorably to the student cause. To be more specific at the time would have put the students and their intermediary in danger of arrest. Suffice it to say that plainclothesmen in crew cuts and matching down jackets loitered outside. Even the building's pay phone was said to be tapped.

We met in a cramped office. I asked a question about philosophy and began scribbling notes furiously. The students spoke of the working class, the ruling class, the military and, of course, the United States. They spoke of "class struggle" and organizing the workers. They talked a lot about "educating" the people and of secretly joining them on the assembly lines. (Detection meant arrest and those arrested for labor-related offenses fared far worse in prison than those who were simply dissidents. Labor meant workers and the government did not want its work force getting the wrong ideas about good wages and decent hours.)

"The people," I was to learn that day and in a succession of numbingly similar conversations, sounded like well-intended but lost sheep in desperate need of the steady hand of the all-knowing shepherd. It was a view best expressed by a Yonsei student who told me, "The people don't know what they want exactly. But if someone points it out to them, they'll know."

That meant the students, whose role it was to remind the nation of what stood between it and something better. And while the populace sometimes wearied of the students—as they were most certainly doing now—and grew sick of the tear gas that always followed the students, they still did not dispute the principle guiding the students' cause. If the students presented them with an issue they believed in, as had happened in June 1987, May 1980 and April 1960, they joined in. Otherwise they shook their heads and went about their business. But these were their children. And children could be indulged, especially if the fruits of the parents' interminable labors had enabled their children to join the privileged elite of the educated class.

On the day of my first encounter with student ideology I listened for an hour or so and then asked if I might interrupt. "Aren't some views you express the ideas of Marx?" I asked rhetorically, not minding if they were, but wanting to hear the response.

"We do not deal in labels," said the lead spokesman.

"But even if you don't, wouldn't you be nervous, hearing these ideas if you were the government?"

"Yes," he said with a smile.

But I did not think the government was nervous so much as annoyed. The students threatened the smooth running of things, the prevailing order and the essential measure of control. The students mucked things up, telling workers that they had a right to a better life, telling people that they should be free of the military and the intelligence apparatus, telling them that the way they were ruled— and ruled they were, not governed—was cruel and punitive and not worthy of a nation approaching universal literacy and where a third of all high-school graduates went to college. Perhaps the government should have been nervous. But in the spring of 1985, when I first encountered the students, the government was smug and content, sure that the middle class was with them and that the students and their dangerous ideas could be easily silenced by tear gas, skeleton police and the faceless men skilled in applying electric shocks to the genitals.

The students and the government continued facing each other time and again in the streets, where the battles approached but never surpassed a mutually acceptable level of violence. Both sides were so well organized, so disciplined. Both were adept, as were all politically oriented Koreans, at the game of political brinksmanship, a wearying exercise played out in the name of purity of motive. Victory was not victory unless it was complete, a lesson brought home at Yonsei a few days after Roh Tae Woo's announcement in June 1987, acceding to protesters' demands that the next president be freely chosen.

I would have thought this a great victory for the students. But then I was thirty-four years old and a Westerner and therefore doomed to be pleased with "pretty good" instead of everything.

"It was a victory, but I don't think it solved our basic inner feelings about Kwangju," said a young woman who identified herself as the "spiritual leader" of the Yonsei student organization. "It was just one announcement. I'll never forgive the violence of the past and the totalitarianism. We want to see the present government go away completely. I don't think this is a complete victory. I think the present government exists because of America. We'll demonstrate against the United States. We believe in the people and they will support us all the way. It's the people's wish to have democracy in Korea."

I asked whether the students had been judicious in changing their tactics, eliminating the harsh anti-American rhetoric that had alienated many people in the past. The forces of moderation within the student movement had prevailed after the previous year's constitutional-reform petition drive was undone, in part by a succession of clashes between students and police.

The question did not interest her.

"That is a foolish question," she said.

I asked it again.

"When you demand something, you don't always say everything together," she said impatiently. "It's not a tactic. We're just putting it in a way that people can understand."

I asked whether she felt the students had made mistakes. This she was willing to address and her response surprised me. It suggested a degree of humility and self-scrutiny that I should have suspected but had not heard before.

"We thought we were ahead of the people," she said.

They weren't that June.

But perhaps they were now.

The speeches on campus were interrupted only by the occasional march of students around the campus, chanting, waving banners, calling out, "Yankee, go home."

Outside an old man in traditional clothing and a straw hat stepped between the ranks of the riot policemen and walked across the highway toward the school. But the riot-police commander did not want him going into the school, so he sent three plainclothesmen to stop him. One young man grabbed the old man by the shoulder and spun him around. The young man was twice the old man's size. He began pulling the old man away and the old man cried out, "What did I do? I'm going to say what I've got to say. I don't care if I die." The plainclothesmen lifted him up and carried him away. The skinny old man tried kicking, but the younger men were too strong. "Are you crazy?" one of them said to the old man. "Try aging well and not like a crazy man." They carried him to a police van, lifted him inside and drove him off.

The students were supposed to begin their march to the border at 10:00, and then at 11:00 and then at 12:00, but the police scuttled their plans. The students had piled their rocks in small clusters around the gate. They were milling near the gate when the skeleton police suddenly dashed across the avenue and began picking up the rocks. They gathered the rocks in their arms and ran back across the avenue. The students retreated to the campus to reassess their strategy.

At 1:30 they began to move. Perhaps it was the loss of the rocks at the hands of the police, and perhaps the students had intended to change strategies all along and let themselves become victims. It was as if the students were listening to what people were trying to tell them, that in the silence of those whose support they were not now enlisting they heard the suggestion that a change in strategies was necessary, that the fighting brought them no sympathetic ears.

The students began marching toward the gate. Musicians and dancers led them. The musicians played drums and cymbals and the dancers danced a folk dance. Now the district was filled with the pulsation of their music, clanging, discordant but electric. The students danced ever closer to the gate. The riot police opened a wide space in their ranks so the rapid-fire launchers could drive through.

The students passed under the gate and were moving out onto the street. They had roped each other together, so that they could not be split up. They formed a circle in front of the gate and the music got louder and faster. Hundreds of students packed close together, moving with the pulse of the music.

The rapid-fire cannon opened fire with a sharp crack and the riot police ran under the cloud of gas toward the students. They descended upon them with feet and fists. The skeleton police beat the fallen students, kicking them in the face, pulling their hair, dragging them along the street. They even ran onto the campus, to pull away those caught in the choking gas.

The students let themselves be arrested. Bound together, they screamed and wailed as the riot policemen dragged them off, huddled them in circles, forced them to kneel and smacked them in the head if they tried looking up. Some students kicked at the riot policemen as they were lifted off the ground and fought as the riot police shoved them into the arrest buses. Inside the buses the policemen beat the students.

Blood soaked through the back of the students' T-shirts and spattered the gray windbreakers of the skeleton police. The commander did not like what he was seeing. He ordered his men to stop the beating. The television cameras were everywhere. When he saw a policeman beating a student, he smacked the man with his swagger stick.

The students regrouped inside the gate and then, once again, tried marching out. And once again the police fired tear gas and ran across the avenue to arrest them. The police did their work quickly and efficiently. Now, in the bright sunshine, groups of students were clustered together and policemen in gas masks were checking their identification cards. The students coughed and wheezed and then, together, sang "The Song of Reunification." They had sung the song time and again last June, when the people who today were enjoying a rare day off were singing along with them.

After the second wave failed, the students retreated to the campus. They returned to the street with rocks. The rock throwing lasted into the afternoon. Chairs were brought over for the riot-police commanders, who sat inside wire-mesh cages. The rocks bounced off the cages. After a while the students' arms got tired and the rocks only bounced and skidded against cages. The commanders did not even take note.

Finally, at 4:20 precisely, there was a cease-fire. The riot policemen walked to the middle of the avenue. So too did the students. They approached the meridian from their respective sides and began collecting the rocks they had thrown. The policemen used their shields to shovel the rocks to their side of the road. The students used boards. They moved away from each other, clearing the road for traffic.

Soon the roadway was free of rocks. The first car through was a taxicab, racing.

Seven students, scraggly in T-shirts and oversized pants, began to chant. One of them called across to the riot police, "We'll leave you alone. We won't hurt you."

"Thank you," replied a riot policeman, and everyone laughed.

Kim Keun Tae's Homecoming

KIM Keun Tae was not released from prison in the year's first amnesty because he was deemed unrepentant. One hundred and twenty-five dissidents were released from prison on February 26, in celebration of Roh Tae Woo's inauguration as president. But Kim, the one the government feared most, was not yet contrite and therefore ineligible.

He was no more repentant and no less adamant in his belief in "mass movements" and a "people's democracy" on June 29, when the government, following the Confucian practice of amnesties to mark significant dates, freed forty-six prisoners convicted of political offenses—this time to mark the first anniversary of Roh's speech of concession to protesters' demands for reform. Roh had promised that political prisoners would be freed. And so Kim, who long before renounced a confession he insisted came during the application of electric shocks to his body and the pouring of red-pepper water down his throat, was set free.

He was not released because he had softened his views. He was released, he said, because the Olympics were approaching and the government wanted outsiders—especially the Americans, who had called for his release—to regard them as merciful and good rulers.

Kim immediately called for the release of the other 600 or perhaps 700 political prisoners still in jail. The government insisted that his figures were wrong. There were only 250 left—proponents of violence, the government said, threats to the state, which is what they had said about Kim too. None was as famous as Kim, who had served two and a half years of a seven-year term for violating the National Security Law.

Kim was found guilty of thinking the wrong ideas and telling others about them. He had espoused ideas that the government deemed dangerously similar to the ideas espoused by North Korea. Kim spoke publicly of class differences and the role of the masses in a society free of corruption and foreign intervention. He was charged with possessing a dangerous book—*Capitalism: Yesterday and Tomorrow* by Maurice Dobb, which the prosecution claimed "advanced the interests of North Korea." He was also charged with organizing and attending meetings "feared to cause social unrest"— eight, was the number cited by the prosecution—where he discussed protests, sympathy strikes and slogans for political fliers. The Supreme Court upheld his conviction.

Amnesty International, however, declared him a prisoner of conscience and both he and his wife, In Jae Keun, were recipients of the Robert F. Kennedy Memorial Award for Human Rights. A noted dissident and labor activist before his imprisonment—he was chairman of the Youth Alliance for Democracy—he was made all the more important in detention when he testified before the Seoul District Court about the nature of torture during the rule of Chun Doo Hwan.

He had been gone for three years and for the four months before his release was kept in virtual isolation. He could not read newspapers or listen to the radio or watch television. And now he was home, sitting on the hardwood floor of his living room. Above him hung a photograph of his ten-year-old daughter and seven-year-old son. His wife slept on the floor in the next room. He pressed his fingers to his head. His head still hurt him, as did his back. A large bottle of Tylenol sat in a cabinet, next to the glasses and dishes.

"There is a change, a lessening of the fear of the government," he said. He had emerged to see people attending rallies without fear of arrest. There were no plainclothesmen in front of his house. He assumed that his phone was tapped and that his trips out of Seoul would be monitored. But now it seemed that people were not quite so afraid of being followed, of being watched and of saying what they thought. And once those fears begin evaporating, he said, it is hard to make people afraid again.

He spoke slowly, in a deep voice. He moved slowly too, peeling and slicing a peach. He wore a light cotton shirt and Bermuda shorts. He was forty-two years old, but his face was still boyish. He smoked almost without pause and said that it was difficult, even now, forty days after his release, to spend much time outside. "Even two or three hours outdoors is difficult for me, especially when I'm in the middle of the street," he said. "When a car passes or when I'm near tall buildings, I get hostile and hysterical and try to overcome this."

His rhetoric, however, had lost none of its passion. "I was disappointed not to see the end of military rule," he said. He spoke of movements, of the "people's democratic movement," the "anti-fascist" and "anti-imperialism" movements and the need to push the opposition politicians to see that foreign governments, most especially the United States, had no place in the nation's affairs.

He did not raise his voice when he spoke about his beliefs. He enunciated his views deliberately. He did not wish to be interrupted, but nor would he speak over a question. He waited until the question was finished and then he continued saying what he wished to say. The floor was his and he spoke like a man so comfortable with that idea that he did not need to impose himself upon his listeners. Indeed, as he spoke in his quiet, patient voice you leaned closer to him. With no apparent effort he could succeed in drawing you in. Only afterward did you realize that, for a moment, you'd been holding your breath.

But then his head would begin to hurt. And once again he felt the past. It was not the memory of the physical pain that haunted him, but what the pain had made him see.

The police came for Kim Keun Tae at dawn, on September 4, 1985. They had detained him many times before, for three days and sometimes ten days, for distributing literature critical of the government and for "spreading groundless rumors." But now they took him to the National Police Agency's Anti-Communism Bureau. The electric shocks and water torture began immediately.

The sessions lasted for five hours. He was stripped naked and tied to a rack. His torturers mocked him. They pointed at his penis and said, "What is this? You call even that a penis?" They bound his heels, knees, thighs and chest and poured water on his chest, head and groin to help conduct the electricity. Then they turned up the radio, so that no one could hear his screaming. After half an hour of screaming the radio was not necessary because no sound came out of his mouth.

Some days they tortured him only once and on others they tortured him twice. Sometimes his torturers talked about their families as they worked, about life for a newly married daughter and college entrance examinations for a son. Sometimes they smiled. One day a broad-shouldered man came to his cell. The man carried torture implements in his briefcase. He told Kim, "Our undertaking business is about to start. Now it's your turn."

Between the torture sessions they beat him. A scab formed on his heel where he had cut himself on the torture rack, thrashing under the tight restraints. He tried saving the scab as evidence of his torture because otherwise there would be no proof. But the guards took it away. From the time of his arrest until ten days before the opening session of his trial on December 10, his lawyers could not see him. His lawyers went to the National Police Headquarters to see him but were told, each time, that he was at the prosecutors' office, which was often the excuse heard by lawyers of political prisoners. Kim asked to see a doctor five times but instead was punished with the loss of his reading, letter-writing and visiting privileges. On Friday, September 13, his jailers told him, "This is the Last Supper for you. Today is going to be a funeral for you." That day they tortured him twice with electric shocks.

"I remember an autobiography written during the Nazi era," Kim said. He lighted another cigarette and sipped a glass of barley tea. "The man was taken into the torture chamber by the Gestapo. These were people he looked at with contempt. But as they decided whether he would live or die that feeling toward them transformed into that of a pathological love object. As I read this, I saw a person trying to recover his dignity and I can say that I've gone through a similar kind of experience."

He paused and lowered his head. He slowly ran his fingers through his hair and in a soft voice said, "I'd like to continue.

"I've been to the cemetery in Kwangju two times and I've pledged that I would die for my beliefs in democracy. I told myself that to be an activist in Korea I should never surrender my beliefs in the face of violence and torture because my death would not be wasted. So when I was taken in, they wanted me to answer questions. But I didn't cooperate. In all that time I never completely gave in. But during the torture I reached a point where it occurred to me, I am dying. And I thought, This is a wasted life, a meaningless life. Not only was I surrendering, but my dignity was gone. I was no better than an animal. I was naked, on my knees and I begged them to kill me. I would talk if they let me die in comfort. But they said, 'You are still resisting,' and I suppose I was. But I felt no better than an animal."

Outside a junk man passed, clanging his thick, metal shears. A child cried. Someone was practicing the piano. Someone else, with dragging feet, passed under Kim's window. He had not heard these sounds for years.

He was not quite used to possibilities of freedom, although even in the much-changed present there were familiar and dark reminders of the past: Just before his release there was a robbery in Kim's home, but he did not believe the work was done by thieves; besides the theft of a watch, the burglers took dissident periodicals and a video recording of an interview he had given. The intruders left behind a knife, stuck in the floor.

But now, with the government made accountable in the National Assembly—and with its new understanding of the need to please the electorate if it hoped to regain the power it had lost—Kim had discovered that such attacks were the exception. Since his release he had been left alone. He was not stopped from attending a rally on behalf of political prisoners, even though that was the sort of thing that had happened in the past, that and the house arrests and preventive detention—detaining someone, often opposition politicians who the police thought might commit the crime of attending a banned rally.

Now the government that used to speak of "cleansing the nation of impure elements" was considering dropping the "contempt of state" law, which punished those who criticized the state to foreigners. In August, shortly after another thirty-six political prisoners were released, the head of the powerful and much-feared Army Intelligence Command was fired for his involvement in a knife attack against a journalist who had criticized the army. Two other generals and a major were arrested. In Inchon a policeman accused of sexually molesting a female defendant was put on trial again, this time by order of the Supreme Court, which ruled that a lower court was wrong when it dropped charges against him.

The victim, Kwon In Suk, was a former university student convicted of falsifying her academic background to obtain work in a factory—presumably to organize workers. She was released before the end of her eighteen-month sentence and filed a $150,000 lawsuit against the government for the psychological trauma suffered when Senior Patrolman Mun Kwi Dong pursued his interrogation by ordering her to strip, fondling her breasts, rubbing his penis against her and then forcing her to kneel down and take his penis into her mouth. The Inchon prosecutor's office insisted that Mun had only beaten her and had done so "out of his eagerness to carry out an effective probe." Dismissed from his job, Mun had tried opening a shoe manufacturing company, but the business failed. Now he was reluctant to go back to his apartment. He was said to be afraid of hectoring questions by reporters, who were suddenly free to write far more of what they wanted. The reporters were no longer afraid of arrest and imprisonment, not as they had been in the past.

Even the torture had stopped, or so it appeared to Kim Keun Tae. His final months in prison were spent in the exclusive company of prison guards who occasionally broke the rules and talked with him. He told them about his ideas, his dangerous ideas, and the guards listened to him. Sometimes, knowing that he wanted to write, they brought him pens, even though this was forbidden. On the morning of his release a friend began shoving a guard outside the prison gate. Kim came over and stopped his friend and shook the guard's hand. He had walked out of prison with his fist in the air.

But Kim was tired. People invited him to their meetings and rallies to speak. He declined and asked them to wait until he was physically able to be outdoors and in the presence of many people. Besides, as the fear dissipated and life improved, as there was more money to be spent and more things to buy, he wondered how large an audience his words might command. People seemed contented and this concerned him. If people were happy, they would not be inclined to listen to someone who wanted them to join him in changing their world. Contented people were people with things to lose, tactile things like cars and televisions, and potentially tenuous things like jobs that might be lost in the uncertain times that change would bring.

Who would listen to Kim Keun Tae, who other than the believers? Each time I looked about me and saw people in clothing more fashionable than the time before and driving new cars their parents could not have afforded, I wondered whether Kim Keun Tae was destined to be remanded to the periphery. The government, with its new and more palatable look—the smiling Roh Tae Woo was not nearly as easy a target as the forbidding Chun Doo Hwan—and with its newly discovered wisdom in avoiding issues that might galvanize the population, had done just what Kim feared it might. It had convinced people that the struggle was done.

But in Korea I'd discovered that that sort of thinking was not only deceptive but dangerous. For years the government insisted that the students could wail and scream, but they would do so alone because people, middle-class people, were contented. And then, last June, middle-class people showed they were not nearly as contented as the government had said. Despite all the very reasonable claims the government could make in helping bring the good life to the nation, the one weapon a dissident like Kim Keun Tae could still deploy was the promise of more.

For all they had, people still felt cheated, and the feeling compounded their han. Someone, be it the man next door or an unpopular relative, had more. Someone always had more. Someone always had what you did not have. I remember a Korean friend, a courtly man who thought himself a citizen of the world, telling me how he felt when as a young man he saw someone with a pack of American cigarettes. My friend may have just finished his last precious Lucky Strike. But when he recalled seeing someone else with a new pack of Marlboros, he said, "I just hated him." He spat the words, "I hated him," hated because he had something that my friend had had the day before and did not have now. That was all it took for my friend to decide he hated this stranger, hated him with a rage born of discontentment and bitterness.

People may have been feeling an end to their fears. They may have been outfitting themselves with the trappings of a better life. But I could not help but feel that given the chance to have more, to have that which they lacked and coveted, they could become first angry and then receptive to someone who could tell them how to get it. Though I could not envision streams of office and shipyard workers joining the campaign for a "people's" Korea, I could not dismiss the rage that came when people felt that, once again, they were being denied. The feeling—be it based on a reality or the perception of that reality—bubbled and bubbled and then it exploded; and as it ran its angry course, any voice of reason, any plea for moderation, any attempt to soften the mood was as audible as a whisper in a gale.

Of course Kim Keun Tae was not selling consumer goods. He was selling ideas. But having seen what a formidable passion han could be, I wondered what might happen if people saw a correlation between Kim's abstract ideas about "the masses" and "class struggle" and the possibility of taking more for themselves from the undeserving—from the hoarders, the rich folk, the politicians' friends whom they were sure benefited not through hard work but through chicanery. Perhaps that was why the government had taken Kim away and tortured him and tried very hard to destroy his humanity—because the government, contemptuous as it could be of the people it ruled, was still keenly aware of what happened when bitter people, discontented people, had someone to point the way.

Kim, meanwhile, wanted people to see that his struggle was not done, that the Americans still played too great a role in their life and that the people who ran the country were many of the same people whom they had feared. He would wait until they listened. He would wait because he was in his early forties and had had no other life.

"I still haven't forgotten what it felt like to be living as an animal," he said that afternoon in his living room. "It still haunts me. My personality was destroyed. But I still resisted. I still refused to answer in interrogation. I found the will to stand up. I felt a destiny. I had an obligation to overcome this, not only for my own sake, but for the Korean people."

Kim Keun Tae spoke of his past when asked about it. He preferred speaking of the future. But the past gave his words their force. The past did not have to be embellished or resurrected. People could see how he carried it with him.

He still suffered the pain of tormenting memories. But by sacrifice he could reconcile the man he wanted to be with one he still recalled, naked and on his knees, begging his tormentors to kill him. He was ready to lead again, if there were those willing to follow. He needed time to see where the nation was heading. "It's not that easy and simple," he said.

He walked outside. It was a warm afternoon. In the market street women were shopping. Children were riding bicycles and making noise. He stayed outside for a few minutes and then stepped back in, closing the metal gate behind him. He would be out again soon. His nose had already gotten red from the sun.

Marriage, Divorce and the Big Brother

D IVORCE saddened Pak Chang U and he did not care to speak of it. Why ask about divorce, he said, when we are talking about marriage. Marriage both pleased and profited Pak and he smiled as he spoke of the couples who came to his office each day seeking documentation, for a fee. Pak, as district representative for the Bum Heung Foundation's Itaewon branch, eased the paperwork, checked identifications, secured visas, assisted with passports and provided airline tickets for the American soldiers and Korean women on their way to America, ring fingers bound in gold.

Business was not good for Pak Chang U. There were fewer marriages and more divorces. The success of the Bum Heung Foundation was predicated on the good feelings between Korea and America. But feelings between the two countries, or at least Korean feelings toward America, were not good. The estrangement seemed inevitable, as it does when one partner in an unequal marriage tires of the inequality and cannot seem to make the other understand that things must change. Feelings turn nasty. The slightest insult seems to trigger the greatest hurt. Words are exchanged. The past, which felt so good, is hardly remembered. The relationship has to run a rocky course if it is going to be good again. But the rocky times seem to go on forever.

Itaewon was an appropriate place for Pak Chang U to ply his trade in marriage and divorce, because it was in Itaewon, loud and vulgar Itaewon, that Korea and America were at their worst with one another. Once a poor and shabby place, Itaewon had become prosperous, primarily by catering to the Americans. Itaewon still needed the

Americans. But it did not love them, not without question, not anymore. In many places in Korea love for America was turning to hate, and if not to hate then to the frustration and bitterness that accompanies doubt and confusion.

In Itaewon passions of various sorts were on constant display. In Itaewon the strains were becoming obvious, despite Pak Chung U's boosterish talk of marital bliss.

"They look like perfect couples," he said, smiling the sort of smile that fits as easily on a justice of the peace as on a mortician. Pak used to sell love, or something close to it, when he ran an introduction service for lonely GIs and Korean women who wanted them. The women left photographs and copies of their identity cards. The GIs came in and looked at the pictures and if they found a face that looked appealing, Pak arranged a meeting in his shabby, cluttered office, where the woman could interview her prospective husband about his potential earnings. But Pak disbanded this service, he said, when those Korean women desperate to leave realized that it was both easier and cheaper to hang around the main gate of the U.S. Eighth Army's Yongsan base and catch the eye of a soldier far from home.

His foundation had chosen for its Itaewon location a corner surrounded on all sides by bars where young Korean hostesses sat and waited for young American men to come and buy them drinks. The women did not like the men to buy them beer because beer was cheap and the house made no profit. Wine was better. A highball was best. The hostesses, hair teased and lips glossed, often wore the same outfits, which were satin, bright, revealing and offset by dark stockings. They sat together until the men arrived, whereupon they descended upon the men, put their arms around their shoulders and ran their fingers along their neck. The men then bought them highballs.

Itaewon sat at the edge of Yongsan, which sat in, or rather spread itself across, a prime swath of real estate in central Seoul. The post contained an eighteen-hole golf course and the only neighborhood in Seoul where the homes were set back from the street and had front lawns, lawns tended by Korean gardeners. Itaewon was Yongsan's discount shopping center and playpen. A generation before the district had been a series of huts and tents selling cheap souvenirs. The sidewalks were still lined with pushcarts loaded with T-shirts and miniature M-16 rifles.

But now there were a thousand shops in Itaewon selling, at an unrelenting scream, imitation Louis Vuitton bags (as seen, still wrapped in plastic, on the arm of then-Treasury Secretary James Baker's wife as the couple was leaving Kimpo Airport), Lacoste tennis shirts, down jackets, baseball mitts, made-to-order shoes, mink coats, antique furniture, brass bed frames, Los Angeles Laker warmup suits, celadon lamps and Reebok sneakers. There were six hundred garment shops, fifty leather shops and tailor shops, where the touts grabbed passersby by the arm, badgering them into buying custom-made suits. When Ronald Reagan came to Seoul in 1983, he went to Itaewon and had two suits made by a tailor who called himself U.S. Kim.

There were two kinds of people in Itaewon—buyers and sellers— and though the streets were a jumble, the lines between them did not blur. Three-quarters of the buyers were foreign—most of them American, many of the Americans, GIs—and the sellers were Koreans who provided the soldiers with what they needed in clothing and cuisine: Pizza Hut, Baskin-Robbins ice cream, Wendy's hamburgers. The foreigners, in turn, provided the merchants of Itaewon with an estimated $500 million in annual sales, swelling real estate prices to $2,500 a square foot and generating profits sufficient to pay the more aggressive touts $425 a month, plus room and board.

Still, neither side distinguished itself in Itaewon. The soldiers were loud and aggressive and the Koreans were their equal. This was especially so after dark, when Itaewon turned to drink and what, in army and port towns from Subic Bay to San Diego, was offered as an approximation of romance. In Itaewon cross-cultural couples whose attachment was genuine shared the crowded sidewalks with those whose connection was billed by the hour. Itaewon's prostitutes ran up to you on the street, grabbed an arm and would not let go. Middle-aged women in baggy pants emerged from the clothing stalls and came close enough to whisper in your ear, "Come to Charlie house. Best girls. You see. Such big titty."

Itaewon had 270 bars, bars with names like Georgetown and Pennsylvania and Lady Luck, where the come-on sign read MY PLACE OR YOURS? There were places where only Koreans were welcome and others restricted to foreign clientele. There were ten gay bars, where transvestite employees were tested for the AIDS virus. There was Sam's Place and Sam's Place II, the Kangaroo Club, Club Bavaria, Lucky Club and the King Club, where in early August three waiters were hospitalized after being throttled by a group of GIs who'd been refused admission because a woman in their company insisted upon bringing her dog inside. The King Club was for foreigners only, although the club's bouncer was famous for kicking and punching expatriate men and women who he decided did not belong.

The incident in the gaudy doorway of the King Club—flanking the glass doors were two six-foot-tall black birds of prey, oversized ringers for the Maltese falcon—was only another in a series of nasty confrontations between Koreans and Americans after nightfall. Something had gone wrong in Itaewon. Everyone was supposed to have a good time, even if it cost a bit. But feelings hatched on the campuses had spread, slowly at first and now with increasing speed, to those of various backgrounds and stations who decided they did not like the Americans anymore.

For years they had, and very much so. They had liked the Americans for coming to fight for them in 1950 at the cost of fifty-four thousand American lives and they liked the Americans when they were starving children and the Americans came to their schools and served powdered milk. Their experience with Americans at the time was still limited. The Americans had come first in 1866, aboard the merchant ship *General Sherman*, whose voyage up the Taedong River ended with the death of all hands when the ship was burned by a mob at Pyongyang. Korea was then a closed country, the Hermit Kingdom, and foreigners entered at their peril. Missionaries had come late in the nineteenth and early in the twentieth centuries and made many converts, in good measure because Christians had led the resistance to the Japanese colonial government. But it was not until 1945, when the American army of occupation landed at Inchon and went in desperate search of anyone who could speak English that Koreans saw Americans in great numbers.

The occupation commander was John Hodge, a general whose experience with Asians was limited to fighting them. The fall of Japan had led many Koreans to believe, erroneously, that their independence was at hand. The Americans had little interest in Korea. The Soviet Union was concerned with protecting its southern flank and regarded Korea as a useful, though not essential acquisition. Franklin Roosevelt had talked of "trusteeships" for Japan's colonies, with the idea that after a Big Power stewardship of fifty years or so these states might indeed be ready for independence. But then Roosevelt died, the Russians entered the war against Japan and descended quickly into the Korean peninsula and Harry Truman decided that America's best course was not "trusteeship" but "containment."

A line was drawn at the thirty-eighth parallel, a proposal hastily made—as the Russians advanced—by two American officers, one of them a future secretary of state, Dean Rusk. Years later, on the campuses, Koreans would still talk of how the Americans looked at the map and drew the line dividing their country. That the Russians had occupied the North and agreed to the split did not matter; the Americans drew the line that ended the dream of a united and independent Korea. It was America, the students argued, that was responsible for the han of the nation's division. And that was only the beginning of what they viewed as America's contribution to the national bitterness.

But in 1945 the question was not so much the line as who might be in charge of the half that remained contested. The North belonged to the Communists and, eventually, to Kim Il Sung. The South had in the days after the surrender been under the loose control of a left-leaning coalition called the People's Republic. The People's Republic began administering the countryside at the same time that the rightists were coming home. The South turned in on itself, as faction and subfaction fought, savagely, for power.

The Americans, knowing nothing about Korea, turned to the Japanese, who in defeat were only too happy to whisper in their conqueror's ear, telling them whom to trust. Collaborators fared well, especially those who'd worked for the Japanese colonial police and who now did the Americans' dirty work, as they had so assiduously for the Japanese. The Americans, in turn, provided them not only with the means and the training, but with an ideology, a reactive ideology, but a belief nonetheless: anti-communism.

The People's Republic was dismantled. Syngman Rhee, a foe of the left who had spent the previous generation in and around Washington courting useful friends, returned from America. Kim Ku, his more militant rival for the right, returned from China. Plots and assassinations ensued. (Kim's would not come until 1948, when Rhee, who was alleged to be behind his killing, had already been accompanied into the National Assembly by Douglas MacArthur as the Republic of Korea's first president.) American MPs, meanwhile, were issued orders to hit Koreans seen riding on the outside of a crowded streetcar. People had been getting hurt and the Americans decided a firm hand was required.

Still, for a long time Koreans thought that Americans could do anything. On the night in 1960 when Syngman Rhee surrendered the presidency as the nation turned against him—scores were killed in demonstrations against his corrupt and ineffective rule—a great crowd gathered outside the American embassy and cheered because people believed that it was the Americans who had coerced Rhee to resign. But the good feeling did not last. When General Park Chung Hee ousted the short-lived and ineffectual civilian government that succeeded Rhee, the Americans turned the other way, just as they would amidst reports of arrests, torture and various abuses of human rights.

The Americans looked so strong and yet they did nothing to make things better. Only in 1977, when Jimmy Carter threatened to withdraw American troops if Park did not curb the abuses, did the American government take so firm a stand. But that was temporary. The abuses continued; the troops remained. After Chun Doo Hwan ordered his paratroopers into Kwangju, many Koreans were convinced that the Americans, if not tacitly behind the killings, certainly could have stopped them. The Americans never bothered explaining the limits imposed upon their military commander by the Status of Forces Agreement.

So on the campuses the blame for Kwangju was shared. Chun may have done the killing. But the Americans let him. That the Americans had intervened to save the life of Kim Dae Jung, whom Chun planned to execute for sedition, was not mentioned, not by the students and not, in the years that followed, by Kim.

American strength became as despised as it was admired. In the interests of "stability" the United States had tolerated decades of cruelty and fear. Yet people still wanted America to interfere in their lives if that interference could be useful in bullying the powerful men who bullied them. Otherwise, the Americans were to stay out of their affairs. America was perceived as abusing its role as older brother, a role it had played to an increasingly unenthusiastic nation forty-eight hundred years its senior, a nation that nonetheless quaked when Americans suggested it was time to begin withdrawing its troops.

America now wanted Korea to buy its beef, so farmers took to the streets in provincial towns, burning American cars. America also wanted to sell cigarettes to Korea, thereby both poisoning the lungs of the nation's youth and encroaching upon the domain of the Korean Tobacco Monopoly, which had been doing a handsome business in a nation where three-quarters of the population smoked. A campaign began against the American cigarettes, a nationwide movement launched with the ceremonial burning of gifts from American tobacco companies. Tobacco growers rallied in Seoul chanting, "We cannot sit idle, lamenting the sorrow of the weak. Let's stand up and make all-out efforts to restore national pride and build up national strength and survive."

Korea wanted the American troops, but then it didn't. It liked the taste of Marlboros but deemed their purchase treasonous. Korea wanted America out of its life but not out of its shops. America, which once could do no wrong, could do no right.

Even in Itaewon there was distaste and resentment of the swagger, boldness, loud voices and late-night rebel yells of the most obvious and numerous Americans: the soldiers. Even those who profited handsomely from trade with the Americans carped about their attitude—their rudeness, crassness and penchant for speaking in less-than-humble language to their elders. The policemen in Itaewon complained about the trouble they had, late at night, with drunk Americans. Cab drivers filed complaints against Americans who refused to pay their fare.

The Americans had been providing grist for any number of stories, some true, some false, some a mix: American servicemen had commandeered a bus in Pohang and forced the driver, at knife point, to take them to the bar district; a group of American soldiers had gang-raped two Korean women during maneuvers. The American military spokesman, who rarely commented on such reports, felt obliged to deny both publicly, if only because the rumor of the rapes had spread so far and so quickly that American diplomats were being hounded about the incident at every Korean reception they attended. The problem for the spokesman was that while there was a good deal of false talk about, there was also truth to allegations of American soldiers' committing any number of crimes, murder among them.

That the bus driver who'd accused the Americans of taking his bus later recanted his story and admitted that he had made up the part about the knife was no longer the issue. People had decided that the Americans were no good, not any more. The white ones were bad enough. But the black ones were cocky and crude and if you were white, that is what you were told. You were taken into the confidence of people like the salesman I encountered one afternoon in an Itaewon shoe shop when a young African man walked in. He looked at the samples, somewhat bewildered, stayed for a minute or so and then departed. And as he walked through the door, the young and eager salesclerk looked at me and said in English, confidentially and knowingly, "African. Smell." He held his nose and screwed up his face to emphasize a point that I'd soon discover was hardly his alone.

Still, there remained shop owners in the district who spoke of the Americans in the most flattering way, especially when they came in to buy a leather jacket or a pair of designer sweats. "I can speak for all the shop owners here—no one resents the Americans," insisted Kim Sam Soon, who owned the American Club, where Americans, both servicemen and civilians, could come to drink beer and eat fries and, on quiet Sunday afternoons, watch such patriotic movies as *Uncommon Valor* on the television. The bar was dark and wagon-wheel fixtures hung from the ceiling. There were, of course, girls in the American Club, waitresses dressed in red who sat by a man's side and danced when he wanted to dance and drank with him. I asked Kim Sam Soon about her girls and she brought me up short. "Contrary to your misconception, most of the waitresses are very well educated and have college degrees," she said. "Our waitresses are not here to sell their bodies. In the smaller clubs they're not educated. This is a legitimate career. Even our dishwashers are high-school graduates and very well mannered."

Kim had met her first American nineteen years ago: the date, she later explained, coincided with the conception of her son. She was married to an American. Her bar, which served Wild Turkey bourbon and Budweiser beer, was festooned with the sorts of suggestive slogans that could remind her patrons of home: NO PLACE BUT TEXAS, and VIRGINITY CAN BE CURED. Her disc jockey played country-and-western music. He even played a disparaging song that the Americans could laugh about. "You picked a fine time to burn me, Miss Lee," went the lyric. "Four days to port call and a dose of VD . . ."

"This entire area exists for the Americans," said Kim Sam Soon. "We built our shops for the Americans."

The American Club sat on a corner across from the dingy office of the Bum Heung Foundation, where Pak Chang U, who had been in the matrimonial trade for twenty-five years, still helped bring young people together. A secretary brought his coffee and Pak reflected upon the American men who came to him, Korean women on their arms. "The servicemen, they're lonesome," he said. "They leave their families behind. They work in the compound. They find Korean girls, get married here. I see a lot of GIs. After they get married, they run around. Then they go back to the States, where they can see their parents, their mothers and sisters. In time they get tired of the Korean girls."

And so some of the marriages that looked so promising to Pak ended in divorce. If the couple remained in Korea, he was available, of course, to assist with the paperwork. Pak did a divorce or two a month. "The American men give Korean women a hard time. Korean women have a special character: If her husband is very faithful, a Korean woman never argues or complains. American men don't come home every night. It is always the American men's fault."

But luckily, he said, Korean women were getting smarter. They were going to school. If they married Americans and their husbands were unworthy, the wives could drop them, especially if they had moved to the States, where they might find it easier securing decent jobs. Besides, Pak said, Korean women could see what America looked like on the television and in the movies and were beginning to believe that America did not look so inviting anymore. He recognized, unfortunately, that business, which was not as good now as it had been five years ago, would suffer even more: Why, after all, would a Korean girl want to marry an American when she might instead enjoy a promising future with a local boy?

In the crowded street near Pak's office three heavy U.S. Army tractor trailers were stuck in an alley. They were trying to negotiate their big rigs between the parked cars. The owners of the cars stood and watched, as did patrons from the Korean restaurant and the sales-clerks from a high-fashion boutique. The drivers pulled in their mirrors and drove very slowly, until they were past the cars.

And only then did the owner of a new, white car emerge from the laughing crowd with his keys in his hand. His car sat in the section of the alley the truckers found most treacherous. He opened the door and got in his car and waited until the rigs were gone before he pulled away.

"You mother f——," a well-dressed young man called after the truckers. But the Americans were too far away to hear him.

The Refugee

KIM Young Chull wanted to have a big party at his mother's house and his four brothers left it to him to draw up the guest list. When they saw who Young Chull invited, they told him he was crazy.

The home of their aging mother sat in the hills above Seoul, in a neighborhood where the city's wealthy people could live away from the noise and congestion below them. It was a large stone house with a wide yard in the back. The cooks set up tables and lights and a long row of chafing dishes. The dishes were filled with meat and vegetables, grilled and barbecued. Waiters circulated, serving whiskey, beer and wine. It was a warm night and the men slipped off their suit coats and began to drink.

The yard was crowded with guests and young women who were there for decorative purposes. There were businesspeople, college professors, journalists and officials from the government, one of whom—an especially powerful man—had, in the harsher times, helped arrange for the arrest of one of these professors. "How could you invite both of them?" Young Chull's brothers had asked. There were other people in the yard who did not like each other. The college professors snubbed the journalists. The journalists cozied up to the politicians and the young women smiled at everyone.

The professor who went to prison avoided the man who helped send him there. Young Chull's brothers were worried, but not Young Chull, who wanted the evening to be a time for lively conversation. Young Chull was a talker and he liked being with people who liked to talk. Young Chull moved among his guests, smiling. He wore a fashionable, collarless shirt and baggy, pleated slacks. He stopped to talk and then moved on, looking for all the world like a man at ease with himself, although this was not always the case.

That Young Chull and his brothers knew so many prominent people was testimony to what they had accomplished in the twenty-five years since their father's bus company went bankrupt and friends who they had hoped would be patient in recovering their loans instead turned against the Kims, demanding immediate payment. Twenty-five years ago the Kim brothers did not throw parties for their friends and relatives, in part because they could not afford it, in part because they were afraid no one would come and in part because they were ashamed. This shame for the failure of their family's business, however, took the form of han when their friends started hounding them about the money they were owed.

The Kim brothers channeled this han into several ventures they hoped would revive the family fortunes. The miniature wooden shoe business did not work, nor did the paper umbrellas they tried to sell to Polynesian restaurants. The idea about the scraps of fur, however, caught on. Young Chull's younger brother, Young Jin, went to the U.S. embassy, copied down the names of all the furriers in New York and wrote to them, suggesting that if they sent their scraps to Seoul, the Kim brothers would have them sewn into salable items. Young Jin got a reply from a furrier who offered a thousand dollars for ten thousand pom-poms from the scraps he sent. The scraps were sewn by girls who worked for the Kim brothers for twenty dollars a month, 365 days a year, sitting on the floor. From that order other orders followed and Jindo Furs was born.

"We had failed. All those friends treated us like shit. We just couldn't shake it off," Young Chull said of past times, which were nothing like the present times. Jindo now produced more fur garments than anyone else in the world. There were over fifty Jindo salons in Seoul, New York, Frankfurt, West Berlin, London and Hong Kong. A Moscow salon was scheduled to open soon. The Kim brothers flew between these cities, meeting with men who treated them not as their friends had twenty-five years before but as prominent men whose business they wanted.

Young Chull was the second son. He fell between his elder brother, Young Won, who had the necessary political connections, and Young Jin, who had devised the idea that made Jindo so successful—manufacturing furs for a mass market. Young Chull was an affable man, tall, thin and ready, always ready, to talk. Many ideas interested him. He talked about issues of the day and his belief that Korea had to move beyond its national self-absorption and begin thinking about nations other than itself. He talked about Korean music, and composers trying to revive the music of the past.

He also talked about being a refugee—how his family had escaped Pyongyang, fleeing the Russians and the Communists in 1946; how they fled Seoul when the city fell in the early days of the Korean War; how his father, as so many others did, made a living from the money of the American army, repairing U.S. Army jeeps and running a gas station on an army base.

But when Young Chull talked about the past, about the years of starvation and death and fear, he grew curiously nostalgic, not for the suffering, but for the simplicity of the times. His father, like his grandfather before him, was consumed by such simple needs as finding the means for feeding his family. Young Chull did not have to worry about such things. When he flew, he sat in first class. He and his Swiss wife, Louisette, had homes in Seoul, London and Guam. Their son was attending Stanford Law School. Their daughter worked in Europe. Young Chull wore expensive suits and his chauffeur drove him about town in a Mercedes-Benz. When their father died, in 1981, Young Chull and his brothers paid to have an elaborate tomb built in his memory, complete with a chiseled family history. The family had had no tomb at which to pay homage to its ancestors since leaving Pyongyang.

Now that Kim Young Chull had a tomb to visit, he went to his father's grave site every month. Lately he had been thinking of his father and the life his father led. Young Chull wondered whether there was something to be envied in the harsh but simple lives of men like his father. Wealth, it seemed to him, brought many complications and doubts.

Of all the doubts that plagued Kim Young Chull at the age of fifty, the most perplexing was the one that he confronted each morning, in the mirror, as he prepared to shave. He would look at the reflection of his tanned face and think of the life that he and his brothers had built for themselves and their children. And then he would say to himself, "You really screwed up."

* * *

In 1965 Kim Young Chull came back to Korea because his father needed him. He had been gone for eight years, living in America. He had left home at nineteen to go to Cowley County Community College in Arkansas City, Kansas, the school where his older brother had gone.

When Young Chull was growing up at a refugee center in Pusan— where the family had fled when the Communists took Seoul—and then in a Seoul destroyed in the war, he believed that the best job a young man could find was as a houseboy to an American soldier. A houseboy could learn English and maybe go to America. Americans were tall, strong, uniformed men who tossed their unwanted C rations to Korean children. Young Chull and his friends always took the cheese out of the C rations because they had never seen cheese before and thought it was rotten butter.

"America was the land of Sears," Young Chull said. "The PX had a Sears catalog with nail clippers, can openers and LP records." Korea had only old 78s. Americans had tins of pineapples they could afford to throw out. They had money. Young Chull wanted to go to America very badly and through a distant cousin working on an army base got the names of people to write to, asking for a scholarship so he could go to college in America. He wrote five hundred letters before he found a sponsor.

He lived in the home of his teacher, Dr. Johnson. Young Chull did not speak much English when he came to live with Dr. Johnson and his family. Sometimes, when the family was out and Young Chull was home alone, the phone rang and Young Chull made believe he did not hear it because he was afraid he would not understand what the caller was saying. When Dr. Johnson told him that he should try to answer these calls, Young Chull answered the phone but took no messages when he could not understand a caller's name. There was an old man who lived near the Johnsons and every morning he greeted Young Chull with words that Young Chull now understands were "How's it goin'?" The words came out in a blur that Young Chull could not fathom. He hid when he saw the old man.

Eight years later, when Young Chull returned to Seoul, he was married, a father of two, an English speaker and the disappointed entrepreneur who, after seeing a machine that sold sanitary napkins, thought of bringing disposable sanitary napkins to Korea. He was told by an American familiar with Korea that his plan was doomed to fail because Korean women were unaccustomed to disposable sanitary napkins. Instead, Young Chull had worked part-time jobs in America until he received a call from his brother telling him that their father wanted him to come home. Young Chull wanted Louisette to feel good about moving to Korea. He told her that his father owned a prosperous business and that the waters of the Han River were blue.

They arrived in August. They flew over dirt roads and then over the Han, which was brown and murky. Young Chull's father had gone into business manufacturing buses for the city of Seoul. Government regulations prohibited his importing the necessary scrap and so he was dependent upon the U.S. Army for supplies. He could not build the buses fast enough. He was going broke. When Young Chull arrived in his father's office and saw the walls lined with army-surplus filing cabinets and the clutter and inefficiency, he announced that the time had come to modernize so that things would be as they were in America. Young Chull wanted a filing system. But the business failed the following year and the Kims' creditors began descending with outstretched arms and open palms. The Kims were left only with each other because no one else was going to help them. Young Chull's father had always told his sons how important it was for a family to stay together.

Young Chull thought about the events surrounding the failure of his father's company and the birth of Jindo Furs and said that it was easy for the family to risk failure. "We didn't know what business was all about," he said. "We didn't have time to train. We weren't tarnished by old habits." In this way his family was no different from all the families around them, both the families that failed and the families that became fabulously wealthy. "Risk is easy when you have nothing," he said.

Young Chull and his brothers worked long hours, as did the women who sewed the furs they sold and worked for a small percentage of the profits that the Kim brothers were beginning to earn. The Kims made friends in the government and in banking circles and were able to borrow the money they needed to build their company—this at a time when the government of Park Chung Hee was granting tax breaks and loans to growing companies in the hope of making Korea something other than a country dependent on American aid.

But as Jindo prospered and there were increasing demands on

Young Chull's time—both at the office and after work, entertaining the men with whom they did business—he grew apart from his family in ways that were then easy to ignore.

"Five years ago when the doorman saluted me, I'd say to myself, 'You've got it made,' " he said. "Now I need recognition when I look in the mirror. When I look at my reflection, I see a lot of hypocritical things I've done, using business and earning money as an excuse. Now I look at myself and say, 'It's bullshit.' The family used to be our religion, for my father and for my brothers. But now our religion is the business. We worship business."

Of course Young Chull's view was clear now, a clarity that is one of success's benefits. Young Chull and his brothers still worked hard—the company was always opening new shops—but Young Chull had the time to think, a gift to go along with his big new office overlooking the Printemps department store in downtown Seoul. The office was lined with posters of racing cars. Music from the opera *Carmen* played on a small stereo. Lately, as Young Chull thought unkind things about himself and the choices he had made in his life, he began writing his memoirs. He did not talk of himself as a man who made the choices he did because he had no other options—the family was broke; the family knew what it meant to be destitute; the family knew what it meant to feel the shame of failure and would show its doubting creditors how wrong they had been. Instead, he saw a man who by doing what had to be done alienated the people his father told him mattered most.

"I have a friend from grade school," Young Chull said. "He owns a small company. His wife can't afford a maid. He drives a five-year-old Maepsy. When he pulls up to a hotel in that car, the doorman tells him to get lost. My friend takes his family out once a week. On Sundays they go to church. He goes home every night. I used to go to geisha parties. I thought he envied me."

Young Chull's wife could travel. His son did not have to write five hundred letters begging for a scholarship to America. Young Chull sent him to Tufts. "But it's not a family life like my wife and children wanted," he said. "My son says, 'You've always been so busy with business, you didn't see me grow up.' I tell him, 'I did all these things for you and you tell me this?' "

Young Chull would never have said that to his father. His father was not always a warm or accessible man, but he was the father and was accorded the respect due his position. Young Chull would not have expected more. "It's not that I miss him," he said of his father. "You never have a relationship with your father like in the West— pals. I didn't always feel affection."

Young Chull did not expect more. His children expected more because Young Chull gave them the means to see a world in which more was possible. Young Chull could keep up with this world in wealth and dress and an eye for what was current. But he could not match its easy confidence. He could not forget fleeing his home at the age of eight, running again at twelve, growing up with nothing, seeing his father ruined, feeling the betrayal of friends. When he talked about this dilemma with his prosperous friends, he discovered that they felt the way he felt.

"We still have a refugee mentality," he said. "Do we really have enough to be confident about? In the morning I ask myself, 'Am I doing well enough?' We work hard in order to show others that we can do it. We're still acting like little kids wanting a pat on the back."

Young Chull's wife told him that the older he gets, the more he favors garlic and kimchi in his food. "I want to be a Korean," Young Chull said. He wished his children knew more about what it means to be Korean. But his children speak English and French and for this Young Chull faulted himself. "It was my mistake," he said. "If I taught them, they'd understand me better. Even though they hug me and kiss me, they don't understand me as well as I understood my father."

The world of Young Chull's father was clear. The family stayed together. The family obeyed the father's commands. Now Young Chull had a sister living in Los Angeles and another living in New York. "It's all spreading out," he said of his father's family. If the family had a center, it was Jindo Furs and the tomb that Young Chull and his brothers built for their father. "I go there because it soothes my feelings," he said of the tomb.

Mostly he went alone, although his daughter would join him when she was visiting Korea. She would bow to her grandfather, as Koreans are supposed to do before the graves of their ancestors.

"She reacts even more than the other grandchildren," Young Chull said. "She overdoes it because of me. By doing that she thinks she's showing me her respect. She takes me as a father. But I wonder, 'Does she really know me?' "

Home

I went to the ballpark in Inchon because the Haitai Lions had come to play. Haitai was the best baseball team in the land. Thousands of people from Inchon and nearby Seoul came to see the Lions. They came because the Lions were good, and because they brought a bit of home with them.

Korea was a nation of people away from home. At the Thanksgiving holiday of Chusok and at the New Year, Seoul Station and the intercity bus depot were jammed with people going home to towns and villages where parents or, perhaps, grandparents remained, towns and villages that had offered nothing. But people from Masan remained Masan people, as people from Pusan and Chungju remained people of those towns. In Seoul there were associations of people from the same hometown. Men who had left their home five or ten or twenty years before could sit and talk about how pretty things had looked at home in the spring, when the snow began to melt.

Haitai's hometown was mournful, bitter Kwangju, the capital of distant Cholla Province. Cholla Province was rich in land but not in commerce, which meant that many of its young men and women had left their family's farm and come north, where the money was better. Cholla people were all over Seoul and the port town of Inchon. When the Lions came to play baseball, they came to the ballpark to cheer themselves hoarse.

The cities may have offered work. But they provided few substitutes for home other than the hometown associations and church congregations comprised of people from the same place. The cities also offered baseball.

Baseball had become the most popular substitute for home. It seemed an ironic choice for a nation that sought purity. Baseball, after all, was an imported game introduced at the turn of the century by American missionaries and honed in the spirit of physical culture by the Japanese colonial government. In the seven years since the professional league's inception, the game had become the nation's favorite, eclipsing soccer, boxing and ssirum.

Koreans played baseball well, if somewhat deliberately, more in the one-run-at-a-time pace of the Japanese, who had had longer to impose their approach, than with the abandon of the Americans.

What happened on the field, however, mattered only in that it meant so much to the people who came to watch. The ballpark was home, or rather several homes, one in the stands along the first-base line and another alongside third. The ballpark was a place to celebrate the jong between men who shared the same hometown. They could celebrate home at the ballpark, but not simply for its fancifully recalled glories. At the ballpark the celebration of your hometown meant denigrating someone else's.

Regionalism, this homogeneous society's substitute for racial and religious intolerance, was an animosity rooted as much in the memory of what home had been as in the principle that those who were not from there were somehow deficient, deficient and contemptible.

Outside the ballpark I met Yi Yong Su, who said that he liked being able to sit in the grandstand with strangers who, in the course of nine innings, became fast, if temporary friends.

Yi was twenty-nine and worked in a factory in Inchon. Cholla Province was his home. Luckily Yi had baseball or, rather, the Haitai Lions. Because seating in the ballpark was by allegiance—the hometown people sat behind the home dugout along the third-base line; the visitors sat near first—Yi knew that the stranger sitting next to him, the fellow sharing his bottle of soju or package of dried squid, was also a son of Cholla. Together they could cheer and, when the mood struck them and those around them, rise and bellow caustic words at the men sitting in the grandstand on the other side of the infield, the men from a different hometown.

"When it comes to baseball, we have radios at work and have to listen to the game," Yi said. "Sometimes the game is not on the air. We have to wait and listen for the news or else something for us is not fulfilled. When the opposing team loses, I feel good."

It was a Sunday afternoon, sunny and not too humid. But the rain of recent days had left the field slippery and muddy. The game was postponed until Monday. Yi and other men from Cholla lingered outside while the Inchon Dolphins' pitchers loosened up in the parking lot. The stadium was closed and there was no place else to play.

It was a cozy setting, though a bit run-down. The stadium was surrounded by gray apartment blocks and laundry was hanging from the windows. The parking lot was part cracked cement and part dirt dotted with grass and broken bottles. The pitchers had to watch where they landed their feet on their follow-throughs. People lolled around the clubhouse door, relaxed and smiling—this in marked contrast to their behavior when a game was in progress and a decision hung in the balance.

People got upset at baseball games. Already this summer twenty people had been hurt by flying bottles and fists during ballpark riots, as had ten players. An umpire was attacked by two hundred spectators who ran out on the field and beat him up because they did not like a call he made. And in the worst baseball riot of the season a twenty-nine-year-old man died of a heart attack at Sajik Stadium in Pusan. Twelve people were also injured when Haitai scored five runs in the top of the ninth and beat the Lotte Giants.

The Giants, like all the nation's professional baseball teams, were sometimes loved at home and sometimes detested. Losing was bad enough—Haitai's players knew that: In the team's lean years the fans would not let the players out of the clubhouse after a loss; they set fire to the team bus. But when the Giants lost to Haitai, as they had that sorry night, they were disgracing not only themselves, but all of Kyongsang Province. Of all the many hatreds that festered between Koreans south of the thirty-eighth parallel, none rivaled the animosity that the people of Cholla and Kyongsang felt for each other.

Kyongsang was not supposed to lose to Cholla, not to a province whose people could not control their temper and whose only worthy contribution to the nation was—and this was admitted grudgingly—a skillful hand in preparing barbecued beef. Cholla people responded to such accusations with windy discourses on the refined nature of Cholla artwork and poetry, followed by a scathing imitation of the butchery Kyongsang people performed on the Korean language.

This was a hatred that had long since eclipsed the bounds of reasoned dislike and escalated into an antipathy that knew no bounds. Cholla and Kyongsang hated one another for reasons as passionate as they were nonsensical and that were made apparent during the presidential election, when the opposition had split along regional lines. Kim Dae Jung had dominated Cholla and Kim Young Sam, though forced to compete with Roh Tae Woo in his native Kyongsang, scored well at home. During the campaign both Kims were attacked on the other's turf for no reason other than birthplace.

And while the rivalries were blamed for Roh's victory—of course many blamed the government for reminding everyone how much everyone hated each other—a far more hideous result of the feud came midway through the campaign in a way that had nothing to do with politics but suggested which way the vote would go. A twenty-five-year-old cutter in a Seoul garment factory named Kim Chong Wang wanted to marry a woman with whom he worked, a dressmaker known in the newspapers only as Pak. Kim was from Andong, in Kyongsang Province. Pak was from Sunchon, in southern Cholla. When Pak returned home for Chusok, she asked her parents' permission to marry Kim. Her parents forbade her because Kim was from Kyongsang. Pak returned to Seoul and told Kim that their courtship was over. Kim went to an inn and there he died of a drug overdose.

Newspaper editorials decried the nature of his self-inflicted death and called upon the nation to abandon the feud. The admonitions were ignored. The hatred was left intact.

The rivalry, after all, was twelve hundred years old: The two provinces had been part of separate and sometimes warring kingdoms—Silla and Paekche. Silla, which now encompassed Kyongsang, was the eventual conqueror. Centuries later Cholla would have the farmland but Kyongsang the money and, more important, the power. It was the home of three presidents—Park Chung Hee, Chun Doo Hwan and now Roh. Kyongsang's claim to the men in power had benefited the province mightily in the national economic boom, with development and investment channeled in its direction. Cholla, left with the crumbs, lagged woefully behind. Cholla's capital, Kwangju, was where Chun's troops had done their killing. Cholla exceeded Kyongsang only in han and baseball. The Lions were champions for two years running. The Giants were doormats.

This pleased Yi Yong Su, although he recognized that the pleasure came at a price. "We have people from Kyongsang and Cholla at work and normally we get along well," he said. "But when it comes to baseball, things start to change. We feel a bit estranged. When we talk, things get thorny. When it comes to baseball, regionalism always enters into it. I don't know why, but it does."

It did because you could find home at the ballpark, in the cheap seats, right next to the riot policemen, who waited, stony faced, for the fighting to begin.

But now, a day later and in the course of a game well into the middle innings, all was calm, if a little drunk. The men who came to cheer for Inchon's Dolphins—a neutral player in this internecine hatred, but a reasonable substitute for the Cholla folks to root against—sat together on the cracked, wooden bleachers, arms resting on each other's legs. The men drank beer and soju. One of them offered a pint of whiskey to a group of young soldiers. Small boys climbed over the seats. The women, those few who were there, stood beside the caldrons, where water boiled for instant noodles. The men ate, the children played and the women served. Nothing could have been more like home.

High screens on rusting poles separated the spectators from the field, keeping them safe from both foul balls and the temptation to litter the pitted field with debris should something upset them. Instead they threw empty cans at the chubby man who insisted upon taking the regular cheerleader's place. Teams had cheerleaders who blew whistles and clapped their hands to show them when to cheer. Sometimes people cheered in unison and sometimes they ignored the cheerleaders and did what they wanted. The regular fellow was dressed like a court jester, in yellow and black. The chubby man who took his place led the faithful in victory chants and derogatory refrains about the Cholla people.

Under a salvo of trash he pulled his pants over his generous gut and handed the cheerleader's whistle to still another substitute cheerleader, as if it were an open microphone on amateur night. The new cheerleader was a young man with a broken leg. The young man hopped up and down on his good leg and the men cheered and booed with him, depending on the target.

The men yelled "drop it" when a fly ball descended into an opponent's glove. Recorded trumpet flourishes of the sort heard in movies about the fall of Rome heralded each batter's arrival at the plate. Boys squirmed in their seats. And each time Cholla scored, which they did often enough to win, the men booed.

The two sides took turns taunting each other. Inchon started. They bellowed the equivalent of "Cholla sucks," to which the Cholla people responded in kind. And perhaps because they were second-best finishers in so much else, the Haiti fans' bellow produced far more volume. Their chant of derision cascaded across the infield.

Though the friction was manifest only in words, the riot police still redeployed with one out in the top of the ninth and the home team down by two. They were in position outside the clubhouse doors at the last out, when the partisans of each side started rushing toward the stairways.

The fight began in front of the clubhouse. The defeated home team was leaving the stadium, still in uniform. The players were walking across the parking lot, toward their bus, when a woman from the crowd rushed one of them. She grabbed him by the collar and shook him.

The crowd stopped to watch. The player tried to fight her off, but the woman, apoplectic with rage, would not let go. She tore at his uniform. She screamed in his face. Security guards descended upon her and wrestled her to the ground. She wailed. And as she was being subdued, the Haitai Lions emerged from their locker room to board their bus.

The admirers, their compatriots, looked away from the woman and toward the bus. They turned to watch them board. They waved as it pulled away. And then, in the warm glow of victory and each other's company, they headed for the street.

By bus and car and foot they returned to wives and children, and what now passed for home.

Reunification

MAYBE Min Kyung Nam's parents were alive and maybe they died when he was a young man. He did not know. Min was sixty-seven years old and retired, which meant that he had time to think. Lately he had been thinking about his parents. He had nothing from them, except for a photograph taken of his father and his father's friend. The photograph was old and in bad shape, so Min had a portrait painted from the photograph.

Min had not seen his parents since he left their home for the South to avoid conscription in the North Korean army. "We thought we'd go back and get them," he said. "We didn't know the division would be permanent."

That it was permanent meant that the five million people from the North who had fled to the South were severed from their families forever. No letters could be sent, no calls connected, no visits possible. Only in 1985 could the International Red Cross arrange a meeting between fifty people from the North and fifty of their relatives from the South. This was the one, brief reunion for one in every million families separated since the end of the war.

But now more reunions seemed possible, though the possibility was still remote: North and South Korea had agreed to talk for the first time in three years. Just when it seemed as if the student campaign for reunification was producing little but resentment among those tired of the tear gas and slogans, the government had seized upon the issue. Perhaps it was the coming of the Olympics and the desire to diffuse tension sufficiently to avoid a North Korean–plotted terrorist attack; and perhaps it was the realization that despite the enmity between the two Koreas, people had never stopped dreaming that one day the nation might be whole again.

Between the two states stood a 155-mile-long heavily fortified Demilitarized Zone; political and economic systems based upon seemingly irreconcilable differences; an army of 800,000 men in the North and 650,000 in the South; and an ongoing state of war, at least in a technical sense—only a cease-fire was signed at Panmunjom in 1953. Measured against the illogic of reunification, however, was the belief that division was not natural, that Korea, despite its ancient and angry division into three kingdoms, had nonetheless been a united state for centuries. People, especially students, argued that were it not for the intervention of the United States and—to a lesser degree—the Soviet Union, it might still be. We were a pawn in the game between East and West, they insisted; Korea's destiny should have been its own to decide. That the entire peninsula might have fallen under the control of Kim Il Sung was not the issue, although that might well have happened. What mattered was that Korea was a victim and the price of its weakness was a state split into warring halves that shared nothing but their ancestry.

Those old enough to remember the roundups and executions when Seoul was captured by the Communists suggested letting the students go to North Korea for a while if they wanted to know what Kim Il Sung's sort of communism was about. But that did not mean they had stopped longing for a nation once again called simply Korea. One poll reported that almost nine out of every ten South Koreans wanted reunification with the North, most of them because they believed Koreans on both sides of the border to be "brethren." (Others favored the idea because it lessened the chances of another war, and because it might be good for business.) For decades the government had tried squeezing the nation dry of the slightest favorable sentiment toward the North. North Korea could not be spoken of, except in the official government lexicon of evil and treachery. Those caught trying to expand their knowledge of the North independently—a book perhaps, or an article—risked imprisonment. Police went on campus to tear down wall posters describing the cleanliness and efficiency of the North Korean capital of Pyongyang—traffic was orderly and people lined up for buses, this in marked contrast to the bedlam of Seoul.

But now the forbidden image of the North Korean flag was shown on television, albeit on the uniform of a North Korean table-tennis player being defeated by a South Korean. Television weather maps showed temperatures for the entire peninsula, North and South. Photographs of North Korea were displayed at Yonsei University— old, brightly colored photographs showing happy workers and public works projects. The government was releasing previously censored information about the North. No longer would its emissaries be required to walk out of international gatherings when North Korea's anthem was played or its flag raised. South Korean diplomats were now permitted to offer their namecard to North Korean diplomats. The propaganda that the South had been broadcasting for decades at the North along the Demilitarized Zone was halted in the interest of reducing tensions.

The government also proposed a meeting between its representatives and the North's. North Korea took the overtures a step farther: It invited the entire South Korean National Assembly to Pyongyang for an interparliamentary meeting. The South worried about logistics, but preliminary talks were nonetheless scheduled in Panmunjom. And as the two sides descended from their respective positions upon the truce village, the Red Cross office in Seoul began taking applications for reunions. By the time Min Kyung Nam came in, two thousand people had been to the office. Many had taken hundreds of application forms, to be brought back to relatives who did not make the trip.

The Red Cross office was all but empty when Min came to fill out his application to search for his parents. Along one wall were volunteers who sat behind six desks for each of the six North Korean provinces. Along the other wall were photographs taken during the 1985 reunion: a mother and a son crying; a middle-aged man hugging two other men whose faces, like his, were twisted with sadness. Min came with his wife, Kim Joong Won, and together they sat at the table for Hamgyong Province. The application form provided room for the names of five people who might be located. Min and Kim wrote in the names of their parents. Min was a sturdy man, dressed in white. His wife had a chubby face and curly hair. They dressed casually, in the fashionable clothing of a prosperous couple.

Min completed his form and gave it to the woman at the desk. "I don't expect to find them," he said. But this did not upset him.

"Whether I find them or not is not the point. I came here because

I have this sudden urge to look for them, and quickly. When you're young you think of your parents a certain way, but as you get older you think of them more."

I asked when they thought most of home and Kim said, "I tend to think about my home during festival time, during a full moon or the time when we pray to our ancestors. I want to go and see where I lived. But I don't want to live there."

"I want to go and see, too," said Min. "These days when I dream, I dream of my hometown."

I asked if they could find their homes if they returned. Min said, "Yes, I could find my home. I dream about the roads I used to walk, about the landscape, about the whole place, what it looked like."

Now, however, he was dwelling upon the circumstances of his leaving, about having to run while his parents stayed behind to safeguard their home. "At that time it was a matter of life and death," he said. "Maybe if I had stayed there, it would have been different. I don't know if I did the right thing by leaving. But I couldn't stay. It was a choice where regrets were inevitable."

At the desk for Pyongyang Province sat Lee Dong Sook, who had come from America to look for her daughters. She was seventy-one years old and had not seen her daughters since the second fall of Seoul, in the winter of 1950. The family had escaped to the South, but then the North invaded a second time and people had to flee again. Lee was away from her home when the Communists took Seoul. When she returned, she found her house burned down, her husband gone and her daughters missing. Neighbors told her that the daughters had taken refuge in the basement of a music shop. But she could not find them there. Their grandparents were still in the North. Lee surmised that her daughters had returned there, trying to find them.

For years she thought her daughters might have gotten lost in the chaos south of the thirty-eighth parallel. In 1983 she hoped she might locate them, as so many families had found one another, through the government television network's family-reunion program. The show, which was to have had a brief run, instead stretched on for months. The nation was caught up in search of relatives long missing. People appeared on the air and told how they had lost their parents or siblings or children and offered clues that might bring them together, should those relatives be watching. A thousand families were reunited, families like the wealthy couple who found their grown daughter living in poverty. Lee thought that if her daughters had remained in the South, she might have found them through the show. But they did not appear and now she believed they were alive in the North. Lee had a picture of two of them—it was, she said, all that remained of her home—that showed her eldest and third daughters at a church Christmas pageant.

Lee was angry. She was angry about the Communists and Kim Il Sung and the students who seemed to her pathetically naive about life in North Korea. She wanted to talk about the things that were bothering her and she did not want to be interrupted. She was a short, husky woman in a bright skirt and blouse. She clutched a Louis Vuitton bag. She did not dwell upon the unpleasant or the unclear, such as how she came to live in America. She had, like millions of others, survived. Now she was trying to locate a central part of the life she had led as a young woman. She sat back in her chair and railed. "I can't go to North Korea because I live in America now," she said. "Even people in their fifties don't know what communism is like."

Min and Kim listened politely and then Min suggested that even if the coming talks did nothing to hasten the day of reunification, they might still make it possible to resume contact with loved ones in the North. "I'd be happy with an exchange of letters," he said. "Just to know if they're alive or not."

Lee scoffed at the idea that talks with North Korea might produce anything but frustration. "Do you think Kim Il Sung will give up his power?" she asked. She looked at me and said, "You don't know anything about communism."

But Min was not ready to abandon all hope. "We should not just insist upon resurrecting the past. We have to follow the tide of the time. Who can stop the flow of time? Both sides should be more flexible. There's a good side to the students. They have good intentions, even though their actions are just too much."

"Fly over anyone who wants to go to North Korea," Lee said. "Let them go and see for themselves."

Lee went on about the students and friends of the North and Min did not try to stop her. His application complete, he and his wife headed for the door. The women at the counters looked over their applications. The students may have been the ones speaking loudest about reunification. But it was their parents and grandparents who were connected to the people of the enemy state. Each year they grew older and more of them died and when they did, that connection, the connection of faces remembered and childhoods recalled, became ever more remote. Reunification was an abstract dream for those born after 1953. South Korean students had never seen North Korean students. Their knowledge was limited to the propaganda of both governments and to recollections that had nothing at all to do with ideology but rather with what home had looked like just before the farewells.

"There isn't a day I don't think about my daughters," barked Lee.

"It's my parents," Min said gently. He paused. "My parents. I've been thinking about them."

~~~~~ *FALL*

*F*ALL is Korea's respite between the misery of summer and the gloom of winter that, with the coming of the cool weather, looms ever closer. Summer gives way to temperate days. But the tranquillity is fleeting. The summer flowers, chrysanthemum, azalea and rose of Sharon, begin to fade and wilt. In the mountains the maples, elms and willows turn from green to amber to bright red until the leaves fall away, leaving bare branches to portend winter. There is a quickening sense of change in the weeks before the cold air descends. The days get shorter. Darkness comes by late afternoon. In the countryside rice is harvested. Down coats and heavy sweaters fill the crowded overhead racks in the outdoor markets. The charcoal peddler returns.

The fall of 1988 brought the end of the Olympic Games. The Games ended with fireworks over the Han River. The Olympic flame was extinguished and the flag lowered. The Olympic world vowed to gather again, in 1992, in Barcelona. People bade farewell to Seoul and headed to the airport.

The street sweepers began cleaning the debris and the dust seeped back into the air over Seoul. The pushcart peddlers returned to the market streets and the dog-meat restaurants served dinners again. The elaborate Olympic decorations in front of the city hall plaza— the plaza where families had gathered to look at the Olympic flame on the night before the opening ceremonies—were dismantled. Traffic once again clogged the roadways of central Seoul. Sirens silenced during the Olympics sounded across the nation, signaling the monthly civil defense drills in preparation for the possibility of a North Korean invasion.

I waited for a month after the end of the Games before returning to Seoul. I wanted the time away, away from more angry talk about insulting foreigners and hurt feelings. In the days after the Korean boxing officials attacked the judge from New Zealand—when the reaction of many Koreans turned from embarrassment to rage at NBC for broadcasting the melee over and over again—the mood at the Games had turned ugly, especially where America was concerned.

At the boxing arena American boxers were booed no matter who their rival. I went to the basketball arena to see the Americans and Australians play for the bronze medal—the Soviets had already defeated the favored Americans for the gold. The building was packed and had I closed my eyes, I might have imagined myself in Sydney, for all the enthusiastic support for the Australians. The Korean crowd chanted, "Australia, Australia," drawing out the middle syllable in a hastily composed chant followed by three quick claps. Really, any country would have done. Because every time an American player so much as touched the ball, the boos cascaded down from the cheap seats to the floor. The booing lasted from the opening tip until the final buzzer.

People smiled when they booed the Americans. They were having a wonderful time. I sat with two American friends and none of us felt in any danger. We were not taunted or heckled. It was America people were booing, America and its television station that had been insensitive enough to show Koreans embarrassing themselves. That Americans might have been upset with them for so roundly and gratuitously booing their basketball players did not seem to register. It was OK for Koreans to boo Americans. America deserved to be booed. I shuddered to think what would have happened had an American crowd done the same to the Koreans. The Koreans would not forgive that. Like a person so absorbed with his own pain that the thought of anyone else's pain becomes an intrusion, Korea was so immersed in tabulating the reasons for its bitterness that it seemed incapable of understanding that it too was capable of inflicting pain.

Two American swimmers had just been arrested for stealing a marble carving from a hotel—an idiotic prank that came in the course of a party celebrating a gold medal. Now the full weight of the Korean judiciary was being lowered upon their head. Hundreds called for jailing the Americans, or at least stopping them from leaving the country. The Americans would learn that Korea was not a country to be trifled with, not a place where arrogant young swimmers—gold medalists or not—could come and do as they pleased. The threatened jail terms were dropped after the swimmers were brought before the cameras and treated to a few hours of not undeserved public humiliation. They were then allowed to leave.

As was so often the case in Korea, it was not the action itself that was revealing, but the reaction. The fight was an ugly moment. The reaction in the days that followed, however, showed how simultaneously painful and emboldening the reflection looked when Korea stood before the mirror.

Korea's history, after all, had been one dominated by reacting—to foreign invaders, to powers offering unfair treaties it could not contest, to countries with the muscle it lacked. For centuries Korea had bristled and suffered the humiliation of the conquered, a humiliation that often gave way to a keen sense of knowing who was in charge and how to curry favor. But now Korea was having none of it, not anymore. If the Games proved anything for Korea, they showed that it really was capable of the great things that its government had boasted of. The Games were the apotheosis of all those internationally acknowledged measures of significance—the cars for export, the rising gross national product, the reputation for hard work, the increasing purchasing power, the suggestion that perhaps South Korea was the model for postwar Third World development.

But for all that Korea proved in staging the Games, it was the fall out from the fight at the boxing arena that proved to be the truest moment of the Olympics. It quickly stripped away the veneer the government had tried so hard to create and revealed a nation desperate to be taken seriously. It also showed Korea to be a nation still incapable of blaming itself for its misdeeds and shortcomings, a nation that had played the victim so long that its immediate response to feeling victimized was to seek out a victim of its own. The fight brought out all the maddening ambivalence Koreans felt about their nation—pride and self-pity, triumph and shame. I remember in particular one well-to-do Korean man's reflection on the fight. Why, he asked, couldn't the Americans have protected Korea? Why couldn't they have acted like older brothers and made sure that the world did not get the chance to see the Koreans losing their temper? Of course any suggestion on the part of the Americans that the Koreans were still their younger brother brought an even more bitter response.

In a way never intended the world got the chance to look into the heart of the Olympic host. It witnessed the creation of yet another bit of han. It witnessed the incident, the reaction, the humiliation and the bitterness that always followed the humiliation. All the television specials aired during the Olympic coverage—the reports from the thirty-eighth parallel, the history of "the economic miracle," the features on Seoul after dark—revealed not nearly so much as did the much-resented coverage of Korea losing its temper.

It was not the fight at the arena that drove me away. Rather, it was Korea's capacity in its moment of embarrassment and its need to respond to its suffering with accusations against the very people from whom it so much wanted approval. And because Korea drew the accused into its struggle, it left those it was denouncing confused and tired and rushing to get away.

I returned four weeks later, naively assuming Seoul might still be caught in some post-Olympic glow. But it was as if the Games had not happened. The Olympic flags lining the boulevards were folded and stored. Shopkeepers removed the Hodori tiger mascot dolls from their windows and shelves.

People still mentioned NBC's callousness. But with the departure of the foreigners they stopped talking about the Games. They did not talk about Ben Johnson's disqualification for steroid use after winning the hundred-meter dash. They did not talk about Florence Griffith-Joyner's running, the tiny Naim Suleymanogulu's weightlifting, Matt Biondi's swimming, Greg Louganis's diving, Carl Lewis's jumping and running, Sergei Bubka's pole vaulting and all the gold medals the Soviets and East Germans won. After a few weeks of boasting they even stopped talking about the twelve gold medals won by Koreans, a number far beyond all hopes and expectations.

The Games were over. Fall had come and it was time to let loose the internally directed passions that had been locked away while the guests were present.

In the largest demonstration since the spring of 1987 thirty thousand workers and students marched to the National Assembly to demand more freedom for labor unions.

Six students were arrested for firebombing the thatched-roof house where Chun Doo Hwan was born.

Friends of three students found guilty of tossing firebombs at the American embassy went on a rampage in the courtroom, throwing chairs and a microphone, denouncing Chun Doo Hwan and tearing the verdict report from the court clerk's hand.

Two professors were seized and beaten by their students for their alleged role in a fire at the school's church. The students insisted the fire was unjustly blamed upon them. The students shaved the professors' heads and forced them to pray for the "normalization" of the school.

Riot police stormed a theological seminary after students abducted a riot policeman. The policeman was seized while he was arresting a student gathering signatures calling for the arrest of Chun Doo Hwan. The captured riot policeman and students were released in an exchange of prisoners outside the school's main gate.

The students returned to campus and renewed their call for Chun Doo Hwan's head. Workers talked of a new round of strikes. The opposition returned to the National Assembly to renew its investigations of the Chun years.

Fall would be Korea's season of reckoning. Winter was approaching and life had resumed what for me remained its contradictory path: It was time to move forward and time to go back. It was time to embrace han and cast it off.

My brief leave-taking over, I returned to see what the future held. But in Korea the future was suspect if the past was not resolved. Westerner that I was, I was still caught looking for tidy resolutions. I'd been away for a month. I'd forgotten where I was.

The Future according to
Soh Yun Am

WOMEN who wanted to know the future came to see Soh Yun Am and sometimes he told them what they wanted to hear. Older women came when their husband beat them, when their sons were not promoted, when their daughters were not married, when their investments looked shaky. Young women came to Soh to know the future when they could not conceive or when their mother-in-law was mean to them, perhaps because they were not good housekeepers or perhaps because they could not conceive.

The husky woman in her forties who sat on a silky pillow across a low table from Soh Yun Am told him the year, month, date and time of her birth and explained that she was in the money-lending business and wanted to know when it might be propitious both to sell some real estate and open a public bathhouse in the city of Suwon. She had brought along her husband. He too was husky and his hands, like his wife's, were fleshy. The wife spoke to Soh and her husband leaned against the wall and grunted his approval when she turned to him and went through the charade of seeking his opinion.

"This year's future is good but not next year," Soh said. He had assessed her fortune by checking her birth dates and times with his red paperback volume of Chinese fortune-telling charts. "The business ideas you get next year will not be good. It's better to start now."

The woman checked the calendar that hung above the table and said, "I've got money coming in, on or about the thirtieth."

"You will have no luck if the money comes in on the thirtieth or thirty-first," Soh said. "The days you will have luck on are the twenty-eighth and twenty-ninth. Call and ask the people who owe you this money to pay you back early."

Soh turned to the silent husband, who now wanted to know how he might fare in the public-bathhouse business. Soh checked his numbers and said, "The future shows you are appropriate for that sort of business." He accepted their five thousand won—about seven dollars—for his services and signaled the next customer.

Soh's office was at the end of an alley near the Yongdong-po railway station. Yongdong-po was a working-class neighborhood in western Seoul and to get to Soh's office you passed through a market near the tracks, crossed the bridge over the tracks, walked along another shopping street, turned right at a vegetable stand and looked for the wooden shingle emblazoned with the title he had taken after completing his correspondence course in fortune-telling: PROFESSOR OF PHILOSOPHY.

Soh's house was brick and new. His office sat behind a paper screen door. It was bright and narrow and the walls were lined with diplomas from the various correspondence academies through which he had studied. Soh sat at the far end of the room, flanked by bookshelves, a space heater and a portable stereo. He was a wiry man in a blue suit and gold-framed glasses that he wore low on his nose. He combed his hair straight back and maintained a studious air. His office had no waiting room and those whose turn had not yet come sat on pillows near the door, listening to the stories and problems of those ahead of them.

I asked Soh, "Do people come to you because they are upset or to have you confirm their intentions?"

"Most come in because they have no idea about their future," he said. "Some come in to confirm their hunches, but that's a few. I play three roles: I counsel the distressed. I provide solutions to those who seek. I provide remedies for those with problems."

I asked how it was that he became a fortune-teller, and Soh replied that eighteen years before he lost his government job and went to see a fortune-teller. "I wanted to know about myself and my destiny," he said. "Everybody seems to have a particular destiny that can be good or bad."

The fortune-teller told him that he had a good future as a fortune-teller himself. Soh met another fortune-teller through a friend and the fortune-teller began teaching him about the philosophy of yin and yang, the forces of good and bad, and their relation to man and the universe. Soh augmented this study with the correspondence courses on the reading of Chinese astrological charts.

The people who came to Soh and to the many other fortune-tellers believed that the future could be forecast through the wise interpretation of the charts. Soh had gained a reputation for wisdom and many people, most of them women—as was the case for most fortune-tellers—came to consult him. Fortune-telling was a good business. People were reluctant to take a step without first consulting a fortune-teller. Without a fortune-teller to offer a picture of what the future held any step into the future felt like a leap. But most of the women who came to Soh left disappointed because when he assessed the future, he saw that their destiny was not a happy one.

"Most of us are born with bad fortunes," Soh said. "There's only one president of the company. Everyone else is an employee. There's only one top student in the class. I tell people, 'If you have a bad future there's a reason.' I refer to Buddhist beliefs. I tell them, 'What you have done in the past will come back to you. It's something you did in a past life.' "

When a woman told Soh that her husband beat her, he suggested that perhaps the matchmaker who had introduced her to her husband had done a poor job, or perhaps an abusive husband was her fate. "I tell her, 'Persevere and love your husband even more. Put up with it and respect your husband.' A lot of people come in and don't want to accept a bad future. They want a way out."

But Soh did not believe that the option existed. A bleak future was an unchangeable fate that had to be endured. When childless couples came to Soh to ask whether they might yet have a child, he consulted his charts and if the future did not promise children, he told them to let go of their dreams. "Han," he said, "is inevitable."

That is what Soh told them, that part of life was accepting han and softening its pain through acceptance. But people did not always listen and came to him again and again to see what the future might hold.

When the husky couple rose to leave, two older women took their place on the cushions by Soh's table. One of the women did all of the talking. She was short and chubby and wore a black sweater and slacks. Her hair was short and curly. I asked her whether she was willing to accept bad news if that was what Soh told her.

"I have to accept," she said. "If my future is bad, then it's bad."

"But some people resist," Soh said. "They want to deny."

The woman said that even if the future was bad, it was best to know because that way she could be prepared. She was a talkative woman and today she wanted to ask about many things. First she wanted to know whether her son would get a promotion and then she wanted to know when she should begin looking for a wife for him. She also wanted to know about her daughter's marriage prospects. The woman wanted to know what the future held for her husband. She wanted to know about herself too.

She gave Soh all the necessary dates about herself and her children, but when she got to her husband she could not remember the hour of his birth. Soh asked whether her husband's face was long or round and when she told him it was on the round side, he concluded that he must have been born after eleven o'clock at night because people born in the late evening generally had a rounder face. The other woman sat near the wall and did not say a word. Soh consulted his charts.

"Listen well!" he said in a stern voice. "Next year is not a good one for your husband. He should not travel and should not make any new investments."

"What about the following year?" she asked.

Soh said the following year looked good.

"What about me?" she asked.

"Until next year is over don't lend money. You will have very bad luck."

The woman stopped him. She asked, "Does that mean I won't have good luck with documents?"

Soh told her documents seemed safe for the present year but not for the next. When he was done the woman went into a long and detailed recitation about a property she was buying and the question of the deed and the man with whom she was doing this deal, who did not think she was shrewd because she was a woman, but that she was going to show him.

Soh was getting tired of the woman's story about the deed, which was followed by a story about her daughter who worked in a municipal registry and knew all about deeds. She wanted to know whether

her daughter's enrollment in a five-year correspondence course might interfere with her marriage prospects. Soh assured her it would not.

"Now about your son," he said. "The next three years are good, but he lacks inner strength. His parents and his friends at work have to help him."

"So what about marriage?" she asked. "We've had several offers."

"Out of the question," said Soh. "He'll have no luck with marriage this year. If he marries this year, the marriage will end in separation."

The woman nodded and said that that must explain why all his romances fell apart. "Nothing works out," she said.

"You see. It's better if he starts matchmaking next year."

"How about moving plans?"

"That looks good."

"He wants to come north, from Masan to Suwon."

"He'll have better luck in the north."

"So when I marry him off next year, I'll move him north," the woman said. She dropped her voice so that it took on an intimate quality. "You see, there's this girl who was born in the year of the dragon. He was recently introduced to her."

"Don't bother," said Soh. "You don't need her. Next year a new person will come along and she'll be even better. This girl might look nice, but her inner being is not as good."

Finally her silent partner said, "About this girl who was born in the year of the dragon. It was I who introduced her to the son of this woman."

Soh nodded and sighed, understanding the true nature of the women's visit.

"She's a good girl. Can we ask to see what her prospects are?"

Soh checked her birth dates in his book and then he changed his mind. He decided that he was wrong. Now he saw the good things that the women were waiting for him to see.

"This girl is really good," he said. "She'll have thirty years of good luck. She's respectful of her elders and family. She will be a wise wife and good mother."

The women nodded.

"That's why I was so insistent about this girl," said the mother of the son. "But you told me to forget about her. What do I do?"

"Since her future is so good, keep her around till next year."

"OK, then we keep her till next year."

"Yes, and another thing. If your son goes into his own business, he's going to become a beggar. His future is very good as an employee."

"My son a beggar?"

"If he goes off on his own."

"What's wrong with marrying him off this year? Why can't we hurry this marriage along?"

"If you're in such a hurry, start the courtship in the spring. Your son's future is a little weak. He needs help from others in marriage. If you like the girl, push things along."

"The girl's mother approved my son. I like her too."

The matchmaker, silent but romantic, said, "Who cares if you and the girl's mother like her? They have to like each other."

"If they're not sure, I can encourage them and speed up the process," said the mother, who had a final question.

She had learned about her husband and her son and had decided that a correspondence school was a good thing for her daughter. But something was nagging at her and that was the question of her own fate. She wanted to know more about what the future held for her. She asked, "Will I really have bad luck next year?"

Soh assured her that she would. He said, "Don't be greedy. Don't lend or borrow money."

"Not even a little?" asked the woman, who was hoping to hear something different. Luckily she knew other fortune-tellers. She could consult with them too.

Kuro

*B*EFORE he came to work in Kuro, Kim Chu Song learned to endure in the army, and before the army, in a factory in Osan. Years later he would recall the feeling of metal dust in his lungs, the ringing in his ears and the sight of the head of the man at the machine in front of him. Kim looked at the man's head for twelve hours a day six days a week, and longer if he was working overtime.

When he left the army, Kim came north, to Seoul, and found work at the Shin Han Valve Company, in the Kuro industrial district. Kuro was an ugly place whose dominant color, both on the ground and in the sky, was gray. The work Kim found there was better than it had been in Osan. He ran a machine that snipped the bottom end off the automobile valves that Shin Han sold to big companies, like Hyundai. The factory room was lighted by fluorescent bulbs over the machines and by the dim light that shone through the ceiling window on sunny days. In the vast space under the ceiling the long room was dark. In the winter the best jobs to have were at the two machines that poured the metal; except for the meager warmth of the space heaters they were the only warm places in the room.

The air was dirty whether the factory was cold or sweltering, as it was in the summer. Kim did not like where he worked, or the hours that he worked, or the money he was paid, but he had learned how to endure and keep his mouth shut, at least until the end of the day. Then he and his friends would go to the food pushcarts near the rail station, sit on stools under the tarpaulin cover and drink soju. The soju got them drunk and then they could complain about everything they did not like. The complaining was not enough, but it was all Kim had and he had to be satisfied with it. Sometimes he and his friends wondered what the life of the bosses was like, the men who worked in the office and wore white shirts and ties. They decided that these men had time to play tennis and eat out in expensive restaurants that served Western food.

"They go to hotels to eat. We don't do that," Kim said. He sat in the small office of a workers' advisory office established by the Catholic church in Kuro. The office was on the grounds of a church and outside a group of children were singing "Rudolph, the Red-Nosed Reindeer," led by a young man playing the guitar. Christmas was approaching.

I asked Kim about his feeling toward these men and he said, "Sure there's resentment. We weren't getting the rewards for our labor. But now, with a union, our demands are being met. Before, we shared this vague hope that things would get better. But we didn't think it was possible to change."

"I feel sorry that the underprivileged give up so easily," Peter Mun had told me. Mun was the director of *Love Song of Kuro*, a musical that played for six months during the spring and summer, far longer than the standard run and surprising for a play about the inability of the working class to escape its misery.

Mun was not a political man. He was a composer. He knew little about the life of the men and women who worked in Kuro. So he met with workers and read poems they had written. "We tried to grasp their soul, their feelings," he said. But the more Mun learned, the more upset he became by the way the workers lived miserable lives buoyed only by fanciful dreams that one day, somehow, things would be good. "They are very emotional," he told me. "They lose their temper very easily."

At first I dismissed Mun as another member of the privileged and educated classes—he spoke fluent English; he had his degree—who saw himself as the working class's superior. But the more Mun spoke, the more I sensed that his sympathy had turned to frustration when he began wondering why the workers could not lessen the pain of their han.

Mun placed the workers of *Love Song of Kuro* in a small factory and surrounded them with a cyclone fence. The walls and floor were covered with paper. There was nothing subtle about *Love Song of*

Kuro, and nothing at all farfetched. The workers suffer a cruel boss ("You worship your superior's words like a god's!" he proclaims), twenty-hour-days, industrial diseases, the loss of their much-needed bonus, the quashing of their union, the arrest of their union leader, the firing of his allies. One worker, promised a promotion, turns against his mates. The foreman extracts sexual favors from the young women from the countryside.

The young union organizer is blacklisted and cannot find work. He lives with his girlfriend, who must support him. When he begs to be rehired, the police are called and he is arrested. The foreman says that the girlfriend is the price for his not pressing charges. When the young man is freed, he mistakenly thinks that his girlfriend has given herself to the foreman. He confronts his girlfriend and then the foreman. He has a knife. He stabs the foreman.

He turns on his girlfriend. He is ready to kill her. But he stops himself. "That point is very important to me," Mun told me. The frenzy is over. The girlfriend catches her breath long enough to see that despite the difficulty of the situation, there is an escape other than death. The young man lets his friends tell the police what has happened. He does not try to run. His girlfriend tells him that she will go back to his hometown and there she will wait until his release from prison. She will care for his ailing mother.

"She is thinking of a solution," Mun said, "even though she's at the bottom. I would like to let the laborers know. They do not know themselves. They do not know their enemy."

The first enemy was poverty, which was easy to see because it was everyone's enemy at the end of the war. It was not until the fall of Syngman Rhee in 1960 and the 1961 coup that brought Park Chung Hee to power that any advantage was gained in ending the nation's poverty. Rhee's Korea was poor and corrupt and dependent upon American aid. Park changed that. A remote, austere man, Park is spoken of as an autocrat of a far different sort than Chun Doo Hwan. Park may have come to power by force, countenanced little dissent, had his opponents jailed and tortured, had himself assured of the presidency for life, but people of varying political persuasions still speak respectfully of him. Park, they said, had vision, and while he may have been a cruel man, Korea needed someone like him to rid them of their poverty.

Park did this by inaugurating a series of five-year plans and letting the Korean technocrats with doctorates from American universities run the economy. Slowly at first and then with a speed that became astonishing, Park's Korea was transformed from a rural, agricultural nation to an urban manufacturer whose primary product was goods for export. The government assisted exporting companies with loans and tax breaks. Safety standards and environmental hazards were overlooked in the interest of production. Salaries rose, but labor remained cheap enough for Korean goods to be competitive abroad. And while Korea's work force was willing to endure a great deal, by the late 1970s it began voicing its dissatisfaction in the money it was getting—especially when compared with the money going to its ever-wealthier employers. Workers, having found a new enemy, struck; unrest grew. And in the midst of that unrest Park was assassinated. It was said that his murderer, the head of the KCIA, believed that Park had lost the ability to maintain control.

When Chun Doo Hwan took power, inflation was running so high that the economists were concerned it might wreck the economy. The Park government had invested heavily in industry and while such industries as steel and shipbuilding had become world leaders, others, such as petrochemicals, were money losers. Chun, like Park, deferred to the technocrats on economic matters while providing them with the muscle to accomplish their goals. The government economists recommended wage and price controls. Inflation came under control.

Chun also decided it was necessary to "purify" labor. Union leaders were arrested and imprisoned. Some were sent to the Samchong "reeducation camps." The nation's labor laws, modeled after America's in 1953, were altered so that while unions were still allowed to form, they were tailored to the companies' purposes. Collective-bargaining agreements had to be approved by the government, which also had the power to dissolve unions or demand elections of new officers. When a group of workers wanted to form a union, they had to present an application to the local government. Often a mistake was found on the form and corrections were demanded. The time spent making the corrections was usually sufficient for the company to have loyal employees form a union of toadies, which was quickly recognized as the workers' sole representative. Dissident union organizers—"impure elements" and "dangerous leftists"—were arrested and imprisoned under the National Security Law for advocating rights deemed dangerous to the state. Chun made it easy for working people to see who their new enemy was.

But then, in August of 1987, in the wake of the June demonstrations, workers long embittered by two enemies—management and government—were emboldened by that government's retreat in the face of protest. They demanded that the newly won political reforms be extended to them as well.

Strikes broke out at the leading conglomerates—Hyundai, Samsung, Gold Star and Daewoo. Bus drivers went on strike in Kwangju, Kunsan and Chonju. Striking chambermaids and porters held a sit-in rally at the Lotte Hotel in downtown Seoul. There were strikes in textile factories and shoe factories. Miners went on strike, as did cabbies, shipyard workers, electronics workers and six hundred fishing-boat captains, who shut down the central fish market in Pusan. By mid-summer there had been three thousand strikes at roughly half the nation's companies. The essential demands seldom varied: wages that represented the work forces's fair share of rising profits; the right to form independent unions. Nor did the ritual of the strike: songs of protest, marches toward a phalanx of riot police and the inevitable battle, with firebombs and tear gas.

But now the government was shaken by the June protests and mindful of how potent a force angry workers could be. Not only did it stand back and permit the strikes—in violation of its own draconian labor laws—but even interceded on labor's behalf. When Hyundai shut down its Ulsan shipyard after ten thousand workers went on strike, the government pushed the company's founder and honorary chairman, Chung Ju Yung, to permit wages to rise and a union to form.

The time of the strikes was dizzying, so dizzying and confusing that there were moments when it was hard to tell who the enemy was. Both labor and management were inexperienced in negotiation and compromise. So used was management to being obeyed that when the senior vice-president of Hyundai Heavy Industries confronted a group of workers who ignored his command to stop smoking, he lamented, "these young workers think it is their world now."

Though the world still belonged to management, labor rejoiced in its newly discovered power, even if it could not agree on how to use it. Strikes did not necessarily mean unanimity. Nascent unions faced off against other nascent unions, all trying to win the right to represent various segments of the work force. There were moderate unions and radical unions and instances in which management found itself sealing a pact with one only to wake up the next day to find that that union was out, a new union was in and they had to start all over again.

The political jockeying took on absurd and, in one instance, near tragic form. A twenty-one-year-old Daewoo shipyard worker, Lee Sok Kyu, was killed during a strike on the southern island of Koje. The union leaders seized both Lee's body and the moment, insisting that the remains would not be surrendered until management acceded to their demands. The workers occupied the hospital where Lee had been brought with pieces of a tear gas canister in his chest. The strike organizers began plotting ways to make the most use of his death. A schedule for protest was outlined: 10:00 A.M. to 10:30 A.M. for practicing songs to be sung at the funeral; 10:30 A.M. to 12:30 P.M. for a seminar on the meaning of an independent union; 2:00 P.M. to 4:00 P.M. for an open discussion about Lee's death.

When Lee's mother came to Koje for her son's body, she was told she could not have it. "You'll only live for thirty more years," a union officer told her. "We want to make him a national labor hero. We want to put him where people can visit him." The union favored a martyr's grave in Kwangju and that is where its procession headed on the day of his funeral. The twenty-five-bus caravan, however, was stopped midway by a police roadblock. Police descended from the hillside, commandeered the hearse and directed it to proceed to Namwon, where Lee was buried close by his grieving mother.

There were calls for a general strike to honor Lee Sok Kyu, but these went unheeded. No national labor movement emerged, despite occasional attempts at solidarity by the most politicized elements in the work force.

People were out for themselves, for their factories or for their shops and when they got what they wanted, they went back to work. The strikes continued in places where two months before the workers could not have imagined walking out, let alone winning. The Shin Han Valve Company was one of those places.

"They were so used to giving orders," Kim Chu Song said of the first time the Shin Han union bargained with management. "When we asked questions they didn't seem to understand that their orders were part of the past. We used to obey. But now we demanded our rights. They told us, 'You obeyed before without complaining. Why do you ask so many questions?' They didn't seem to grasp what we were talking about."

The union was formed in the midst of the August strikes. The workers chose Yi Oh Kyu as their union leader even though he was new to the company. Yi had had his own shop and the workers believed that he understood the way a company like theirs might be run. Kim Chu Song became an officer too. The union demanded recognition, the right of collective bargaining and wage increases of 15 percent. Management offered 12 percent. The workers shut down the plant.

They remained peaceful. They painted their signs, sang their songs, beat the drums and banged the cymbals of Korean folk music. "There was not much elation," Yi said. "We tried to restrain ourselves, keep our heads. But we learned that we could close this place down, that with the union we had power."

Management did not call in the police. The workers did not damage the plant. After two days management agreed to recognize the union, permit collective bargaining and grant wage increases of 14 percent. The strike ended. But neither the relatively quiet strike nor the settlement brought trust or good feelings, not after all the bad feelings that had come before.

"We weren't able to express our feelings because then they'd know who was dissatisfied," Kim said. "We felt that human beings shouldn't be treated this way."

"It wasn't as if we looked at them as inanimate objects that moved because we told them to move," Joon Sang Jik said to me. Joon was Shin Han's executive director. "They didn't protest. They were silent. We didn't pay attention to what they wanted."

Joon, a burly man in his late fifties, sat in the company offices in an ornate, wooden chair, next to an equally ornate chair, where Kim Chu Song sat and listened to his boss's version of the events of that summer. The office looked like offices in companies all over Korea. The room was lined with metal desks for the clerks and overstuffed furniture, where the executives sat when they met salesmen. The walls were white and the paint, like the linoleum floor, was faded and cracked. The room was lighted by naked fluorescent bulbs. For fourteen years Joon Sang Jik had spent eight hours a day six days a week in this office, which seemed a long time, except when compared with the ten- and eleven-hour days that Kim Chu Song worked in the factory.

Joon said, "We disapproved of the union. We thought we shouldn't have one. There was a feeling of distrust, of checking each other out. We had no background in the functioning of a union. We didn't know what its purpose was, what it was supposed to do. It came at us out of the blue."

The managers called the union leaders sons of bitches and bastards to their face when they met to negotiate. The union leaders raised their voice in response but did not swear because the men from management were older and profanity would have been rude.

"At first we weren't willing to give in and they wouldn't yield," Joon said. The company had not paid much attention to wages or working conditions, he said, in good measure because they had never heard complaints. "We didn't think they were afraid to speak out. We felt they had needs and demands but that they tolerated things. They were persevering."

Kim, knowing better, did not interrupt.

Joon continued. He admitted that management had given little thought to the life of men and women who worked for them. "To tell you the truth," he said, "until the union was founded, we hardly paid any attention to that."

Still, they were able to settle. But though the strike ended and the union was given office space, the talk between the two sides remained strained and often angry. The following May the union asked for higher wages. Management refused. The union challenged management's power to fire workers at will. Management felt that this encroached upon their power.

The union called a second strike. This time the plant was shut down for five days. But once again there was no violence and once again an agreement was reached.

"We've come to accept most of their demands," Joon said. "They got more selective in their proposals."

That did not mean that the two sides necessarily liked each other. They remained in different worlds, separated by the driveway that divided the factory from the office and by the status of their respective social stations. The managers did not join the union officers for soju at the pushcarts near the railway station. The union officers did not play tennis or go to lunch at the Western restaurants.

It took a year, but they began to trust one another. Joon said he began feeling comfortable with the union when he saw that they were not being influenced by people outside the company. And Kim and Yi said that they had come to regard Joon as a man they could believe.

The Shin Han union office is a small room upstairs from the factory. Workers come there when they are upset about working conditions or the way they are being treated. Yi or Kim will listen to these grievances, walk downstairs and across the driveway and bring these matters to Joon's attention.

The room is cluttered with ceremonial drums and banners from the two strikes. There are old desks and racks filled with brochures about workers' rights. The walls are covered with posters advertising new political plays.

I asked Yi and Kim whether they had heard of *Love Song of Kuro* and its message about the sorry lives of industrial workers.

Yi said he knew about the play, although he had not been able to go into Seoul to see it. "I think there was a time when workers were like that," Yi said. "But that's not true anymore. I think the director was being too abstract and wasn't seeing the real lives. Now workers are out to change their life."

Kim said, "We feel that reality is what we make of it."

The room was filling up with men from the factory. They all wore dark blue jackets. The jackets had their name and the characters of the company stitched over their heart. The jackets represented a recent victory by the union. The managers used to be the only ones who had warm jackets like these. The union demanded that the workers get them too, especially for the winter.

"This jacket is much warmer than the ones we had before," Yi said with a smile.

It was cold outside and getting dark. Kim walked me to the bus stop on the highway. His tenure in the union would end soon. He would soon return to the factory.

We passed another factory, one that manufactured cellular phones. The workers at this factory were on strike. They were beating drums and chanting in the dark. Up the road, massed for a protest march, came another group of workers. Kim said that they were workers from a company in Pusan who had come to Kuro to show support for the strikers. The strikers were making a lot of noise and Kim smiled and recalled how much they looked like the workers at Shin Han when they had gone out.

Winter was approaching and the angry mood that had begun with the strikes of a year and a half before had not abated. There were new strikes at Hyundai, Samsung and the Korean subsidiaries of American companies that had come to a Korea where labor was cheap and manageable. IBM and Tandy were being struck and at Motorola the local management worried that the Americans might pull out, especially after a group of strikers threatened to set themselves and the plant on fire.

The good feelings or, rather, the lessening of bad feelings that had come to Shin Han were proving the exception and not the rule. There was no middle ground and no path for attaining it. There was only the contest for power, which meant that no one believed he could afford to lose even a little bit, for fear of what the victor might do. Trust came slowly, if it came at all, and felt as if it were built on sand. There was anxious talk of a violent spring. Said one labor organizer, "It's hard to play a game where there are no rules."

Kim and I stood on the side of the road and watched the picket line. It snaked through the company parking lot. The strikers marched and danced to their cacophonous music. Their march looked like a celebration. The picket line grew longer and wider as more came along to join.

The Dance Master

THERE was a little war going on in the dance studio of Yi Mae Bong, although Yi did not think there was a war and his students would not admit it. Yi Mae Bong did not want his students taking what he taught them and then, when they left him, making changes that in Yi's view were motivated not by love for dance but by a desire to see their face in the popular magazines.

"I'm concerned about the young generation," said an angry Yi Mae Bong. He lay on the bedding on the floor of his bedroom, surrounded by geegaws and pictures of himself. His doctor had advised him to stay in bed for a while to ease the pain in his legs. Yi was sixty-one years old. He wore pink satin pajamas and a pink terry-cloth robe. He was short and sinewy. He lit a long cigarette and pulled the cigarette out of his mouth with a flourish. He adjusted the heavy silver ring on his finger, tucked a leg beneath him and, in a raspy voice, derided what the young people were doing to the dances he had been dancing since he was seven.

"In the days when I learned, I'd just follow the path of my teacher. There was no other way," he said. "When my teacher said, 'Move your hands like this,' that was what I did. That is what I tell my students, but when they leave my teaching they do what they want. They think a different movement will be more popular. They take what I teach to make money. They think people like these different movements. They want to be famous."

Three young men sat by his bedroom door. Yi wanted another cigarette lighted, so he flicked his thumb like a lighter. Lee Woo Chung, who had left him once and then come back, hurried to light the cigarette. Lee was thirty years old and so loyal to Yi and to the principle of a disciple never eclipsing his master that when Yi asked what dance he had performed for me, he replied with great embarrassment that he had danced the salpuri but had brought me upstairs so that I might see a videotape of Yi himself dancing.

Yi grunted. He was regarded as one of the foremost dancers of the salpuri, the dance performed by women to ease the pain of their han. When he danced the salpuri, Yi danced as a woman.

Lee Woo Chung had been his attendant. He cleaned the studio and ran the errands. Now he was Yi Mae Bong's driver. He had interrupted his tenure, however, to study modern dance. Yi Mae Bong scoffed at modern dance. He would say, "To do classical ballet is very hard; to do modern dance is not." Still Woo Chung left the studio, whose polished wooden floors he had swept—and where the walls, like the bedrooms walls, were lined with photographs of Yi in performance—and embarked upon a course of study far different from that of a dance master's disciple.

No longer was instruction a matter of observation and imitation. Now there was a curriculum. There were steps to learn and then to rehearse. Missing from all of this, at least for Lee Woo Chung, was passion, the passion necessary for making a dance like the salpuri into a true release from han.

Once a reporter for a dance magazine, he had become a dancer, he said, because he had to dance. This need came from a feeling that Woo Chung could express best in dance. He was introduced to Yi Mae Bong by a mutual friend, Lee Jung Tae, who though not a dancer—he was a merchant banker—was a devotee of things traditional, dance among them. Lee Jung Tae had, in turn, met Yi Mae Bong through an introduction provided by the owner of a Seoul restaurant that served vegetarian Buddhist-temple fare (the owner had been a monk), where traditional dances were performed during the dinner hour, sometimes by students of Yi Mae Bong.

It was Lee Jung Tae who explained this complicated network to me during dinner one night at the vegetarian restaurant. The dance segment had just ended and Lee was unimpressed, having found it lacking in spirit. Despite his work in his bank's treasury division, Lee, at age thirty-one, had placed himself among the artists, dancers and singers whose art was the art of the past. He had furnished the study in his apartment with furniture made by a cabinetmaker skilled in traditional furniture making. He had lined the walls of the study with mulberry paper. It was a traditional gentleman's study.

Lee was a celebrant of the past, as were many of his generation. Their parents were, by and large, uninterested, having forsaken or forgotten the art and lore of their parents and instead become admirers of the sentimental music heard on the radio or in nightclubs. The younger people, anxious to imbue their lives with that which was truly Korean, turned to the generation of their grandparents for guidance, although many still opted for Michael Jackson compact discs and bought tickets for Duran Duran when they came to town. Lee Jung Tae, together with his wife and baby daughter, spent occasional Sunday afternoons in the studio of Yi Mae Bong, where his friend, Woo Chung, was caught between celebrating the dance of his master and the need to dance to the music in his own heart.

We sat on rugs on the cold wooden floor. The new attendant served instant coffee and then retreated to another corner of the room so that he would not intrude upon the conversation of Lee Woo Chong, who, as the driver, was his senior.

"I was at the wedding of my wife's cousin's son," Lee Jung Tae began to say, "and afterward we went back to the apartment. We ate and drank and people began playing music. We sang and danced and the way everyone expressed their feelings differed according to age. But there was one elderly aunt in her seventies and she knew traditional dances. Those under sixty sang sentimental songs. I said, 'Stop. There are lots of better Korean songs.' I sang some folk songs and the elderly aunt just started to dance and urged me to dance with her. I couldn't stop. Everyone followed."

"The feeling is in their blood," said Woo Chung. "Whenever they hear that rhythm, they dance. They need to dance."

"It's like an itch in my blood," said Lee Jung Tae.

Woo Chung talked about his time studying modern dance—dances built upon ideas. "But I couldn't feel the emotion," he said. So he returned to Yi Mae Bong.

Yi Mae Bong lay on his mattress brooding. His mood was sour. His legs hurt. Everyone was becoming a dancer now. Young people went to college and learned folk dances and performed these buoyant dances with the other members of their folk-dance clubs. They learned to play the drum and flute and even to do the masked dances that peasants used to dance when most everyone in Korea was a peasant. Young women were studying traditional dance at the universities. Yi Mae Bong knew their teachers because they had been his students. He scoffed at them, as he had scoffed at modern dance and all the people hopping around doing folk dances.

Yi Mae Bong's was a refined art, the art of the kiseng house, where women of rigorous training performed their dances for men who could appreciate their artistry. But even kiseng houses were not the same anymore. They had lost their refinement. Now they were places for bawdy good times. As a young man Yi Mae Bong had danced men's roles. But often he had dressed himself in the long, flowing robes of a woman, lined his large eyes with mascara, covered his hair with a close-fitting hat, bent his long fingers up toward the sky and assumed the role of a woman dancing away her bitterness. He was a magnificent dancer. He danced with such force, such passion that when the salpuri reached its emotional crescendos, his dark, creased face broke into a smile of such sublime pleasure that by watching him you could feel the joy in the salpuri's catharsis.

I saw him dance only on television; now he was too sore to dance in his studio. So instead he slid from his bed to the television and began searching through his videotapes for the recordings of himself. We sat through the performance of a rival, an elderly woman whose form he mocked. Then he cued up the television special on the dancing of Yi Mae Bong. He sat back on his bed and plucked another cigarette from the carton of Parliaments that sat among his trinkets and souvenirs—a sphinx-shaped scotch bottle, a geisha doll encased in glass. The room was dark and the light from the television was harsh and tinted blue.

The young men who served Yi Mae Bong sat by the door as their master perched on his bed. Cigarette smoke rose past his face. We did not talk as Yi Mae Bong stared at himself on the television.

Earlier in the afternoon Yi Mae Bong and Lee Jung Tae, the merchant banker, had gotten into a brief but spirited disagreement about the future of traditional dance. Yi Mae Bong wanted limits maintained and feared for his dances' survival. All he saw about him was greed and selfish dreams of turning skill at these dances toward profit. He did not want many dancers. He wanted a few who understood the responsibility a dancer has to his craft. Dancers did not have to be rich. They did not have to bleed their students, even though that was what some of them did.

"I'm looking for quality, not numbers," Yi Mae Bong insisted. "Now there's more folk art, more people doing farmers' dances. But that's not enough. If we keep going in that direction, we'll lose a lot."

"I disagree," said Lee Jung Tae, contradicting the master. Were he a student he might well have been banished from the studio. But Lee was an observer and that meant he had a certain latitude in expressing his views. "Quantity first. Quality later."

Yi Mae Bong addressed his point, although he could have ignored him. Yi replied that he was less interested in the cause of tradition's revival than he was in maintaining his dances in their purest form: Because if they were sullied, they were not worth reviving. Yi Mae Bong longed for moments of distilled pleasure, not a communal festival. His happiness was in the dance. And the dances, though sometimes danced in groups, could still be danced alone.

"It's all in a state of confusion in salpuri," he said. "These new teachers first came to me so they could say, 'I was a student of Yi Mae Bong.' Almost all the college professors at one time came to me. But none of them can dance my salpuri correctly. These university professors can't dance as well as my students here. Students here are very disloyal. I'm very concerned about this. There aren't any people who can continue what I know."

The apprentice Lee Woo Chung could, or so I assumed. Yi Mae Bong did not look to him: That would have violated the requisite distance between mentor and apprentice. Yi Mae Bong's task was not to praise his students but, rather, to allow them close enough to him to watch him dance, to observe the subtleties and techniques and perhaps to master them well enough to pass them on to students of their own. In return they drove his car, cleaned his studio, lit his cigarettes and did not dispute him, as their friend had, when Yi talked about the curse of youthful enthusiasm for tradition.

Woo Chung listened and then returned to the studio. There, in the long, cold room, he tried to duplicate what his master had done while at the same time lending to these passionate dances something of his own heart—his loyal heart that needed to dance.

Woo Chung danced the salpuri for me and for his friend Lee Jung

Tae and Lee's wife and daughter. The attendant cued the music on the tape player and he and Woo Chung took long, white scarves and walked to the middle of the studio floor. They held out their arms like tall birds preparing for flight. The scarves hung limply from their hands. The music came on in a roar. Lee Jung Tae's baby began to cry. He held her tight and smiled as he watched his friend begin to dance. Lee Jung Tae knew that he lacked the talent to dance himself. But he could not help moving his feet to the music. He danced his private, happy dance with his daughter in his arms as Woo Chung began to glide across the floor.

In tandem with the apprentice Woo Chung spun mournfully. The music was harsh and discordant. Its rhythm was a loud drum and its skittish melody a flute that spat out disconnected notes, whistles and breathy tones that sounded like random, unhappy thoughts.

The men rose up on their toes and sank back to the floor. They moved in quick circles when the tempo heightened. When the music slowed, their feet tightened and shook with tension. Their steps were restrained and deliberate. Then the flutes blew a harsh whistle and the dancers exploded, rushing across the floor, their scarves billowing behind them.

The dance felt like deep breathing—inhaling, holding the breath until the breaking point, exhaling in a rush. The dancers sank to their knees and lowered their heads to the floor before rising again. They held their bodies erect and pointed their fingers upward.

They danced before a mirror. When they turned, they could see reflections of two young men spinning, pointing toward the sky, trying to break free from the earth and fly.

The Future Comes to Sadang

SADANG looked the way all of Seoul had looked when the war ended. Houses were gone and where they had stood lay concrete blocks, roof tiles and, buried in the debris, the scattered reminders of homes once occupied—wash basins, magazines, records and shoes. Sadang rose up along the side of a steep hill. Uneven stone stairways ran down the hillside to the single road through the district. The junk men were on the road now. They arrived with empty carts. They picked through the rubble, helping themselves to rusted pipes and corrugated boxes, which they folded and stacked. They loaded their carts and gingerly navigated their way back down the badly rutted roadway, leaving Sadang to those who still would not leave.

When the wreckers came to Sadang, many families had already left, money in hand. The construction companies had first settled with the landlords. Then they offered compensation to the tenants in the form of vouchers for a portion of an apartment in the new housing complex. A single voucher did not buy an apartment. Three were necessary. But there was money to be made in selling the vouchers to the much-despised real estate speculators, who would profit handsomely on the resale. The going price was said to be the equivalent of ten thousand dollars. And while that was a lot of money, it could not buy you an apartment in the new complex, or any place else in Seoul. With ten thousand dollars you could find a place in the distant suburbs or in the countryside and hope the commute to work was not impossible.

Still, by the time the wrecking crews set up their tents, most of the thirty-six hundred people who had lived in the section of Sadang designated for demolition were gone. The construction companies knew there would be trouble with those who would not leave, as there was each time a wrecking crew came to raze a neighborhood desirable only for the land it occupied.

The construction companies hired teams of thugs to protect the wreckers. The thugs guarded the wreckers with iron pipes. In the first fight with the tenants of Sadang the thugs sent forty people to the hospital. Ten thugs were also hurt and riot police were posted outside the police station, ward office and subway entrances. The night before the wreckers began their work, a band of tenants descended upon their tents and set three on fire. It was not easy for the construction companies to bring progress to the slum neighborhoods of Seoul. People resisted.

The year before, in a similar Seoul neighborhood, Sanggye, the developers had also had to hire thugs. The thugs administered a terrible beating. Many people gave up after that and went away, but a hundred or so families would not leave. They lived in and around the ruins of what was once their homes and called upon the government to provide affordable housing for them in the city. They also insisted that their fight was not merely about accommodations: It was about being poor and being allowed to remain in Seoul. They worked, they said, but did not make enough money to afford the new housing going up so quickly, housing built in clusters of tall, pale-green or tan buildings indistinguishable from one another but for the large identification numbers painted on their sides.

The slum homes, everyone agreed, would have to go if the city was to move itself beyond the physical limits of a once-poor place and provide the housing suitable for an increasingly wealthy people. The city was overfilled. Each year 340,000 people came to Seoul from the countryside. They rented homes in the poorer districts. But then their neighborhood might be designated for redevelopment and the landlords would sell. The city was building housing for them—small apartments in buildings that provided reading rooms in the basement. But the numbers were inadequate: Thirty-seven hundred apartments were to be available in the coming spring in northern Seoul, a number that would barely accommodate the former residents of Sadang alone.

Still, the old homes were small and shabby, with outdoor plumbing and concrete floors. They were heated with charcoal bricks. The new apartments had running water, flush toilets and heated floors. The people of Sadang and Sanggye did not dispute the question of relative comfort: They wanted only to ensure that the comforts accessible to a growing number of their countrymen were not denied them simply because their jobs were not well paying. And so they resisted, holding out for better money, which meant a better home near their job. Those whose plans were stymied by their resistance responded, as so often happened in Korea, with a quick and painful application of force. And because one side used force, the other side did too, which meant that there were injuries on both sides.

After their forced removal the families of Sanggye had, with the assistance of the Catholic church, bought a small tract of land that abutted the Seoul-Inchon Expressway in the suburb of Puchon. It was not a desirable place to live. The truck traffic was loud and heavy. But it was theirs and soon after they arrived with their furniture, they bought wood and built temporary shelters until they could build permanent homes. The city officials of Puchon, however, informed the families that temporary housing was forbidden. Then, to ensure that the families complied with the law, the city government sent over men to tear down the wooden frames. Furniture was piled together. The chairs, cabinets, tables and tall chests were covered with thick plastic. The former residents of Sanggye had no place else to live. So they dug holes in the ground.

They dug one large, deep hole and another smaller one and lined the holes with sleeping bags. They covered the ground and roof of each hole with tarpaulins and placed heaters inside. It was February and bitter cold. The men spent their days by the fire. The women washed vegetables and prepared meals in the one structure that was left standing, a wooden hut. The children ran across the hard ground. They lighted small fires along the edge of the barren land, where their parents had burrowed themselves underground, trying to hold back the future.

It took ten minutes for twenty men to flatten Kim Hyun Sup's house in Sadang. They worked with sledgehammers. Kim had heard that the men might be coming to his house. It was the second day of the demolition. Each house had been assigned a number and the numbers were painted in red on the outside wall. In the morning the wreckers and the thugs appeared on the crest of the hill overlooking Sadang.

Kim Hyun Sup was home when the wreckers came. He heard them taking apart the house next door. He was finishing his packing when the wreckers came through his door and started tossing out his belongings. He told them that he would not resist and asked that they give him time to carry his belongings outside. The wreckers waited and then started their work. The wreckers did not talk to him.

Now Kim stood by a fire that burned near the remains of his home and his neighbors' homes. He fed the fire with the wood from their homes. Nails stuck through the wood. The fire was very hot. In the dark it lighted the face of the men and women huddled around it. Individual lights shone against the dark hill and children played with fires among the ruins. The children were having a great time crawling through and over the rubble. They had the whole hillside to themselves after the junk men left.

"Last night I slept right here," Kim said of the spot where he stood. He had slept on the ground, near his wife and their child. It was getting cold and Kim wore the warmest jacket he owned, the field jacket he took with him when he was discharged from the army.

Ten people huddled close to the fire. They looked like the remnants of a ghost town. Their friends had already left. Some people had been in Sadang for twenty years. They had been displaced from similar neighborhoods when the government decided to build new apartments or clear away homes that might embarrass the nation in the eyes of foreigners. There was such a neighborhood next door to the Seoul Hilton. When the hotel hosted the World Bank and International Monetary Fund, in 1985, the neighborhood was razed and paved over with a parking lot. The lot sat on a steep incline, just as the homes had. The people who'd lived next to the Hilton had moved to remote neighborhoods, like Sadang. But now, three years later, Sadang was no longer a distant place.

Kim Hyun Sup was waiting for his landlord. He had already missed four days of work at his factory but was not leaving until he got back the hefty deposit he had paid. It was common for rents to be paid not on a monthly basis but with a large cash sum that the landlord could invest for the length of the lease. When the tenant left, he received his money back and the landlord kept the profits of his investment. Kim's landlord might come tomorrow and then he could move on to a new home, distant but not yet determined. Kim had lived in Sadang for ten years.

Someone was getting too close to the two blue tarpaulin-covered piles of furniture and clothing that sat on the remains of his home and which represented the Kim family's belongings. "Don't touch that," Kim snapped. The tenants of Sadang who had some savings had gone to those without and offered to buy their vouchers, so that they could move into the new apartments. It was not that people were turning against each other, said those who remained in Sadang; the situation was not as it was after the war, when people in the poor neighborhoods hid their food so that they would not have to share. Now people were simply looking out for themselves—just as Kim Hyun Sup was keeping an eye on his goods, to make sure they were all there in the morning. Kim had no savings. In fact, he had very little and was trying hard to steel himself so that he would not descend into remorse.

"I don't like to indulge in self-pity," he said. "That wouldn't help me anyway." His voice grew emphatic. "But they always say this country is getting democratic. But such democracy seems to apply only to the rich. What good is democracy if it can't help the poor? I live hand to mouth every day. I have a family. I have to control my emotions in a situation like this because self-pity won't help."

Neither would anger, but often that is what people felt. They were angry with the thugs for hitting them with pipes, with the wreckers for breaking apart their homes, with the construction companies for hiring the thugs and wreckers, with the city for designating the area for redevelopment, with the real estate speculators for growing rich with their vouchers, with the government for not providing them with homes and with everyone whose benefit came at their expense. The anger over the inequities in the quality of life was not restricted to the dispossessed. In June, 150 people from the Chamsil section of Seoul attacked the construction site of the massive, gaudy Lotte World shopping center and hotel because, they claimed, not only were they suffering the noise and dust of construction, but they were having problems seeing out their windows because of the glare from the three-story indoor amusement park. The protesters beat on the building with steel pipes and seven people were hurt in the subsequent fight with security guards. That same week, in the city of Kwangyang in Cholla Province, one hundred people who lived near the local Pohong Iron and Steel Company's mill charged into the site, wielding clubs and knives. A mill employee was stabbed in the back. The people were protesting the harmful effects of living close to the mill.

Though the government economists issued reports showing that income was distributed relatively equitably—relative, that is, to other nations with a per-capita income of three thousand dollars and even to nations far wealthier—people did not feel this to be the case. The opposition politicians, sensing the public resentment, made much of the issue of income distribution to show that theirs were the true parties of the people.

The widespread belief that people were being denied the fruit of the nation's increasing affluence went beyond the sometimes opulent displays of sudden wealth—new fast cars, Hermes scarves, diamond pinky rings, homes filled with porcelain geegaws. The greatest concentration of poor people was no longer in the countryside but in the cities. Moreover, the greatest concentration of wealth was in the conglomerates, which meant that those working for them fared better than those employed by small companies. That wealth and poverty were concentrated in the vast basin that was Seoul only exacerbated the bitterness of those who worked sixteen hours a day in a knitting factory, or polished the brass in the subway stations, or found themselves one night sitting in front of a fire kept alive by the wood that was once part of their home.

The Korean War had been the society's great equalizer, making those once part of the ruling classes and those who owned land and those who had nothing all the same. But in the years that followed, when a man who once repaired U.S. Army jeeps could rise to become chairman at Hyundai while others still delivered charcoal, resentment was inevitable. The rich did little to soften the bitterness. You were told, ad nauseam, about the "lower classes," how they were overly emotional and without refinement and not worthy of conversation with a foreigner seeking to know something of Korea. Korea had become a nation of snobs, where the children of the recently wealthy thought nothing of treating a waitress as they might a servant forced to sleep across two chairs in the kitchen.

"If you're poor here, you're unlucky," a government official told me when I asked about the people of Sadang. "You have no chance in this country." The official was sensitive to the plight of the urban poor and was pleased to see that the government had been forced to become sensitive to the issue too. The government's sensitivity, he said with a smile, was recent, dating from the opposition's triumph in the National Assembly elections and the subsequent need on the part of the ruling party to show that it cared.

In the past, he explained, it was easy for the government to strike lucrative deals with landowners and have old neighborhoods razed because the government did as it pleased, especially when it stood to gain all the revenues from the development of new, high-rise apartments. The city government was merely an extension of the national government: The mayor of Seoul was appointed by the president; the city had had six mayors in the past ten years. There was no city council to check the mayor, or at least to provide an outlet for the voices of its constituency. In a sense, the mayor's only constituency was the president, whom he tried to please by spending not on such hidden amenities as sewers, but on roadways and buildings dedicated at ribbon-cutting ceremonies that the president attended and were aired on the evening news.

But now the ruling party recognized that there were far more tenants than there were landowners, and tenants voted. It was the ruling party, he said, that had recently introduced legislation that would bring running water and sewer systems to the poorer neighborhoods, as well as the promise of a desk in public reading rooms for every junior-high- and high-school student. A ban on extensive home improvements was lifted and tenants were free to add a second floor to their cramped home if they liked.

Sadang, however, was a vestige of the past, as were another half-dozen neighborhoods where the landlords had been issued permits for redevelopment before the spring of 1987. The speed of the city's development, at least in a superficial sense, would change. The demolition would stop and the old neighborhoods would be permitted to stand. They would even have indoor plumbing.

The official and I started talking about wealth and power and how friends of his from school were now making far more money than he was. His wife sometimes complained to him about this, but the official said that he was happy in his work. Still, he was aware of how much it meant to keep up, to be doing as well as a relative, or a friend, or the fellow down the block. No one wanted to risk being left behind.

"If you have a little more money than the average person," he said, "if you have a little more power, then this country is heaven."

And everyone wanted a share. Now.

Kim Hyun Sup was gone in the morning. The fire was out and people had dispersed. It was a cloudy, chilly day. The wreckers had not yet appeared on the crest of the hill.

The daylight, dull as it was, exposed the scale of the devastation. I stood at the bottom of the road and looked up at the broad hillside covered with flattened homes. There was one color on the hillside and that was gray, the gray of concrete and cinder block and stone. But more haunting than the sight was the silence. I climbed onto a concrete slab that was once a roof. I listened and heard nothing coming from the hillside.

But then came a dog's barking, and then a rooster's call, and then the sound of the motorcycle of the man delivering heating fuel. And slowly, from homes that still stood among the rubble, people emerged. Children appeared on the stone stairway leading from the hill. They carried their schoolbags. A young woman stepped from a hovel, dressed in a suit. Men in jackets and ties appeared on the road. The egg man was making deliveries. Red peppers were set out to dry on the roofs. Bedding and laundry were hung up to air. In the market at the foot of the hill the peddlers stacked oranges on their carts and the fishmongers sliced squid and eels.

But it all felt like a death postponed. Because now, on the road, appeared the empty trucks heading to the homes scheduled for demolition. One truck stopped in front of house number 751 and the eldest son, a boy of perhaps twelve, came out of the house and showed the driver where he could turn around before he and his mother and father began loading the truck with their belongings.

The boy and his younger brother had helped with the stacking. They carried out boxes, a coat rack, a hobbyhorse and a table to a low wall lined with plants. The house sat alongside the road. It was small and concrete and its roof was fading red tile. It was indistinguishable from many of the other houses still standing. Inside the house the boy's mother and father were walking across the yellow linoleum floor, preparing the furniture. The truck driver came in to help with the cabinets and closets.

First they broke down the front door. The door was wooden and cracked and it broke easily. The boy helped knock out the glass, which smashed on the ground. He climbed onto the truck bed and began stacking the boxes as the men tended to the heavy pieces.

They were still packing when, up the road, came the junk man. He pulled an empty cart. The junk man was short and skinny and lost in his baggy clothes. He wheezed and stopped to catch his breath. He was clanging the long metal shears that in neighborhoods all over the country announced the coming of the junk man. But no one called to him. The junk man looked about him and saw little. He took hold of the cart handle and trudged farther up the road, to find what was left behind.

Salpuri

*T*HE roots of bitterness did not interest Kim Jung Ok as much as he was interested in consoling those whom bitterness saddened. Kim was a theatrical director. In the twenty years since he had lived in Paris and begun looking at Korea from a distance, his Free Theater Group had evolved from a Korean interpreter of Western drama into a modern-day practitioner of the ancient Korean rituals of exorcism. "I've adapted the theme of death in just about every play I've done," Kim said. "Not only the element of death, but that of shamanism."

Shamanists still danced and chanted throughout the day and into the night and kept the omnipresent angry gods at bay. Kim, a slight man with long gray hair and a quick smile, took scripts and contorted them so that the plots disappeared and he was left with an amalgam of events whose cumulative effect was the bitterness and sadness of han. His most recent production was an adaptation of Federico García Lorca's *Blood Wedding*. Rather than show the progression toward tragedy that began with a wayward bride's decision to run off with her former lover, Kim began with García Lorca's ending: the bride and her mother-in-law fighting over the corpses of the lover and the bridegroom. Kim said, "I don't interpret plays in terms of cause and effect."

People were unsettled by Kim's *Blood Wedding* and some walked out during the first ten minutes. Kim's version opened with the two women wailing and screaming, which is what Korean women are expected to do at the graveside. "There are lots of things," he said, "that people want to close their eyes to." Still, most of the audience stayed and together they shared in the ritualized catharsis Kim had arranged. *Blood Wedding* was written during the Spanish civil war and Kim saw in the battle between the two women parallels to the bitterness of Korea's unresolved conflicts: the war, the division, the abuses of the government, the Kwangju killings. "Often I begin with death and work backward to develop my ideas," Kim said. "The consequence is death. I go on to resolve the han of this death."

In the cab I took to meet Kim, the driver had the radio tuned to the opening session of the National Assembly hearings into past wrongdoings. People watched the hearings on television or listened at work or in their cars. More people were watching the hearings than had watched the Olympics and this spoke not only of the Games' limited impact in Korea but also of the seemingly inexhaustible capacity the nation had for unearthing, examining and seeking release from the pain of its past.

For years the ritual of release, traditional rituals and modern ones too, had substituted for genuine release because in the harsh way the nation was ruled, ritual was all that was permitted. But now the opposition controlled the National Assembly. The government party was powerless to stop the hearings and the subpoenas went out.

Kim Jung Ok and his troupe of young actors meanwhile continued providing their pageantry of release. "Most of my plays are about victims," he said. "The causes that lead to the han are diverse and do not necessarily follow from one to the next. I want to console the spirit."

Kim's actors sang and danced and each played various parts in a confusing spectacle whose desired result was a theatrical version of salpuri, the cathartic dance that women performed to ease the pain of han. Their performance mirrored the progression of the fall, a season that felt like a collective rendering of the salpuri—in the succession of hearings and in the ritualized reenacts of painful times that appeared with increasing frequency on television and on the stage.

This salpuri began when the Olympics ended and the government could no longer use the responsibility of the host as an excuse for delay. The dance unfolded slowly. And as it did, it grew more passionate, which is the way salpuri must be danced.

The first person called before the investigating committee was Chang Se Dong. A year before he was the most feared man in South Korea.

Chang was director of the Agency for National Security Planning—the euphemistic name that the Korean Central Intelligence Agency had given itself. The name change fooled no one. The agency was still the arbiter of right and wrong and employed thousands of agents and informers to ensure that the populace did not veer in the slightest from the course toward "purity" that Chun Doo Hwan had plotted when he seized power. Chang did Chun's dirty work so efficiently that for seven years millions of people were afraid of what might slip out of their mouth.

But now the cab driver laughed at Chang Se Dong. From ten in the morning until midnight Chang defended the Chun government's multi-million-dollar shakedown scheme that was gloriously called The Ilhae Foundation. Ilhae was Chun's pen name. The foundation, as portrayed by Chang, was a research institute dedicated to the reunification of the peninsula, as well as to world peace. It was established in 1983, he said, on the flight back from Rangoon, after a North Korean bomb killed several members of the South Korean cabinet. Businessmen wanted to give money to the bereaved families. The idea seemed so good that businessmen kept on giving and giving long after the mourning ended. They gave, Chang said, because they wanted to give to the president's foundation. The businessmen, some of the most prominent in the country, insisted that they gave because they were forced to give. If they gave, they enjoyed government loan assistance and government contracts. If they displeased the government, as the Kukje-ICC group did when its chairman angered Chun by arriving late to a presidential party, the firm, charged the opposition, was allowed to go bankrupt.

Chang stuck to his story, even though a former Chun aide admitted the former president had actually ordered some collections himself. Chang remained the loyal second in command, insisting that Chun did not intend to move from the presidential residence into the foundation villa upon his retirement, but instead planned to use the villa as a meeting place where he might pass along all that he had learned as head of state. Chun had other homes. He had a villa in Cholla Province and another set on a lake in Chungju. The government tried to stop the opposition from touring the lakeside villa, insisting that the security of the president and the nation might be endangered. The government was new to the game of damage control and resorted to the ways of the past. Soldiers armed with submachine guns stood at the villa gate and would not let the legislators pass.

The spring and fall had been a messy time for both the government and the Chun family. By the time the hearings began, Chun's younger brother was in prison for extorting millions of dollars from the national rural redevelopment project he had headed. Chun's older brother and brother-in-law were arrested for embezzlement; his cousin was arrested for accepting bribes; and another brother-in-law was arrested for tax evasion and influence peddling. Fourteen members of his family were prohibited from leaving the country.

Chun himself was in seclusion. He had planned to go to the Olympics but stayed at home when it was clear how angrily people would react should they see him. Riot policemen had to guard his home because students tried to attack it with firebombs. The students, not content with his arrest alone, called for his execution.

Chun had been out of power for eight months and people could not stop thinking about him. They wondered what he wanted— whether he might take the government down with him if he was indicted; whether he might implicate his protégé, the president, Roh Tae Woo; whether he would be forced to leave the country; whether he might go to prison; whether there were elements in the army still loyal to him.

There were Chun stories and rumors: that Chun had stashed millions abroad; that he had heliports in his homes; that he had three airlines with pilots on a twenty-four-hour alert should he need to flee the country. There were stories, too, about his wife, Lee Soon Ja, who was accused, among other acts of corruption, of squeezing donations from hospitals for the New Generation Heart Foundation that she chaired.

Chun said nothing. He was not seen. His name dominated conversation.

"We have complete freedom to satirize anybody," said Kim Chong Sik, star of the television variety show "Angels of the City." The show was the most popular in the country. "But we restrain ourselves because we don't want to confuse this freedom and let it get out of hand."

Kim sat in the communal dressing room dressed in shorts and knee socks. His short pony tail was tied in a black ribbon with gold sparkles. Kim wanted to look silly. On the air he spoke in a little boy's voice, a Korean Pee-wee Herman with a penchant for well-disguised social satire. The dressing room was littered with cigarette butts and scripts. The members of the cast put on their makeup and one of them played with a toy—a helium balloon that made one's voice small and tinny. Everybody laughed at the sound of the voice.

Men were dressing in army uniforms. The show had begun a segment on the army called "Attention!" This week's episode was about a sergeant's hazing a recruit until the captain comes in, discovers the recruit is from his hometown, and stops the hazing. Hazing was common in the army, as was the beating, kicking and slapping of recruits. A friend told me that when he was in the army, he slept fitfully unless he had been hit before he went to bed: He knew that sometime in the middle of the night he would be woken up to be slapped or kicked. The corporal who did a lot of this hitting was a short man a few years his junior who outranked him because he had started his army tour straight from high school, while my friend was a college graduate. One night, on a remote island, my friend could stand no more. The corporal was berating him for being a college boy. As the corporal screamed at him, my friend calculated how close they stood to the side of a mountain. He wondered whether anyone would doubt his story about the corporal's accidentally falling to his death. In the end, however, he just listened until the screaming was done.

The hazing on "Attention!" however, involved only the forced singing of songs, but it seemed enough to suggest that a recruit's life was not a happy one. The sergeant enjoyed making the recruit feel bad.

The skit's happy ending aside, no one had dared satirize army life before. The closest the cast of "Angels of the City" could get before "Attention!" was a skit on the life of a foot soldier during the Yi dynasty. Otherwise the government censors would have cut the script, or canceled the show. "Angels of the City" aired on the Korean Broadcasting System, which the government controlled. Now Kim was enjoying the chance to make fun of powerful people on the government network. But he did not want to lose this freedom by pushing the limits of expression.

"There's so much expectation," he said. The actor sitting next to him was in a great mood so he put his arm around my interpreter's shoulder and asked her to marry him. There was a lot of laughing in the dressing room. "This show makes people feel good," Kim said.

"We're dealing with people from such a wide spectrum and want to draw them toward the middle. In the past people didn't have very high expectations. They just took things and didn't expect they could release their frustrations through comedy."

During the presidential campaign "Angels of the City" poked fun at Roh Tae Woo, who had invited the parodies to show that he was a man of the people. A set of oversized ears was found in the prop room—Roh's large ears were the stuff of caricature—and "Angels of the City" aired a segment about a man with big ears who hears but does not listen to what people are saying. The troupe also made fun of the opposition candidates, satirizing them as men who talked about nothing.

While people were at first tentative about making fun of Chun himself, they were now seizing upon his brother, the recently imprisoned Chun Hyung Hwan. Baby Chun, as he now was called, made a fine surrogate. He looked like his older brother. He was an accessible target. At his arrest people crowded around him calling, "Kill him!" A man reached out from the crowd and slapped his face. The man said he did this because "Baby Chun did not show any sign of contrition or remorse."

"Angels of the City," sensing the public's desire for more abuse of the younger Chun—and, by extension, his brother—performed a skit called "Thieves' Vacation," in which a group of burglars break into the home of a man with political connections. The man is away and the phone rings. A thief answers the call, which is from a man who wants a favor. The thieves move into the house and make believe they own it. When the police come, the thieves are sure they will be arrested. But the police are not after the thieves. They want the owner, Kim said, who is supposed to be Chun Hyung Hwan.

"What was indirectly expressed in the past is now expressed directly," Kim said. The Yonhee Clown Group, for instance, was performing "Hey, Mr. President! That's Not the Case," which shows a bespectacled, bald-headed chief of state tortured with electric shocks and sent to a reeducation camp when he is mistakenly accused of being a spy. There were the new Chun comic books, like *The Ordinary Gorilla, First Lady You Have Gone Too Far* and *Please Wake Up Your Majesty.*

All of it had been unimaginable a year before. A year before only a few people dared poke fun at powerful people and even then they had to do so in the most roundabout ways. One of them, Kim Hyong Kon, was down the hall rehearsing another segment of "Dear Chairman."

The remarkable thing about Kim Hyong Kon was that he had managed to avoid prison. Kim was careful, but he had also maintained an edge to his humor, even during the Chun years. He was twenty-nine years old and portly and looked like a man several years his senior. Kim played the chairman of a fictitious company. Each week for the past two years the show had parodied the nation's politicians and tycoons. For a while people thought Kim's character was a takeoff on Chung Ju Yung, the honorary chairman of Hyundai.

This got Kim in trouble. There were threatening phone calls. The censors threatened to cancel the show. When the censors wanted segments dropped, they were dropped because Kim could do nothing to stop them. Even during the presidential campaign the censors were threatening to halt the show because "Dear Chairman" parodied the opposition for being unable to field a single candidate. The show did not mention the government, Kim said, but the government decided that the show implicitly supported the opposition. The censors wanted the show taken off the air, but people in the media, who were enjoying the freedom to report and write what they wanted, protested on Kim's behalf.

The biggest risk Kim ever took came in the show he did on the torture and death of Park Chong Chol. One of the chairman's lieutenants breaks a vase. The sound the vase makes when it breaks is the same sound that the police said Park Chong Chol made when his windpipe was broken. "I never thought I'd get away with it," Kim said.

But now many people were doing what Kim had done when the risk was great. He did not begrudge the rise in popularity of "Angels of the City." Instead, he wanted to take his show to a higher level of sophistication. "I'm not hasty. I'll go step-by-step," he said. "We'd like to have a show that appeals to intellectuals. You probably can't understand our show unless you read the newspapers."

Two years before it was hard for many people to know what Kim was trying to tell them. Even if they read the newspaper, they learned only what the government had decided was permissible to learn.

* * *

Facts, confirmable and reliable, were now accessible. The facts appeared on the television and radio and in the newspapers and the government was now making it possible for people to know what they were long prevented from knowing. One of the facts that people were now aware of was the way they had been systematically lied to for years.

People had sensed this and had often relied upon rumor as their source of information because the printed and electronic sources could not be trusted. The Chun government called its control of information "a plan to purify mass media." To accomplish this "purification" 44 newspapers were either shut down or merged and 933 journalists were fired. Those fired were considered "problem journalists," who had protested against martial law. Those who were allowed to keep their job were joined in their newsrooms by representatives of the government, who were on hand to ensure that the government's 688 directives on the reporting, writing and editing of news were carried out.

Reporters who resisted were brought to the Agency for National Security Planning. Some were arrested and some were tortured. Each day the government issued directives on the way certain stories were to be written, their length, the size of the photograph to accompany the story and the placement of the story in the paper. Kim Dae Jung's face could not appear in a newspaper. The front pages belonged to the president. There were stories about the important things he had done for the nation that day as well as photographs capturing him in noble and flattering poses. It was impossible to know from these photographs that Chun Doo Hwan was a short man because no one ever seemed taller than Chun.

Huh Moon Do was one of the men in charge of this work. He was a thin man with a pleasant face. Huh was Chun's senior secretary and he admitted that, yes, he did call on editors and seek their "cooperation" on "sensitive matters." Huh did not think there was anything unusual in this. He told the assembly committee that every government in the world did the same thing. "The Chun government's only fault was that it handled the matter coarsely," he said. The opposition people laughed at him when he said this.

The newspapers reported Huh's brief humiliation as well as the nature of the censorship he supervised. It printed transcripts of testimony by former newspaper publishers who told of being brought before martial-law commanders—on the pretext of having dinner together—and forced to sign documents relinquishing control of their newspaper. Men whom the government favored were placed in control of television networks and newspapers. And journalists whom the government trusted were placed in newsrooms so that they could supervise the staff.

Despite all the attempts to curb knowledge people still heard about the Samchong reeducation camps but did not know how many young men were sent there for forced labor, how many were hurt and how many died. They had heard about torture and arrests of dissidents but were told that these people were enemies of the state.

They had heard about Kwangju. They did not believe what the government told them—that only 191 people died. And they did not believe the United States government when it said that it had nothing to do with the killings.

Kwangju was brought to the stage of a small theater near Yonsei University. The cast was young, as was the audience that filled the bleachers on the Friday night I went to watch. The production told the story of a family of four, a mother and father, son and daughter. The father is a pushcart peddler. The mother and her friends work in the outdoor market. They are poor but they smile when they work. The daughter is young and innocent, the son enthusiastic. The son tries to tell his parents about politics but they do not listen until the soldiers come to the market and beat an old woman to death. Then the parents and their friends begin painting anti-government placards so that they can join the protests against martial law.

The killings were depicted in a slide show that showed mutilated faces and bodies thrown together. Interspersed with the gruesome pictures were slides of Chun Doo Hwan and Roh Tae Woo in uniform. The sounds of shooting, screaming and protest songs accompanied the slide show.

The son staggers home, bewildered. The father goes to fight the soldiers, but he returns safely. The son is given a gun and decides to join his mates who have taken over the provincial capitol. The students in the building want to surrender to the soldiers, but the townspeople are angry now and vow to fight to the death. The students stay with them. The son escapes long enough to return home on the night before the assault on the capitol. His sister calls out to him, sure that he is home to stay. When his mother sees him, she pleads with him not to go back. But the son cannot abandon his mates.

When his mother sees his body after the troops storm the provincial capitol, she waits until her husband has a moment of quiet mourning. He kneels next to his son and strokes the boy's hair. Then the mother throws herself on his body and wails. People in the audience cried. The theater went black and protest songs played. People sang along, punching the air with their fists. The actors waited by the door to thank the members of the audience for coming. They nodded and shook hands and looked drained.

Kwangju was then brought before the nation on the television and ratings were high. In the Kwangju intercity bus terminal people crowded around a television to watch. Kim Dae Jung testified on the first day and got the chance to renounce the confession that the government had used as proof of his organizing the uprising. The confession—that Kim had met and paid a student leader, instructing him to begin the protests—came, he said, after being held with little sleep for sixty days in a windowless room in the basement of the KCIA headquarters. Kim blamed the killings on Chun. The former defense minister testified the following day that the military had declared martial law to protect the country from a threatened invasion by North Korea.

There was nothing startling or new. The opposition blamed Chun. The people who had worked for Chun said that while they felt terrible about the killings, it was necessary to send in the army because things had gotten out of hand. There was no agreement on causes, or numbers, or on the role the United States had played. Chun's people said the Americans had nothing to do with what happened, but Kim Dae Jung criticized the United States Army for not standing between the Korean army and the people of Kwangju.

On the day Kim testified a group of thirty students broke into an American army compound and destroyed five cars with steel pipes and firebombs. No one was injured and the students fled. They chanted, "U.S. imperialists out."

The Deep Sleep was supposed to open in the late summer. The script had been approved, even though the subject of the play was the torture of dissidents.

The play told the story of a young dissident named Lee, modeled loosely on Kim Keun Tae. Lee is in hiding and the police try to get his mother to tell them where he is. The police torture his sister, trying to force her to tell where he is. The sister dies. Lee is arrested and tortured. His mother dies. He is filled with guilt because of the death of his mother and sister. But he does not surrender to his pain and suffering. He endures. The play was written by Chun Gi Joo.

"I write plays about the workers and the alienated classes," Chun told me. "I write about things that touch me as I live, things that I need to write about."

The programs for *The Deep Sleep*, printed posters showing the young man on the torture rack, had been posted in the Kuro industrial district, where the theater was located. Then thirteen men came by to take down the roof of the theater. There were apparently problems with the roof and with the placement of a theater in a long, wide corridor between a warren of shops. A small stage had been built, as well as low risers, where the audience could sit on the red, carpeted floor. There were no windows, but there were two ceiling fans.

Everything had been proceeding well. The man who appeared to have been sent by the police stopped by every day during rehearsals to say hello and ask about the play. But then there was the problem with the roof, which coincided with the presentation of a slide show on North Korea. Reunification had become an open topic and Chun Gi Joo wanted to show what he knew to be an overly flattering portrait of North Korea, just so people could see the propaganda for themselves. Shortly before *The Deep Sleep* was to open, the thirteen men came in to take down the section of the roof over the theater. The opening was canceled. The cast hoped that the matter of the roof would only delay the presentation of *The Deep Sleep*.

"When they took off the roof, I was really sad," said Song In Ja, who was to play the mother. "I want to do this play. I hope it can be a source of consolation to the young people."

Song sat in the small, stuffy theater greenroom with the two other members of the cast and Chun Gi Joo. She was thirty-two years old and a mother too, which made her feel for the character she played. Her husband supported her decision to appear in the play. But Song's relatives told her not to get involved with a political play. There might be trouble.

It was not easy earning a living as a stage actor in Korea. "The pay is bad," said Jin Myong Sun, who played the dissident's wife. "The play is not understood by my family. I want to go ahead with it. I'm not getting much support from my friends."

"There are some things an actor has to do that are serious and some that are just fun," said Shin Yong Chul, who played the torture victim. "But for me acting is a medium in which I can speak on behalf of the nation. Through acting I can express what our nation is facing."

"I felt that by doing this kind of play I was putting the pain of the young people on stage," Song said. "The older generation has a negative view of students and young people. But this is a play about a family."

Shin said, "I'm Korean and I want to show the pain of the Korean people by looking at them, by hearing them, by listening to their pain."

Shin was twenty-five years old and a college graduate. He knew little of lives like the one he was portraying until he was cast in the play. He read about Kim Keun Tae's torture and tried to imagine what Kim had endured. The others were also removed from the life of the dissidents and from the people in Kuro. The one who did know was Chun Gi Joo.

Chun used to work as an electrician at a Kuro factory. He had only a high-school education, having been forced to leave school before college. His father died and he had to support his mother and brother. "I work in Kuro because it is far from the center of the city and I have more freedom," he said. "It's also culturally isolated. I want to let people here know what they ought to know. This slide show is very innocent. If they don't let us show it in our theater, we'll show it in a church. Why don't they let us show it? You can't stop something that's begun to flow."

But even the shop owners in Kuro complained about the slide show. They worried about the show causing problems. They said it would be bad for business.

When I met Chun, he thought his play might still open. But it never did.

Until the morning of his apology Chun Doo Hwan was not seen in public. People were shocked when they saw him on television. He was drawn. He was not haughty anymore, not the way he had appeared on television to make announcements to the nation.

"For the past nine months I have lived with bitter repentance and bone-aching remorse," he said. "I thought I had to keep silent to be modest and believed that the silence would be accepted as my apology. But that was my mistake."

For the month since the hearings began, people wondered whether Roh could get Chun to apologize. The apology was necessary if the anger of the past was to dissipate and if Roh was to show that he was not simply Chun's toady. Chun was being threatened with indictment for various offenses. There were rumors that he was willing to apologize, then of his refusal to apologize, then of his implicating Roh in the wrongdoings of which he was accused. Chun could still make people afraid of what he might do. And then, at 9:30 in the morning, he appeared on television and did not look so frightening anymore.

"I tried to do my best in my own way during my years of service," he said. "But the seven and a half years when I ruled are now condemned as an age of authoritarianism and irregularities. I am responsible for this."

He spoke about the revelations in the assembly investigations, of the purge of journalists and the Samchong reeducation camps. He said, "I frankly admit that those are the result of trial and error of my rule."

He said that his heart ached when he thought about Kwangju.

He apologized for the crimes of his relatives and for the way money was raised for The Ilhae Foundation. He surrendered his villas and his ski-resort condominium, his three million dollars in assets and the twenty million dollars left over from political contributions.

"I will not shrink from any punishment from you the people and if you insist upon my departing, I am ready to go wherever you want, except out of the fatherland."

He would leave his home and together with his wife live in a Buddhist monastery, for a "period of self-reflection."

"My fellow countrymen," he said in closing, "I am very sorry."

Two days later Roh called for clemency. But he did not issue a pardon. Some people said they were satisfied to see Chun apologize and that it would be unseemly to send a former president to prison. But others said that it was not enough. They said the damage was not repaired. The students called for his arrest. The opposition politicians tried to gauge the nation's feelings.

The Chuns retired to their monastery and waited until it was safe to go home.

The Free Theater Group's presentation of *Blood Wedding* was preceded by the historical drama *If the Rooster Doesn't Call, Let the Hen Do It.* Kim Jung Ok wanted the play to show the slow destruction of Korea in the late nineteenth century.

As in *Blood Wedding,* Kim did not choose a logical approach. Instead he presented the harsh moments of the past in random order—the assassination of the Korean queen Min by the Japanese in 1895, the military uprising of 1882, the formal annexation of Korea by Japan in 1910. "It's about the death of a country," Kim said, "how a country is slowly dying. It takes thirty years to die. I'm trying to console the spirit of this country."

It was his years in Paris that taught Kim about Korea or, rather, that provided the distance he found necessary for seeing Korea stripped of its Western trappings. It was also in Paris that he discovered the theater of the absurd and where he began thinking of bringing that illogical theater and the plays of Korea's past together to form a theater that was neither Western nor a resurrection of tradition.

Kim often cast his actors as itinerant jesters who traveled through the countryside putting on funny plays. That the jesters had lived difficult lives too made them an appropriate vehicle for portraying the sorrow of victims. Young people came to see the Free Theater Group's plays and Kim noticed that many more young men were joining the young women who had always come to his theater. He assumed that many came because they wanted to see theater that was somehow Korean. Kim could be hard on his audiences, pushing them to see the nation whole, even when it was easiest to see Korea only as a victim whose sorry fate was never its own to decide.

For all that Korea had suffered at the hands of outsiders, Kim still did not feel the nation to be blameless. "It wasn't just external forces," he said on the day of Chang Se Dong's appearance before the National Assembly, when the televised hearings began. "The fault lies within ourselves. It could be many things inherent in us. Sometimes the plays can be unpleasant. I can provide a different perspective. We can be cruel sometimes because we're dealing with subjects that people want to avoid."

But as much as people wanted to avoid sadness, they recognized that life could not exist without it. Kim did not want to make the sadness disappear. He only wanted to make sad people feel a little better.

"My theater has a privilege," he said. "We don't have much power, but we have privilege when we deal with a subject like death. Korean people approach death with solemnity. But we can laugh at death."

The laughter of *If the Rooster Doesn't Call, Let the Hen Do It,* the songs and dances of the jesters, served a purpose, the same purpose as the jesters' tears.

"The whole play," said Kim Jung Ok, "is salpuri."

The Mountaintop

THROUGHOUT the winter Chun Doo Hwan remained cloistered in a Buddhist monastery. Yi Man Gi remained the Strongest Man under Heaven. Kim Young Chull began writing his memoirs. Shin Hye Ra entered college. Chung Hee, the coffee-shop lady, disappeared into the countryside. And In Seok, facing a deadline for finding a bride, began thinking more and more of the woman he loved. She was in America. She still cared for him. Her friends told him to call her. He resisted. Then he relented and called. He thought she would have already married someone else. She thought that he'd have married. Each confessed to having prayed for the other's happiness.

She came to Korea for a friend's wedding. In Seok brought her to see his parents. His parents accused him of treachery. His father took ill, complaining of high blood pressure. In Seok resisted his parents, resisted until his father surrendered. In Seok and the woman he loved went to Hong Kong and Bangkok for their honeymoon.

Kim Keun Tae, recovered from the physical pain of his imprisonment and torture, resumed the life of a dissident. He joined other opponents of the government in forming a new political coalition. Kim would not consider himself a candidate for elective office. He preferred maintaining the position of a moral force for change.

By December Kim was a changed man. His stride had regained its vigor. He now walked the way he spoke—like a young man with purpose. We arranged to meet for dinner.

We walked to the restaurant through an underground arcade. At the top of the stairway to the street stood an old woman. She was lost and cold and alone. Kim Keun Tae stopped when he saw her. He asked where she wanted to go. The woman said she was trying to get to a neighborhood on the outskirts of Seoul. She asked Kim where the bus stopped. Kim tried to explain, pointing and giving directions. But he could see that the woman did not understand. He turned from the woman and apologized to me for the coming delay. He took the woman's arm and began walking her to the traffic circle, several blocks away.

It was a bitter cold night and Kim and the old woman walked slowly. He asked the woman, "Do you know who I am?" but the woman did not recognize his face or his name. He told her who he was and what had happened to him. When he told her about the things he believed in, the woman listened and wrote down his name on her shopping bag.

At the crowded bus stand Kim Keun Tae searched for the woman's bus. People watched him helping the old woman and when they saw him doing this, they offered to help too. They pointed to where her bus stopped and helped her get on the bus. The driver said he would make sure she got off at the right place.

The scene at the bus stand did not last very long. It took place at night and in the cold on a street crowded with people who had thing on their mind other than the fate of an old woman on her way to a distant home. But in that moment Kim Keun Tae, through little more than his presence, had enlisted volunteers who could not seem to do enough to help the old woman. For a moment they were listening to him. But then the moment ended and life on the street resumed its hectic pace. Kim Keun Tae was another person on the street, fighting through the crowd.

Kim did not begin talking seriously until dinner was over. It would have been inappropriate to interrupt the dinner with conversation. He ate in silence broken only by my questions, to which he smiled and did not respond until the waitress came with the tea. Then he spoke about the present. He was not entirely pleased.

"It's all very unclear, fluid," he said. Change had come, but it was insufficient. Democratic reforms had been enacted, but the instruments of oppression—the state security apparatus—still existed. Labor had been allowed to organize, but the middle class was not nearly as interested in their plight as it had been in following the students in June of 1987. Kim was disappointed in the middle class. He called them "selfish." He was upset that those with a little more continued looking down on those with a little less.

The past, both recent and distant, continued to stand between Korea and the democracy that Kim Keun Tae envisioned. Authoritarianism was a vestige of a feudal past that had never been eradicated: The Japanese had simply taken over at the turn of the century and feudalism was never repudiated. Nor were the ways of the Fifth Republic, not to Kim's satisfaction. Chun Doo Hwan may have apologized and endured his public humiliation. But Kim did not believe that Roh Tae Woo had separated himself from the man he once served. The past had not been sufficiently unearthed. It remained unresolved. Punishment was called for, most especially for Chun. Kim Keun Tae believed that the future would be marred unless the past was made right. He said, "Only when they're punished can we have a firm foundation upon which to build a democracy."

He had heard that the man who conducted his torture—the man nicknamed the Master of Water Torture—was being sought by the police. But the police reported that the man was missing. They could not find him. Kim smiled as he told this story. He did not wish to dwell upon his own past. Instead he wanted to talk about the lingering causes of the nation's han.

With all the change of the past year—change that was unimaginable before the June protests—with all the possibilities of a Korean democracy with a government accountable to its people, with the prospect of a work force that had a voice in its future, with a populace that no longer lived in fear, with all that had happened to Korea since the spring of 1987, the bitterness endured.

I knew that the pain of han could be eased. I knew that the dissidents had a formula for ending the bitterness. Kim Keun Tae repeated the catechism for me: the departure of the American troops, the end of great-power meddling in Korea's life, settling the abuses of the past and, of course, reunification. By now the words had taken on a numbing familiarity. The Americans might one day leave, but great powers are, by nature, meddlers. The past could be examined and settled. But I doubted that everyone would be satisfied. And I could not envision a reunified Korea, certainly not until the death of the North Korean president Kim Il Sung and the ensuing political vacuum.

I had seen how han could propel that nation and I had seen how it held it back. But because I was an American, I had trouble resisting the inclination to see han as a series of conflicts to be resolved. If enough of the causes of bitterness could be undone, then perhaps the bitterness might ease enough for Koreans to one day be happy.

But happiness, as an abstract concept, is an American idea—the idea of life as an exercise directed in the pursuit of happiness. It was, in Kim Keun Tae's view, a foolish idea. "If you keep searching for happiness," he said, "you'll end up unhappy."

Happiness was not waiting at the end of Kim Keun Tae's rainbow. But hope was. "You're saying that han is suffering as well as triumph," he said. "But han can make sense only if you remember that with han there is also the hope. Without hope, han perishes. Without hope han is destructive. It becomes what we call wan han, 'vengeance.' The hope makes han dynamic."

Kim was not interested in punishing Chun Doo Hwan for the sake of seeing Chun suffer. Chun had to be punished by Roh Tae Woo so that Roh could demonstrate the sincerity of his break with the past. Kim was anxious to see the Americans leave not because he did not like them but because he saw their armed presence as an obstacle to unifying the peninsula. Kim knew that so much stood between a union of the North and South. But he believed that it was essential to hope.

He had studied the Bible and had taken a particular interest in the story of the Exodus of the Jews from Egypt. He saw in that story of flight from bondage a parallel with his country's desire to be whole again. Reunification would be Korea's deliverance. It would be a deliverance born out of pain and bitterness. And when it came, the nation would at last be redeemed.

But while Kim Keun Tae hoped, he continued living in the here and now. Around him he saw struggle and tension and bitterness on a personal scale. The problem with Korea, he explained, was that it allowed no escape from the struggle. "In the West if you don't like someone, you go your separate ways," he said. "But not here. Here you go on being together. You accept it as your destiny. You find a way to fulfill your hopes and dreams. When a vase breaks, it is broken. But here you glue it back together. You go on mending. Han begins and ends with relationships. And the source of maintaining those relationships is jong."

Just as there was good han and bad han—the han of progress, the han of anger—so too was there good jong and bad jong. But if in the West an equivalent of bad jong—a sour relationship, a hatred—was resolved by separation, in Korea it meant something very different. In Korea, Kim said, "You still go on together."

You go on together, even with your enemies. Kim Keun Tae understood these men. He understood the pain they felt because it was his pain too. When I told him my friend's theory about Park Chung Hee—that Park's han was born out of his being a small man who became president of a small country—Kim said, "Of course Park Chung Hee had han." Then he said, "So does Chun Doo Hwan."

Kim Keun Tae smiled as he spoke of his enemy, an enemy with whom he knew he shared a hope as well as a bitter past, a past from which their common destiny sprang.

The end of han meant the end of hope. So the han did not go away.

On my last Sunday in Korea I went mountain climbing with a group of men who had been friends since high school. Every Sunday morning they laced on their boots, pulled on their rucksacks and like men and women all over Seoul, hiked in the nearby mountains.

It was a sunny day, bright and crisp. It was the middle day of a three-day weekend and many people had returned to the countryside. The hiking trails, often jammed, were deserted. The group split between the fast and the slow walkers. The slow walkers waved the fast ones ahead and assured them that they would see them at the bottom of the trail in time for a hot bath and lunch.

We walked along the rocky trail, picking our way around the boulders. We climbed higher. There was snow along the trail and slippery spots in the shaded places, where the ice was thick. The men chatted for a while. But soon they grew silent. We stopped every now and then to look back at the city. Mountains enveloped Seoul. They were dark and craggy. A layer of clouds hung over the city and hid it from view. The clouds felt like a heavy blanket muffling the city. Seoul felt distant and quiet.

We turned back to the trail. The mountainside was still. The only sound was our forced breathing in the chilly air. We climbed higher. Then I heard the screaming.

It was a man's scream. It came from a nearby ridge. I tried to find the source, but the trees blocked my view. The sound of the scream reverberated against the mountainside. It was not a fearful scream. It was not a call for help. It sounded like the scream of a man who had filled his lungs with air, opened his mouth wide and forced the air from his lungs like a bellows. Each scream was followed by another. The man paused for a moment and then screamed again. The screams lasted for a few seconds and then dissipated in the cold air.

I asked what the screaming was about. One of the men in our group smiled. Every Sunday, he explained, men hike to the top of these mountains. And when they reach the top, they scream. They scream away their week, he said. They scream away their frustrations, their anger. They scream away a bit of their han.

And then, when they are finished screaming, they pick up their rucksacks and make their way back down the mountain. They hike back to the city, now shrouded in clouds, prepared to resume their passionate life, a life filled with sadness and hope.

Postscript: New York, Winter 1990

*T*HE news from Korea is not good.

Kim Young Sam and Kim Jong Pil have joined the government party to form a coalition that will control the National Assembly. If the coalition remains intact—there is still the delicate and unprecedented problem of dividing the spoils of power—the government stands to reverse all that it lost in the 1988 assembly elections and, for that matter, undo all that was won in the streets in the spring of 1987.

Kim Dae Jung, left as the sole political opponent to the government, has called upon Roh Tae Woo to dissolve the assembly and hold new elections as a referendum on the new order. Roh had approached Kim Dae Jung with a similar offer, but Kim insisted that their ideological differences were too vast to form an alliance. Kim Dae Jung has warned the government that people might once again take to the streets. But others are not so sure. The students may demonstrate. But the middle class is tired of conflict, tired of unrest. There is no sense of outrage, at least not for the moment.

I called a Korean political scientist who knew both Kim Dae Jung and Kim Young Sam. He was not so much enraged by the news of Kim Young Sam's defection—Kim Jong Pil, after all, had been second in command of a military dictatorship—as he was weary of a political opposition that believed in nothing but the preservation of its own bit of power. Another scholar said that the merger was little more than a consolidation of Kyongsang Province's domination over Cholla Province. Roh and Kim Young Sam are both from Kyongsang, and he feared that their agreement would only worsen the animosity between the regions.

Roh remains the elusive target. During the presidential election campaign he promised to hold a referendum on his rule. But he has announced that there will be no vote, because leftists might use the referendum to cause social unrest. The question of the referendum was dropped by the opposition, who sensed that perhaps the time was not right for challenging the president at the ballot box.

The three opposition parties controlled the assembly for almost two years but failed to use their power to eradicate the instruments of repression. The assembly debated but never abolished the laws and agencies that made South Korea a police state. The Agency for National Security Planning is still intact, as is the Defense Security Command. The National Security Law has not been revised. And the government is again showing a willingness to use the instruments at its disposal to quash dissent.

In August Amnesty International reported that eight hundred political prisoners were being held—six hundred more than in December of 1988. This figure did not include the thousands who were detained for taking part in demonstrations. Dissident students were arrested. Dissident offices were raided. Police seized leaflets deemed favorable to North Korea or leftist in tone.

It was as if nothing had changed. Once again there are reports of beatings, torture and prisoners held for weeks without being allowed to see a lawyer.

In Kwangju a dissident student was found drowned. It was said that he was fleeing the police and fell in a lake. Although the drowning was officially listed as the cause of death, a physician present at the autopsy challenged the results. The face and body of the student, Lee Chol Kyu, were covered with bruises. Dissidents claimed that Lee was tortured and killed by the police. A National Assembly investigation produced no evidence of foul play. The authorities did not permit a visiting American forensic pathologist to perform a second autopsy.

In Pusan seven riot policemen were burned to death when they stormed a university library to rescue five policemen held hostage by students. The students had taken the hostages after police detained several students who demonstrated in front of a police station. The students had then covered the library floor with paint thinner.

When the police raided the library the students set the room on fire. Four students were charged with murder.

The government was once again sending in riot police to break up strikes. Union leaders were arrested, but the strikes did not stop. Teachers tried to organize. But the government banned their union, insisting that it was a front for leftist ideology. Fifteen hundred teachers were fired or suspended for joining the union. Dozens of teachers were jailed.

Moon Ik Kwan, a dissident pastor, was sentenced to ten years for making an illegal trip to North Korea. So, too, was a National Assemblyman, Suh Kyong Won, a member of Kim Dae Jung's party. Kim himself was arrested and charged, under the National Security Law, with secretly knowing of Suh's trip and not informing the authorities.

The four policemen who Kim Keun Tae accused of torturing him went on trial. The complaint had been filed in 1985. The prosecutor's office had decided against pursuing the case, but in late 1988 the Seoul Court of Appeal ordered the trial. The first hearing was held in June of 1989. The second hearing was scheduled for July. But Kim Keun Tae was not there. The police had issued a warrant for his arrest for his involvement in his newly formed dissident group. A year after his release from prison, and two years after the demonstrations that had heralded the beginning of a new South Korea, Kim Keun Tae was said to be in hiding.